Workshop on New Frontiers in Summarization 2017

Copenhagen, Denmark
7 September 2017

ISBN: 978-1-5108-4761-3

Printed from e-media with permission by:

Curran Associates, Inc.
57 Morehouse Lane
Red Hook, NY 12571

Some format issues inherent in the e-media version may also appear in this print version.

Copyright© (2017) by the Association for Computational Linguistics
All rights reserved.

Printed by Curran Associates, Inc. (2017)

For permission requests, please contact the Association for Computational Linguistics
at the address below.

Association for Computational Linguistics
209 N. Eighth Street
Stroudsburg, Pennsylvania 18360

Phone: 1-570-476-8006
Fax: 1-570-476-0860

acl@aclweb.org

Additional copies of this publication are available from:

Curran Associates, Inc.
57 Morehouse Lane
Red Hook, NY 12571 USA
Phone: 845-758-0400
Fax: 845-758-2633
Email: curran@proceedings.com
Web: www.proceedings.com

Workshop on New Frontiers in Summarization 2017

Copenhagen, Denmark
7 September 2017

EMNLP 2017

Workshop on New Frontiers in Summarization

Workshop Proceedings

September 7, 2017
Copenhagen, Denmark

©2017 The Association for Computational Linguistics

Introduction

Can intelligent systems be devised to create concise, fluent, and accurate summaries from vast amounts of data? Researchers have strived to achieve this goal in the past fifty years, starting from the seminal work of Luhn (1958) on automatic text summarization. Existing research includes the development of extractive and abstractive summarization technologies, evaluation metrics (e.g., ROUGE and Pyramid), as well as the construction of benchmark datasets and resources (e.g., annual competitions such as DUC (2001-2007), TAC (2008-2011), and TREC (2014-2016 on Microblog/Temporal Summarization)).

The goal for this workshop is to provide a research forum for cross-fertilization of ideas. We seek to bring together researchers from a diverse range of fields (e.g., summarization, visualization, language generation, cognitive and psycholinguistics) for discussion on key issues related to automatic summarization. This includes discussion on novel paradigms/frameworks, shared tasks of interest, information integration and presentation, applied research and applications, and possible future research foci. The workshop will pave the way towards building a cohesive research community, accelerating knowledge diffusion, developing new tools, datasets and resources that are in line with the needs of academia, industry, and government.

The topics of this workshop include:

- Abstractive and extractive summarization

- Language generation

- Multiple text genres (News, tweets, product reviews, meeting conversations, forums, lectures, student feedback, emails, medical records, books, research articles, etc)

- Multimodal Input: Information integration and aggregation across multiple modalities (text, speech, image, video)

- Multimodal Output: Summarization and visualization + interactive exploration

- Tailoring summaries to user queries or interests

- Semantic aspects of summarization (e.g. semantic representation, inference, validity)

- Development of new algorithms

- Development of new datasets and annotations

- Development of new evaluation metrics

- Cognitive or psycholinguistic aspects of summarization and visualization (e.g. perceived readability, usability, etc)

In total we received 23 valid submissions (withdrawns are excluded), including 14 long papers and 9 short papers. All papers underwent a rigorous double-blind review process. Among these, 13 papers (7 long, 6 short) are selected for acceptance to the workshop, resulting in an overall acceptance rate of about 57%. We appreciate the excellent reviews provided by the program committee members, and we are grateful to our invited speakers who enriched this workshop with their presentations and insights.

Lu, Giuseppe, Jackie, Fei

Organizers:

Lu Wang (Northeastern University, USA)
Giuseppe Carenini (University of British Columbia, Canada)
Jackie Chi Kit Cheung (McGill University, Canada)
Fei Liu (University of Central Florida, USA)

Program Committee:

Enrique Alfonseca (Google Research)
Asli Celikyilmaz (Microsoft Research)
Jianpeng Cheng (University of Edinburgh)
Greg Durrett (The University of Texas at Austin)
Michael Elhadad (Ben-Gurion University of the Negev)
Benoit Favre (Aix-Marseille University)
Katja Filippova (Google Research)
Wei Gao (Qatar Computing Research Institute)
Shafiq Joty (Qatar Computing Research Institute)
Mijail Kabadjov (University of Essex)
Mirella Lapata (University of Edinburgh)
Junyi Jessy Li (University of Pennsylvania)
Yang Liu (The University of Texas at Dallas)
Annie Louis (University of Essex)
Daniel Marcu (University of Southern California)
Gabriel Murray (University of the Fraser Valley)
Jun-Ping Ng (Amazon)
Hiroya Takamura (Tokyo Institute of Technology)
Simone Teufel (University of Cambridge)
Kapil Thadani (Yahoo Inc.)
Xiaojun Wan (Peking University)

Invited Speakers:

Katja Filippova (Google Research, Switzerland)
Andreas Kerren (Linnaeus University, Sweden)
Ani Nenkova (University of Pennsylvania, USA)

Table of Contents

Workshop Program

08:45–10:30 **Morning Session 1**

08:45–08:50 *Opening Remarks*

08:50–09:50 *Invited Talk*
Andreas Kerren

09:50–10:10 *Video Highlights Detection and Summarization with Lag-Calibration based on Concept-Emotion Mapping of Crowdsourced Time-Sync Comments*
Qing Ping and Chaomei Chen

10:10–10:30 *Multimedia Summary Generation from Online Conversations: Current Approaches and Future Directions*
Enamul Hoque and Giuseppe Carenini

10:30–11:00 *Break*

11:00–12:30 **Morning Session 2**

11:00–12:00 *Invited Talk*
Katja Filippova

12:00–12:15 *Low-Resource Neural Headline Generation*
Ottokar Tilk and Tanel Alumäe

12:15–12:30 *Towards Improving Abstractive Summarization via Entailment Generation*
Ramakanth Pasunuru, Han Guo and Mohit Bansal

12:30–14:00 *Lunch*

14:00–15:30   Poster Session

Video Highlights Detection and Summarization with Lag-Calibration based on Concept-Emotion Mapping of Crowdsourced Time-Sync Comments
Qing Ping and Chaomei Chen

Coarse-to-Fine Attention Models for Document Summarization
Jeffrey Ling and Alexander Rush

Automatic Community Creation for Abstractive Spoken Conversations Summarization
Karan Singla, Evgeny Stepanov, Ali Orkan Bayer, Giuseppe Carenini and Giuseppe Riccardi

Multimedia Summary Generation from Online Conversations: Current Approaches and Future Directions
Enamul Hoque and Giuseppe Carenini

Combining Graph Degeneracy and Submodularity for Unsupervised Extractive Summarization
Antoine Tixier, Polykarpos Meladianos and Michalis Vazirgiannis

TL;DR: Mining Reddit to Learn Automatic Summarization
Michael Völske, Martin Potthast, Shahbaz Syed and Benno Stein

Low-Resource Neural Headline Generation
Ottokar Tilk and Tanel Alumäe

Topic Model Stability for Hierarchical Summarization
John Miller and Kathleen McCoy

Learning to Score System Summaries for Better Content Selection Evaluation.
Maxime Peyrard, Teresa Botschen and Iryna Gurevych

Revisiting the Centroid-based Method: A Strong Baseline for Multi-Document Summarization
Demian Gholipour Ghalandari

Towards Improving Abstractive Summarization via Entailment Generation
Ramakanth Pasunuru, Han Guo and Mohit Bansal

Reader-Aware Multi-Document Summarization: An Enhanced Model and The First Dataset
Piji Li, Lidong Bing and Wai Lam

A Pilot Study of Domain Adaptation Effect for Neural Abstractive Summarization
Xinyu Hua and Lu Wang

15:30–17:15   Afternoon Session

15:30–16:30   *Invited Talk*
Ani Nenkova

16:30–16:50   *Reader-Aware Multi-Document Summarization: An Enhanced Model and The First Dataset*
Piji Li, Lidong Bing and Wai Lam

16:50–17:10   *Learning to Score System Summaries for Better Content Selection Evaluation.*
Maxime Peyrard, Teresa Botschen and Iryna Gurevych

17:10–17:15   *Closing Remarks*

Video Highlights Detection and Summarization with Lag-Calibration based on Concept-Emotion Mapping of Crowd-sourced Time-Sync Comments

Qing Ping and Chaomei Chen
College of Computing & Informatics
Drexel University
`{qp27, cc345}@drexel.edu`

Abstract

With the prevalence of video sharing, there are increasing demands for automatic video digestion such as highlight detection. Recently, platforms with crowdsourced time-sync video comments have emerged worldwide, providing a good opportunity for highlight detection. However, this task is non-trivial: (1) time-sync comments often lag behind their corresponding shot; (2) time-sync comments are semantically sparse and noisy; (3) to determine which shots are highlights is highly subjective. The present paper aims to tackle these challenges by proposing a framework that (1) uses concept-mapped lexical-chains for lag-calibration; (2) models video highlights based on comment intensity and combination of emotion and concept concentration of each shot; (3) summarize each detected highlight using improved SumBasic with emotion and concept mapping. Experiments on large real-world datasets show that our highlight detection method and summarization method both outperform other benchmarks with considerable margins.

1 Introduction

Every day, people watch billions of hours of videos on YouTube, with half of the views on mobile devices[1]. With the prevalence of video sharing, there is increasing demand for fast video digestion. Imagine a scenario where a user wants to quickly grasp a long video, without dragging the progress bar repeatedly to skip shots unappealing to the user. With automatically-generated highlights, users could digest the entire video in minutes, before deciding whether to watch the full video later. Moreover, automatic video highlight detection and summarization could benefit video indexing, video search and video recommendation.

However, finding highlights from a video is not a trivial task. First, what is considered to be a "highlight" can be very subjective. Second, a highlight may not always be captured by analyzing low-level features in image, audio and motions. Lack of abstract semantic information has become a bottleneck of highlight detection in traditional video processing.

Recently, crowdsourced time-sync video comments, or "bullet-screen comments" have emerged, where real-time generated comments will be flying over or besides the screen, synchronized with the video frame by frame. It has gained popularity worldwide, such as niconico in Japan, Bilibili and Acfun in China, YouTube Live and Twitch Live in USA. The popularity of the time-sync comments has suggested new opportunities for video highlight detection based on natural language processing.

Nevertheless, it is still a challenge to detect and label highlights using time-sync comments. First, there is almost inevitable lag for comments related to each shot. As in Figure 1, ongoing discussion about one shot may extend to next a few shots. Highlight detection and labeling without lag-calibration may cause inaccurate results. Second,

---

1 https://www.youtube.com/yt/press/statistics.html

1

Proceedings of the Workshop on New Frontiers in Summarization, pages 1–11
Copenhagen, Denmark, September 7, 2017. ©2017 Association for Computational Linguistics

time-sync comments are sparse semantically, both in number of comments per shot and number of tokens per comment. Traditionally bag-of-words statistical model may work poorly on such data.

Third, there is much uncertainty in highlight detection in an unsupervised setting without any prior knowledge. Characteristics of highlights must be explicitly defined, captured and modeled.

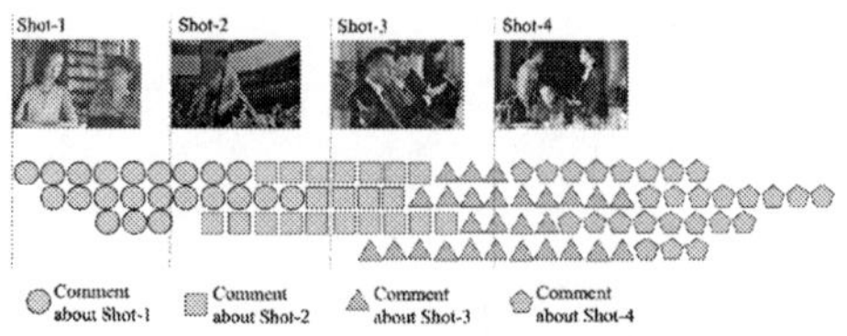

Figure 1.Lag Effect of Time-Sync Comments Shot by Shot.

To our best knowledge, little work has concentrated on highlight detection and labeling based on time-sync comments in unsupervised way. The most relevant work proposed to detect highlights based on topic concentration of semantic vectors of bullet-comments, and label each highlight with pre-trained classifier based on pre-defined tags (Lv, Xu, Chen, Liu, & Zheng, 2016). Nevertheless, we argue that emotion concentration is more important in highlight detection than general topic concentration. Another work proposed to extract highlights based on frame-by-frame similarity of emotion distribution (Xian, Li, Zhang, & Liao, 2015). However, neither work proposed to tackle the issue of lag-calibration, emotion-topic concentration balance and unsupervised highlight labeling simultaneously.

To solve these problems, the present study proposes the following: (1) word-to-concept and word-to-emotion mapping based on global word-embedding, from which lexical-chains are constructed for bullet-comments lag-calibration; (2) highlight detection based on emotional and conceptual concentration and intensity of lag-calibrated bullet-comments; (3) highlight summarization with modified Basic Sum algorithm that treats emotions and concepts as basic units in a bullet-comment.

The main contribution of the present paper are as follows: (1) We propose an entirely unsupervised framework for video highlight-detection and summarization based on time-sync comments; (2) We develop a lag-calibration technique based on concept-mapped lexical chains; (3) We construct large datasets for bullet-comment word-embedding, bullet-comment emotion lexicon and ground-truth for highlight-detection and labeling evaluation based on bullet-comments.

2 Related Work

2.1 Highlight detection by video processing

First, following the definition in previous work (M. Xu, Jin, Luo, & Duan, 2008), we define highlights as the most memorable shots in a video with high emotion intensity. Note that highlight detection is different from video summarization, which focuses on condensed storyline representation of a video, rather than extracting affective contents (K.-S. Lin, Lee, Yang, Lee, & Chen, 2013).

For highlight detection, some researchers propose to represent emotions in a video by a curve on the arousal-valence plane with low-level features such as motion, vocal effects, shot length, and audio pitch (Hanjalic & Xu, 2005), color (Ngo, Ma, & Zhang, 2005), mid-level features such as laughing and subtitles (M. Xu, Luo, Jin, & Park, 2009). Nevertheless, due to the semantic gap between low-level features and high-level semantics, accuracy of highlight detection based on video processing is limited (K.-S. Lin et al., 2013).

2.2 Temporal text summarization

The work in temporal text summarization is relevant to the present study, but also has differences. Some works formulate temporal text summarization as a constrained multi-objective optimization problem (Sipos, Swaminathan, Shivaswamy, & Joachims, 2012; Yan, Kong, et al., 2011; Yan, Wan, et al., 2011), as a graph optimization problem (C. Lin et al., 2012), as a supervised learning-to-rank problem (Tran, Niederée, Kanhabua, Gadiraju, & Anand, 2015), and as online clustering problem (Shou, Wang, Chen, & Chen, 2013).

The present study models the highlight detection as a simple two-objective optimization problem with constraints. However, the features chosen to evaluate the "highlightness" of a shot are different from the above studies. Because a highlight shot is observed to be correlated with high emotional intensity and topic concentration, coverage and non-redundancy are not goals of optimization any more, as in temporal text summarization. Instead, we focus on modeling emotional and topic concentration in present study.

2.3 Crowdsourced time-sync comment mining

Several works focused on tagging videos shot-by-shot with crowdsourced time-sync comments by manual labeling and supervised training (Ikeda, Kobayashi, Sakaji, & Masuyama, 2015), temporal and personalized topic modeling (Wu, Zhong, Tan, Horner, & Yang, 2014), or tagging video as a whole (Sakaji, Kohana, Kobayashi, & Sakai, 2016). One work proposes to generate summarization of each shot by data reconstruction jointly on textual and topic level (L. Xu & Zhang, 2017).

One work proposed a centroid-diffusion algorithm to detect highlights (Xian et al., 2015). Shots are represented by latent topics by LDA. Another work proposed to use pre-trained semantic vector of comments to cluster comments into topics, and find highlights based on topic concentration (Lv et al., 2016). Moreover, they use pre-defined labels to train a classifier for highlight labeling. The present study differs from these two studies in several aspects. First, before highlight detection, we perform lag-calibration to minimize inaccuracy due to comment lags. Second, we propose to represent each scene by the combination of topic and emotion concentration. Third, we perform both highlight detection and highlight labeling in unsupervised way.

2.4 Lexical chain

Lexical chains are a sequence of words in a cohesive relationship spanning in a range of sentences. Early work constructs lexical chains based on syntactic relations of words using the Roget's Thesaurus without word sense disambiguation (Morris & Hirst, 1991). Later work expands lexical chains by WordNet relations with word sense disambiguation (Barzilay & Elhadad, 1999; Hirst & St-Onge, 1998). Lexical chains is also constructed based on word-embedded relations for disambiguation of multi-words (Ehren, 2017). The present study constructs lexical chains for proper lag-calibration based on global word-embedding.

3 Problem Formulation

The problem in the present paper can be formulated as follows. The input is a set of time-sync comments, $C = \{c_1, c_2, c_3, \dots, c_{|T|}\}$ with a set of timestamps $T = \{t_1, t_2, t_3, \dots, t_{|T|}\}$ of a video v, a compression ratio $\tau_{highlight}$ for number of highlights to be generated, a compression ratio $\tau_{summary}$ for number of comments in each highlight summary. Our task is to (1) generate a set of highlight shots $S(v) = \{s_1, s_2, s_3, \dots, s_n\}$, and (2) highlight summaries $A(v) = \{I_1, I_2, I_3, \dots, I_n\}$ as close to ground truth as possible. Each highlight summary comprises a subset of all the comments in this shot: $I_i = \{c_1, c_2, c_3, \dots, c_{n_i}\}$. Number of highlight shots n and number of comments in summary n_i are determined by $\tau_{highlight}$ and $\tau_{summary}$ respectively.

4 Video Highlight Detection

In this section, we introduce our framework for highlight detection. Two preliminary tasks are also described, namely construction of global time-sync comment word embedding and emotion lexicon.

4.1 Preliminaries

Word-Embedding of Time-Sync Comments

As pointed out earlier, one challenge in analyzing time-sync comments is the semantic sparseness, since number of comments and comment length are both very limited. Two semantically related words may not be related if they do not co-occur frequently in one video. To compensate, we construct a global word-embedding on a large collection of time-sync comments.

The word-embedding dictionary can be represented as: $D\{(w_1: v_1), (w_2: v_2), \dots, (w_{|V|}: v_{|V|}),$ where w_i is a word, v_i is the corresponding word-vector, V is the vocabulary of the corpus.

Emotion Lexicon Construction

As emphasized earlier, it is crucial to extract emotions in time-sync comments for highlight detection. However, traditional emotion lexicons cannot be used here, since there exist too many Internet slangs that are specifically born on this type of platforms. For example, "23333" means "ha ha ha", and "6666" means "really awsome". Therefore, we construct an emotion lexicon tailored for time-sync comments from the word-embedding dictionary trained from last step. First we manually label words of the five basic emotional categories (*happy, anger, sad, fear and surprise*) as seeds (Ekman, 1992), from the top frequent words in the corpus. Here the sixth emotion category *"disgust"* is omitted because it is relatively rare in the dataset, and could be readily incorporated for other datasets. Then we expand the emotion lexicon by searching the top N neighbors of each seed word in the word-embedding space, and adding a neighbor to seeds if the neighbor meets at least percentage of overlap $\gamma_{overlap}$ with all the seeds with minimum similarity of sim_{min}. The neighbors are searched based on cosine similarity in the word-embedding space.

4.2 Lag-Calibration

In this section, we introduce our method for lag-calibration following the steps of concept mapping, word-embedded lexical chain construction and lag-calibration.

Concept Mapping

To tackle the issue of semantic sparseness in time-sync comments, and to construct lexical-chains of semantically related words, words of similar meanings should be mapped to same concept first. Given a set of comments C of video v, we first propose a mapping $\mathcal{F}$ from the vocabulary V_C of comments C to a set of concepts K_C, namely:

$$\mathcal{F}: V_C \rightarrow K_C \quad (|V_C| \geq |K_C|)$$

More specifically, mapping $\mathcal{F}$ maps each word w_0 into a concept $k = \mathcal{F}(w_0)$:

$$\mathcal{F}(w_0) = \mathcal{F}(w_1) = \mathcal{F}(w_2) = \cdots = \mathcal{F}(w_{|top\_n(w)|}) =$$
$$\begin{cases} k, \ \exists k \in K_C \ and \ \dfrac{|\{w|w \in top\_n(w_0) \wedge \mathcal{F}(w)=k\}|}{|top\_n(w_0)|} \\ \qquad\qquad\qquad \geq \phi_{overlap} \\ w, \ otherwise \end{cases} \quad (1)$$

and $top\_n(w_0)$ returns the top n neighbors of word w_0 based on cosine similarity. For every word w_0 in comment C, we check percentage of its neighbors already mapped to a concept k. If the percentage exceeds the threshold $\phi_{overlap}$, then word w_0 together with its neighbors will be mapped to k. Otherwise they will be mapped to a new concept w_0.

Lexical Chain Construction

The next step is to construct all lexical chains in current time-sync comments of video v, so that lagged comments could be calibrated based on lexical chains. A lexical chain l_{ij} comprises a set of triples $l_{ij} = \{(w,t,c)\}$, where w is the actual mentioned word of concept k_i in comment c, t is the timestamp of the comment c. A lexical chain dictionary $D_{lexical\ chain}$ for time-sync comments C of video v: $L_{lexical\ chain} = \{k_1: (l_{11}, l_{12}, l_{13} \ldots), k_2: (l_{21}, l_{22}, l_{23} \ldots), \ldots, k_{|K_C|}: (l_{|K_C|1}, l_{|K_C|2}, l_{|K_C|3} \ldots)\}$, where $k_i \in K_C$ is a concept, and l_{ij} is the jth lexical chain of concept k_i. The algorithm for lexical chain construction is described in Algorithm 1.

Specifically, each comment in C can be either appended to existing lexical chains, or added to new empty lexical chains, based on its temporal distance with existing chains controlled by Maximum silence l_{max}.

Note that word senses in the lexical chains constructed here are not disambiguated as most traditional algorithms do. Nevertheless, we argue that lexical chains are still useful, since our concept mapping is constructed from time-sync comments in its natural order, a progressively semantic continuity that naturally reinforces similar word senses for temporally close comments. This semantic continuity together with global word embedding ensures that our concept mapping is valid in most cases.

Algorithm 1 Lexical Chain Construction

```
Input time-sync comments C. Word-to-concept
mapping F. Maximum silence l_max.
Output A dictionary of lexical chains
L_lexical chain.
Initialize L_lexical chain ← {}
for each c in C do
    t_current ← t_c
    for each word in c do
        k ← F(word)
        if k in L_lexical chain then
            chains ← L_lexical chain(k)
            t_previous ← t_chains[last]
            if t_current − t_previous ≤ l_max then
                chains[last] ← chains[last] ∪ c
            else
                chains ← chains ∪ {c}
            end if
        else
            L_lexical chain(k) ← {{c}}
        end if
    end for
end for
return L_lexical chain
```

Table 1. Lexical Chain Construction.

Comment Lag-Calibration

Now given constructed lexical chain dictionary $L_{lexical\ chain}$, we can calibrate the comments in C based on their lexical chains. From our observation, the first comment about one shot usually occurs within the shot, while the rest may not be the case. Therefore, we calibrate the timestamp of each comment to the timestamp of first element of the lexical chain it belongs to. Among all the lexical chains (concepts) a comment belongs to, we pick the one with highest score $score_{k,c}$. $Score_{k,c}$ is computed as the sum frequency of each word in the chain weighted by its logarithm global frequency $\log(D(w).count)$. Therefore, each comment will be assigned to its most semantically important lexical-chain (concept) for calibration. The algorithm for the calibration is described in Algorithm 2.

Note that if there are multiple consecutive shots

```
Algorithm 2 Lag-Calibration of Time-Sync Comments

Input time-sync comments C. Word-to-concept
mapping   F.   Lexical   chain   dictionary
L_lexical chain. Word-embedding dictionary D.
Output Lag-calibrated time-sync comments C'.
Initialize C' ← C
for each c in C' do
    chain_best,c ← {}
    score_best,c ← 0
    for each word in c do
        k ← F(word)
        chain_k,c ← L_lexical chain(k)[c]
        score_k,c ← 0
        for (w, t, c) in chain do
            N(w) ← D(w). count
            score_k,c ← score_k,c + 1/log(N(w))
        end for
        if score_k,c > score_best then
            chain_best,c ← chain_k,c
        end if
    end for
    t_c ← t_chain_best,c[first]
end for
return C'
```

Table 2. Lag-Calibration of Time-Sync Comments.

$\{s_1, s_2, \ldots, s_m\}$ with comments of similar contents, our lag-calibration method may calibrate many comments in shots $s_2, s_3, \ldots, s_m$ to the timestamp of the first shot s_1, if these comments are connected via lexical chains from shot s_1. This is not necessarily a bad thing since we hope to avoid selecting redundant consecutive highlight shots and leave opportunity for other candidate highlights, given a fixed compression ratio.

Shot Importance Scoring

In this section, we first segment comments by shots of equal temporal length l_{scene}, then we model shot importance. Then highlights could be detected based on shot importance.

A shot's importance is modeled to be impacted by two factors: comment concentration and commenting intensity. For comment concentration, as mentioned earlier, both concept and emotional concentration may contribute to highlight detection. For example, a group of concept-concentrated comments like "the background music/bgm/soundtrack of this shot is classic/inspiring/the best" may be an indicator of a

highlight related to memorable background music. Meanwhile, comments such as "this plot is so funny/hilarious/lmao/lol/2333" may suggest a single-emotion concentrated highlight. Therefore, we combine these two concentrations in our model. First, we define emotional concentration $C_{emotion}$ of shot s based on time-sync comments C_S given emotional lexicon E as follows:

$$C_{emotion}(C_S, s) = \frac{1}{-\sum_{e=1}^{5} p_e \cdot \log(p_e)} \quad (2)$$

$$p_e = \frac{|\{w | w \in C_S \wedge w \in E(e)\}|}{|C_S|} \quad (3)$$

Here we calculate the reverse of entropy of probabilities of five emotions within a shot as emotion concentration. Then we define topical concentration C_{topic}:

$$C_{topic}(C_S, s) = \frac{1}{-\sum_{k=1}^{|K_{C_S}|} p_k \cdot \log(p_k)} \quad (4)$$

$$p_k = \frac{\sum_{w \in C_S \wedge F(w)=k \wedge w \notin E} n_w / \log(N_w)}{\sum_{k \in K(C_S)} \sum_{w \in C_S \wedge F(w)=k \wedge w \notin E} n_w / \log(N_w)} \quad (5)$$

where we calculate the reverse of entropy of all concepts within a shot as topic concentration. The probability of each concept k is determined by sum frequencies of its mentioned words weighted by their global frequencies, and divided by those values of all words in the shot.

Now the comment importance $\mathcal{I}_{comment}(C_S, s)$ of shot s can be defined as:

$$\mathcal{I}_{comment}(s) = \lambda \cdot C_{emotion}(C_S, s) + (1 - \lambda) \cdot C_{topic}(C_S, s) \quad (6)$$

where λ is a hyper-parameter, controlling the balance between emotion and concept concentration.

Finally, we define the overall importance of shot as:

$$\mathcal{I}(C_S, s) = \mathcal{I}_{comment}(C_S, s) \cdot \log(|C_S|) \quad (7)$$

Where $|C_S|$ is the length for all time-sync comments in shot s, which is a straightforward yet effective indicator of comment intensity per shot.

Now the problem of highlight detection can be modeled as a maximization problem:

$$Maximize \quad \sum_{s=1}^{N} \mathcal{I}(C_S, s) \cdot x_S \quad (8)$$

$$Subjective\ to \quad \begin{cases} \sum_{x=1}^{N} x_S \leq \tau_{highlight} \cdot N \\ x_s \in \{0,1\} \end{cases}$$

5 Video Highlight Summarization

Given a set of detected highlight shots $S(v) = \{s_1, s_2, s_3, \ldots, s_n\}$ of video v, each with all the lag-calibrated comments C_S of that shot, we are attempting to generate summaries $A(v) = \{I_1, I_2, I_3, \ldots, I_n\}$ so that $I_s \subset C_s$ with compression ratio $\tau_{summary}$ and I_s is as close to ground truth as possible.

We propose a simple but very effective summarization model, an improvement over SumBasic (Nenkova & Vanderwende, 2005) with emotion and concept mapping and two-level updating mechanism.

In the modified SumBasic, instead of only down-sampling the probabilities of words in a selected sentence to prevent redundancy, we down-sample the probabilities of both words and their mapped concepts for re-weighting each comment. This two-level updating mechanism could: (1) impose a penalty for sentences with semantically similar words to be selected; (2) still select a sentence with word already in the summary if this word occurs much more frequently. In addition, we use a parameter *emotion bias* $b_{emotion}$ to weight words and concepts when computing their probabilities, so that frequencies of emotional words and concepts will increase by $b_{emotion}$ compared to non-emotional words and concepts.

6 Experiment

In this section, we conduct experiments on large real datasets for highlight detection and summarization. We will describe the data collection process, evaluation metrics, benchmarks and experiment results.

6.1 Data

In this section, we describe the datasets collected and constructed in our experiments. All datasets and codes will be made publicly available on Github[2].

Crowdsourced Time-sync Comment Corpus

To train the word-embedding described in 4.1.1, we have collected a large corpus of time-sync comment from Bilibli[3], a content sharing website in China with time-sync comments. The corpus contains 2,108,746 comments, 15,179,132 tokens, 91,745 unique tokens, from 6,368 long videos. Each comment has 7.20 tokens on average.

Before training, each comment is first tokenized using Chinse word tokenization package Jieba[4]. Repeating characters in words such as

---

[2] https://github.com/ChanningPing/VideoHighlightDetection
[3] https://www.bilibili.com/
[4] https://github.com/fxsjy/jieba

"233333", "66666", "哈哈哈哈" are replaced with two same characters.

The word-embedding is trained using word2vec (Goldberg & Levy, 2014) with the skip-gram model. Number of embedding dimensions is 300, window size is 7, down-sampling rate is 1e-3, words with frequency lower than 3 times are discarded.

Emotion Lexicon Construction

After the word-embedding is trained, we manually select emotional words belonging to the five basic categories from the 500 most-frequent words in the word-embedding. Then we expand the emotion seeds iteratively using algorithm 1. After each

	Happy	Sad	Fear	Anger	Surprise
Seeds	17	13	21	14	19
All	157	235	258	284	226

Table 3. Number of Initial and Expanded Emotion Words.

expansion iteration, we also manually examine the expanded lexicon and remove inaccurate words to prevent the concept-drift effect, and use the filtered expanded seeds for expansion in next round. The minimum overlap $\gamma_{overlap}$ is set to be 0.05, and minimum similarity sim_{min} is set to be 0.6. The selection of $\gamma_{overlap}$ and sim_{min} is selected based on grid search in the range of [0,1]. The number of words for each emotion initially and after final expansion are listed in Table 3.

Video Highlights Data

To evaluate our highlight-detection algorithm, we have constructed a ground-truth dataset. Our ground-truth dataset takes advantage of user-uploaded mixed-clips about a specific video on Bilibli. Mixed-clips are a collage of video highlights by the user's own preferences. Then we take the most-voted highlights as ground-truth for a video.

The dataset contains 11 videos of 1333 minutes in length, with 75,653 time-sync comments in total. For each video, 3~4 video mix-clips about this video are collected from Bilibili. Shots that occur in at least 2 of all the mix-clips are considered as ground-truth highlights. All ground-truth highlights are mapped to the original video timeline, and the start and end time of the highlight are recorded as ground-truth. The mix-clips are selected based on the following heuristics: (1) The mixed-clips are searched on Bilibli using the keywords "video title + mixed clips"; (2) The mixed-clips are sorted by play times in descending order; (3) The mix-clip should be mainly about highlights of the video, not a plot-by-plot summary or gist; (4) The mix-clip should be under 10 minutes; (5) The mix-clip should contain a mix of several highlight shots instead of only one.

On average, each video has 24.3 highlight shots. The mean shot length of highlights is 27.79 seconds, while the mode is 8 and 10 seconds (frequency=19).

Highlights Summarization Data

We also construct a highlight-summarization (labeling) dataset of the 11 videos. For each highlight shot with its comments, we ask annotators to construct a summary of these comments by extracting as many comments as they see necessary. The rules of thumb are: (1) Comments of the same meaning will not be selected more than once; (2) The most representative comment for similar comments is selected; (3) If a comment stands out on its own, and is irrelevant to the current discussion, it will be discarded.

For 11 videos of 267 highlights, each highlight has on average 3.83 comments as its summary.

6.2 Evaluation Metrics

In this section, we introduce evaluation metrics for highlight-detection and summarization.

Video Highlight Detection Evaluation

For the evaluation of video highlight detection, we need to define what is a "hit" between a highlight candidate and reference. A rigid definition would be a perfect match of beginnings and ends between candidate and reference highlights. However, this is too harsh for any models. A more tolerant definition would be whether there is an overlap between a candidate and reference highlight. However, this will still underestimate model performance since users' selection of beginning and end of a highlight can be quite arbitrary some times. Instead, we propose a "hit" with relaxation ε between a candidate h and the reference $\widehat{H}$ as follows:

$$hit_\varepsilon(h,\widehat{H}) = \begin{cases} 1, & \exists \widehat{h} \in \widehat{H} : (s_h, e_h) \cap (s_{\widehat{h}} - \varepsilon, e_{\widehat{h}} + \varepsilon) \notin \emptyset \\ 0, & otherwise \end{cases} \tag{9}$$

Where s_h, e_h is the start time and end time of highlight h, and ε is the relaxation length of reference set $\widehat{H}$. Further, the precision, recall and F-1 measure can be defined as:

$$Precision(H,\widehat{H}) = \frac{\sum_{h=1}^{|H|} hit(h,\widehat{H})}{|H|} \tag{10}$$

$$Recall(H,\widehat{H}) = \frac{\sum_{\widehat{h}=1}^{|\widehat{H}|} hit(\widehat{h},H)}{|\widehat{H}|} \tag{11}$$

$$F1(H,\widehat{H}) = \frac{2 \cdot Precision(H,\widehat{H}) \cdot Recall(H,\widehat{H})}{Precision(H,\widehat{H}) + Recall(H,\widehat{H})} \tag{12}$$

In present study, we set the relaxation length to be 5 seconds. Also, the length for a candidate highlight is set to be 15 seconds.

Video Highlight Summarization Evaluation

We use ROUGE-1 and ROUGE-2 (C.-Y. Lin, 2004) as recall of candidate summary for evaluation:

$$ROUGE\text{-}n(C,R) = \frac{\sum_{\widehat{S} \in R} \sum_{n\text{-gram} \in \widehat{S}} Count_{match}(n\text{-}gram)}{\sum_{\widehat{S} \in R} \sum_{n\text{-gram} \in \widehat{S}} Count(n\text{-}gram)} \tag{13}$$

We use BLEU-1 and BLEU-2 (Papineni, Roukos, Ward, & Zhu, 2002) as precision. We choose BLEU for two reasons. First, a naïve precision metric will be biased for shorter comments, and BLEU can compensate this with the BP product factor:

$$BLEU\text{-}n(C, R) = BP \cdot \frac{\sum_{S \in C} \sum_{n\text{-gram} \in S} Count_{1V1-match}(n\text{-}gram)}{\sum_{S \in C} \sum_{n\text{-gram} \in S} Count(n\text{-}gram)} \tag{14}$$

$$BP = \begin{cases} 1, & if\ |C| > |R| \\ e^{(1-|R|/|C|)}, & if\ |C| \leq |R| \end{cases}$$

Where C is the candidate summary and R is the reference summary. Second, while reference summary contains no redundancy, candidate summary could falsely select multiple comments that are very similar and match to the same keywords in reference. In such case, the precision is extremely overestimated. BLEU will only count the match one-by-one, namely the number of match of a word will be the minimum frequencies in candidate and reference.

Finally, the F-1 measure can be defined as:

$$F1\text{-}n(C,R) = \frac{2 \cdot BLEU\text{-}n(C, R) \cdot ROUGE\text{-}n(C,R)}{BLEU\text{-}n(C, R) + ROUGE\text{-}n(C,R)} \tag{15}$$

6.3 Benchmark methods

Benchmarks for Video Highlight Detection

For highlight detection, we provide comparisons of different combinations of our model with three benchmarks:

- **Random-selection.** We select highlight shots randomly from all shots of a video.
- **Uniform-selection.** We select highlight shots at equal intervals.

- **Spike-selection**. We select those highlight shots who have the most number of comments within the shot.
- **Spike+E+T**. This is our method taking into consideration of emotion and topic concentration without the lag-calibration step.
- **Spike+L**. This is our method with only the lag-calibration step without taking into consideration of content concentration.
- **Spike+L+E+T**. This is our full model.

Benchmarks for Video Highlight Summarization

For highlight summarization, we provide comparisons of our method with five benchmarks:

- **SumBasic.** Summarization that exclusively exploits frequency for summary construction (Nenkova & Vanderwende, 2005) .
- **Latent Semantic Analysis (LSA).** Summarization of text based on singular value decomposition (SVD) for latent topic discovery (Steinberger & Jezek, 2004).
- **LexRank**. Graph-based summarization that calculates sentence importance based on the concept of eigenvector centrality in a graph of sentences (Erkan & Radev, 2004).
- **KL-Divergence.** Summarization based on minimization of KL-divergence between summary and source corpus using greedy search (Haghighi & Vanderwende, 2009).
- **Luhn method**. Heuristic summarization that takes into consideration of both word frequency and sentence position in an article (Luhn, 1958).

6.4 Experiment Results

In this section, we report experimental results for highlight detection and highlight summarization.

Results of Highlight Detection

In our highlight detection model, the threshold for cutting a lexical chain l_{max} is set to be 11 seconds, the threshold for concept mapping $\phi_{overlap}$ is set to be 0.5, threshold for concept mapping top_n is set to be 15, and the parameter λ to control balance of emotion and concept concentration is set to be 0.9. A parameter analysis is provided in section 7.

The comparisons of precision, recall and F1 measures of different combinations of our method and the benchmarks are in Table 4. Our full model (Spike+L+E+T) outperforms all other benchmarks on all metrics. The precision and recall for Random-selection and uniform selection are low since they do not incorporate any structural or content information. Spike-selection improves considerably, since it takes advantage of the comment intensity of a shot. However, not all comment-intensive shots are highlights. For example, comments at the beginning and end of a video are usually high-volume greetings and goodbyes as a courtesy. Also, spike-selection usually condenses highlights on consecutive shots with high-volume comments, while our method could jump and scatter to other less intensive but emotionally or conceptually concentrated shots. This can be observed by the performance of Spike+E+T.

We also observe that lag-calibration (Spike+L) alone improves the performance of Spike-selection considerably, partially confirming our hypothesis that lag-calibration is important in time-sync comment related tasks.

	Precision	Recall	F-1
Random-Selection	0.1578	0.1587	0.1567
Uniform-Selection	0.1775	0.1830	0.1797
Spike-Selection	0.2594	0.2167	0.2321
Spike+E+T	0.2796	0.2357	0.2500
Spike + L	**0.3125**	0.2690	0.2829
Spike+L+E+T	0.3099	**0.3071**	**0.3066**

Table 4. Comparison of Highlight Detection Methods.

Results of Highlight Summarization

In our highlight summarization model, the emotional bias $b_{emotion}$ is set to be 0.3.

The comparisons on 1-gram BLEU, ROUGE and F1 of our method and the benchmarks are in Table 5. Our method outperforms all other methods, especially on ROUGE-1. LSA has lowest BLEU, mainly because LSA favors long and multi-word sentences statistically, however these sentences are not representative in time-sync com-

	BLEU-1	ROUGE-1	F1-1
LSA	0.2382	0.4855	0.3196
SumBasic	0.2854	0.3898	0.3295
KL-divergence	0.3162	0.3848	0.3471
Luhn	0.2770	0.4970	0.3557
LexRank	0.3045	0.4325	0.3574
Our method	**0.3333**	**0.6006**	**0.4287**

Table 5. Comparison of Highlight Summarization Methods (1-Gram).

ments. The SumBasic method also performs relatively poor since it considers semantically related words separately unlike our method that use concepts instead of words.

The comparisons on 2-gram BLUE, ROUGE and F1 of our method and the benchmarks are in Table 6. Our method also outperforms all other methods.

From the results, we believe that it is crucial to perform lag-calibration as well as concept and emotion mapping before summarization of time-sync comment texts. Lag-calibration shrinks prolonged comments to its original shots, preventing inaccurate highlight detection. Concept and emotional mapping works because time-sync comments are usually very short (7.2 tokens on average), the meaning of the comment is usually concentrated on one or two "central-words" in the

	BLEU-2	ROUGE-2	F1-2
SumBasic	0.1059	0.1771	0.1325
LSA	0.0943	0.2915	0.1425
LexRank	0.1238	0.2351	0.1622
KL-divergence	0.1337	0.2362	0.1707
Luhn	0.1227	0.3176	0.1770
Our method	**0.1508**	**0.3909**	**0.2176**

Table 6. Comparison of Highlight Summarization Methods (2-Gram).

comment. Emotion mapping and concept mapping could effectively prevent the redundancy in the generated summary.

7 Influence of Parameters

7.1 Influence of Shot Length

We analyze the influence of *shot length* on $F1$ score for highlight detection. First from the distribution of highlight shot lengths in golden standards (Figure 2), we observe that most of the highlight shot lengths lie in the range of [0,25] (seconds), with 10 seconds as the mode. Therefore, we plot the $F1$ score of all four models at different shot lengths ranging from 5 to 23 seconds (Figure 3).

From Figure 3 we observe that (1) our method (Spike+L+E+T) consistently outperforms the other benchmarks at varied shot lengths; (2) however, the advantage of our method over Spike method seems to be moderated as the shot length increases. This is reasonable, because as the shot length becomes longer, the number of comments in each

shot accumulates. After certain point, shot with significantly more comments will signify as highlight, no matter of the emotions and topics it contains. However, this may not always be the case. In reality, when there are too few comments, detection totally relying on volume will fail; on the other hand, when there are overwhelming volumes of comments evenly distributed among shots, spikes may not be a good indicator since

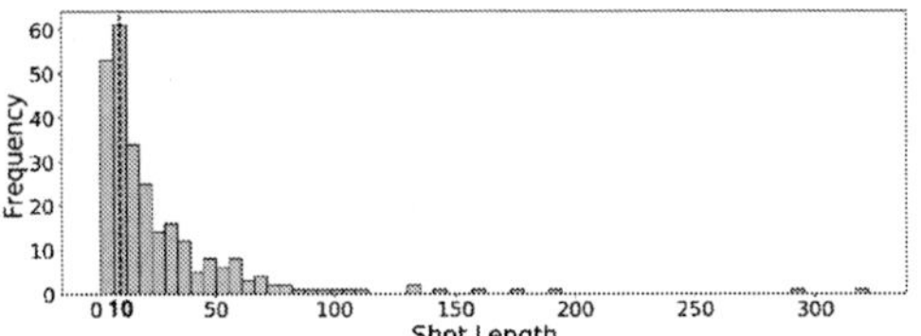

Figure 2.Distribution of Shot Lengths in Highlight Golden Standards.

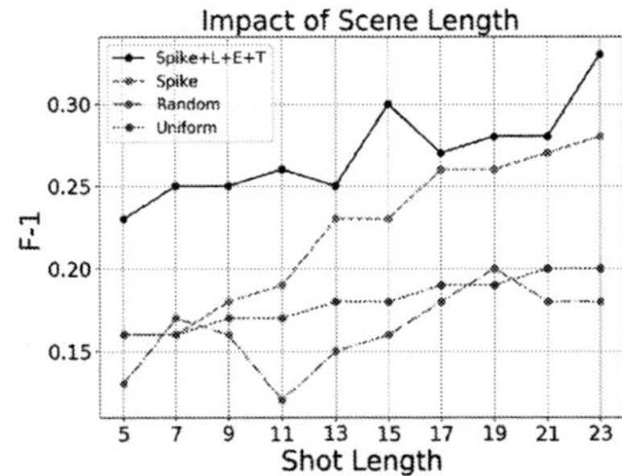

Figure 3.Influence of Shot Length on F-1 Scores of Highlight Detection.

every shot has equally large volumes of comments now. Moreover, most highlights in reality are below 15 seconds, and Figure 3 shows that our method could detect highlights more accurately at such finer level.

7.2 Parameters for Highlight Detection

We analyze the influence of four parameters on recall for highlight detection: maximum silence for lexical chains l_{max}, the threshold for concept mapping $\phi_{overlap}$, the number of neighbors for concept mapping top_n, and the balance of emotion and concept concentration λ (Figure 4).

From Figure 4, we observe the following: (1) when it comes to lag-calibration, there seems to be an optimal *Max Silence Length*: 11 seconds as the longest blank continuance of a chain for our dataset. This value controls the compactness of a lexical chain. (2) In concept mapping, the *Minimum Overlap with Existing Concepts* controls the threshold for concept-merge, the higher the threshold the more similar the two merged concepts are. The recall increases as overlap increase to a certain point (0.5 in our dataset), and will not improve further after such point. (3) In concept mapping, there seems to be an optimal *Number of Neighbors* for searching (15 in our dataset). (4) The balance between emotion and concept concentration (*lambda*) is more on the emotion side (0.9 in our dataset).

7.3 Parameter for Highlight Summarization

We also analyze the influence of *emotion bias* $b_{emotion}$ on ROGUE-1 and ROGUE-2 for highlight summarization. The results are depicted in Figure 5.

From Figure 5, we observe that when it comes to highlight summarization, emotion plays a moderate role (emotion bias = 0.3). This is less significant than its role in the highlight detection task, where emotion concentration is much more important than concept concentration.

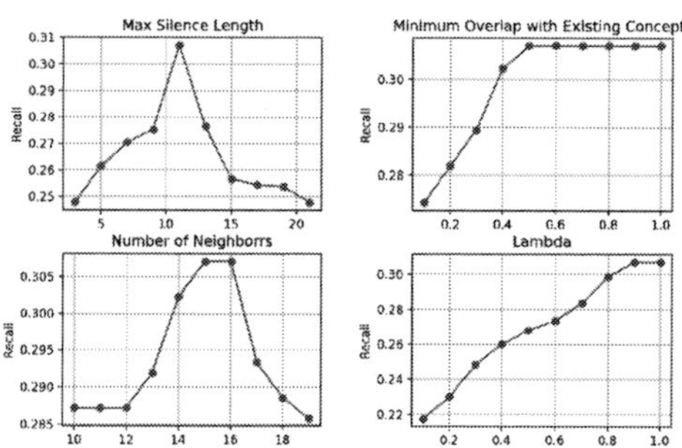

Figure 4. Influence of Parameters for Highlight Detection.

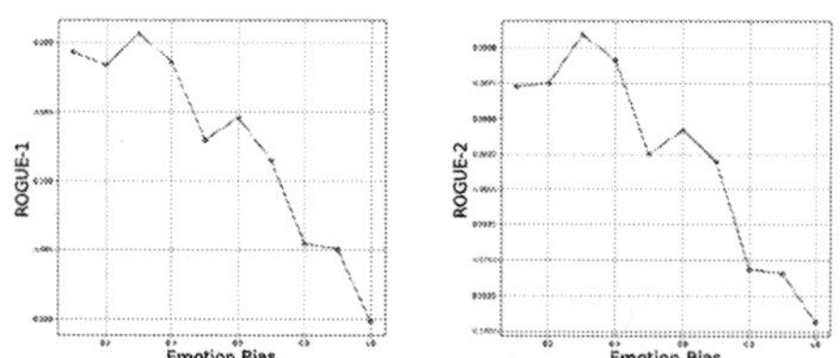

Figure 5. Influence of Parameter for Highlight Summarization.

8 Conclusion

In this paper, we propose a novel unsupervised framework for video highlight detection and summarization based on crowdsourced time-sync comments. For highlight detection, we develop a lag-calibration technique that shrinks lagged

comments back to their original scenes based on concept-mapped lexical-chains. Moreover, video highlights are detected by scoring of comment intensity and concept-emotion concentration in each shot. For highlight summarization, we propose a two-level SumBasic that updates word and concept probabilities at the same time in each iterative sentence selection. In the future, we plan to integrate multiple sources of information for highlight detection, such as video meta-data, audience profiles, as well as low-level features of multiple modalities through video-processing.

References

Barzilay, R., & Elhadad, M. (1999). Using lexical chains for text summarization. Advances in automatic text summarization, 111-121.

Ehren, R. (2017). Literal or idiomatic? Identifying the reading of single occurrences of German multiword expressions using word embeddings. Proceedings of the Student Research Workshop at the 15th Conference of the European Chapter of the Association for Computational Linguistics, 103–112.

Ekman, P. (1992). An argument for basic emotions. Cognition & emotion, 6(3-4), 169-200.

Erkan, G., & Radev, D. R. (2004). Lexrank: Graphbased lexical centrality as salience in text summarization. Journal of Artificial Intelligence Research, 22, 457-479.

Goldberg, Y., & Levy, O. (2014). word2vec explained: Deriving mikolov et al.'s negativesampling word-embedding method. arXiv preprint arXiv:1402.3722.

Haghighi, A., & Vanderwende, L. (2009). Exploring content models for multi-document summarization. Paper presented at the Proceedings of Human Language Technologies: The 2009 Annual Conference of the North American Chapter of the Association for Computational Linguistics.

Hanjalic, A., & Xu, L.-Q. (2005). Affective video content representation and modeling. IEEE transactions on multimedia, 7(1), 143-154.

Hirst, G., & St-Onge, D. (1998). Lexical chains as representations of context for the detection and correction of malapropisms. WordNet: An electronic lexical database, 305, 305-332.

Ikeda, A., Kobayashi, A., Sakaji, H., & Masuyama, S. (2015). Classification of comments on nico nico douga for annotation based on referred contents. Paper presented at the Network-Based Information Systems (NBiS), 2015 18th International Conference on.

Lin, C., Lin, C., Li, J., Wang, D., Chen, Y., & Li, T. (2012). Generating event storylines from microblogs. Paper presented at the Proceedings of the 21st ACM international conference on Information and knowledge management.

Lin, C.-Y. (2004). Rouge: A package for automatic evaluation of summaries. Paper presented at the Text summarization branches out: Proceedings of the ACL-04 workshop.

Lin, K.-S., Lee, A., Yang, Y.-H., Lee, C.-T., & Chen, H. H. (2013). Automatic highlights extraction for drama video using music emotion and human face features. Neurocomputing, 119, 111-117.

Luhn, H. P. (1958). The automatic creation of literature abstracts. IBM Journal of research and development, 2(2), 159-165.

Lv, G., Xu, T., Chen, E., Liu, Q., & Zheng, Y. (2016). Reading the Videos: Temporal Labeling for Crowdsourced Time-Sync Videos Based on Semantic Embedding. Paper presented at the AAAI.

Morris, J., & Hirst, G. (1991). Lexical cohesion computed by thesaural relations as an indicator of the structure of text. Computational linguistics, 17(1), 21-48.

Nenkova, A., & Vanderwende, L. (2005). The impact of frequency on summarization. Microsoft Research, Redmond, Washington, Tech. Rep. MSR-TR-2005, 101.

Ngo, C.-W., Ma, Y.-F., & Zhang, H.-J. (2005). Video summarization and scene detection by graph modeling. IEEE Transactions on Circuits and Systems for Video Technology, 15(2), 296-305.

Papineni, K., Roukos, S., Ward, T., & Zhu, W.-J. (2002). BLEU: a method for automatic evaluation of machine translation. Paper presented at the Proceedings of the 40th annual meeting on association for computational linguistics.

Sakaji, H., Kohana, M., Kobayashi, A., & Sakai, H. (2016). Estimation of Tags via Comments on Nico Nico Douga. Paper presented at the Network-Based Information Systems (NBiS), 2016 19th International Conference on.

Shou, L., Wang, Z., Chen, K., & Chen, G. (2013). Sumblr: continuous summarization of evolving tweet streams. Paper presented at the Proceedings of the 36th international ACM SIGIR conference on Research and development in information retrieval.

Sipos, R., Swaminathan, A., Shivaswamy, P., & Joachims, T. (2012). Temporal corpus summarization using submodular word coverage. Paper presented at the Proceedings of the 21st ACM international conference on Information and knowledge management.

Steinberger, J., & Jezek, K. (2004). Using latent semantic analysis in text summarization and summary evaluation. Paper presented at the Proc. ISIM'04.

Tran, T. A., Niederée, C., Kanhabua, N., Gadiraju, U., & Anand, A. (2015). Balancing novelty and salience: Adaptive learning to rank entities for timeline summarization of high-impact events. Paper presented at the Proceedings of the 24th ACM International on Conference on Information and Knowledge Management.

Wu, B., Zhong, E., Tan, B., Horner, A., & Yang, Q. (2014). Crowdsourced time-sync video tagging using temporal and personalized topic modeling. Paper presented at the Proceedings of the 20th ACM SIGKDD international conference on Knowledge discovery and data mining.

Xian, Y., Li, J., Zhang, C., & Liao, Z. (2015). Video Highlight Shot Extraction with Time-Sync Comment. Paper presented at the Proceedings of the 7th International Workshop on Hot Topics in Planet-scale mObile computing and online Social neTworking.

Xu, L., & Zhang, C. (2017). Bridging Video Content and Comments: Synchronized Video Description with Temporal Summarization of Crowdsourced Time-Sync Comments. Paper presented at the Thirty-First AAAI Conference on Artificial Intelligence.

Xu, M., Jin, J. S., Luo, S., & Duan, L. (2008). Hierarchical movie affective content analysis based on arousal and valence features. Paper presented at the Proceedings of the 16th ACM international conference on Multimedia.

Xu, M., Luo, S., Jin, J. S., & Park, M. (2009). Affective content analysis by mid-level representation in multiple modalities. Paper presented at the Proceedings of the First International Conference on Internet Multimedia Computing and Service.

Yan, R., Kong, L., Huang, C., Wan, X., Li, X., & Zhang, Y. (2011). Timeline generation through evolutionary trans-temporal summarization. Paper presented at the Proceedings of the Conference on Empirical Methods in Natural Language Processing.

Yan, R., Wan, X., Otterbacher, J., Kong, L., Li, X., & Zhang, Y. (2011). Evolutionary timeline summarization: a balanced optimization framework via iterative substitution. Paper presented at the Proceedings of the 34th international ACM SIGIR conference on Research and development in Information Retrieval.

Multimedia Summary Generation from Online Conversations: Current Approaches and Future Directions

Enamul Hoque and **Giuseppe Carenini**
University of British Columbia, Canada
{enamul,carenini}@cs.ubc.ca

Abstract

With the proliferation of Web-based social media, asynchronous conversations have become very common for supporting online communication and collaboration. Yet the increasing volume and complexity of conversational data often make it very difficult to get insights about the discussions. We consider combining textual summary with visual representation of conversational data as a promising way of supporting the user in exploring conversations. In this paper, we report our current work on developing visual interfaces that present multimedia summary combining text and visualization for online conversations and how our solutions have been tailored for a variety of domain problems. We then discuss the key challenges and opportunities for future work in this research space.

1 Introduction

Since the rise of social-media, an ever-increasing amount of conversations are generated every day. People engaged in asynchronous conversations such as blogs to exchange ideas, ask questions, and comment on daily life events. Often many people contribute to the discussion, which become very long with hundreds of comments, making it difficult for users to get insights about the discussion (Jones et al., 2004).

To support the user in making sense of human conversations, both the natural language processing (NLP) and information visualization (InfoVis) communities have independently developed different techniques. For example, earlier works on visualizing asynchronous conversations primarily investigated how to reveal the thread structure of a conversation using tree visualization techniques, such as using a mixed-model visualization to show both chronological sequence and reply relationships (Venolia and Neustaedter, 2003), thumbnail metaphor using a sequence of rectangles (Wattenberg and Millen, 2003; Kerr, 2003), and radial tree layout (Pascual-Cid and Kaltenbrunner, 2009). However, such visualizations did not focus on analysing the actual content (i.e., the text) of the conversations.

On the other hand, text mining and summarization methods for conversations perform content analysis of the conversations, such as what topics are covered in a given text conversation (Joty et al., 2013b), along with what opinions the conversation participants have expressed on such topics (Taboada et al., 2011). Once the topics, opinions and conversation structure (e.g., reply-relationships between comments) are extracted, they can be used to summarize the conversations (Carenini et al., 2011).

However, presenting a static/non-interactive textual summary alone is often not sufficient to satisfy the user information needs. Instead, generating a multimedia output that combines text and visualizations can be more effective, because the two can play complementary roles: while visualization can help the user to discover trends and relationship, text can convey key points about the results, by focusing on temporal, causal and evaluative aspects.

In this paper, we present a visual text analytics approach that combines both text and visualization to helps users in understanding and analyzing online conversations. We provide an overview of our approach to multimedia summization of online conversations followed by how our generic solutions have been tailored to specific domain problems (e.g., supporting users of a community question answering forum) . We then discuss further

Proceedings of the Workshop on New Frontiers in Summarization, pages 12–19
Copenhagen, Denmark, September 7, 2017. ©2017 Association for Computational Linguistics

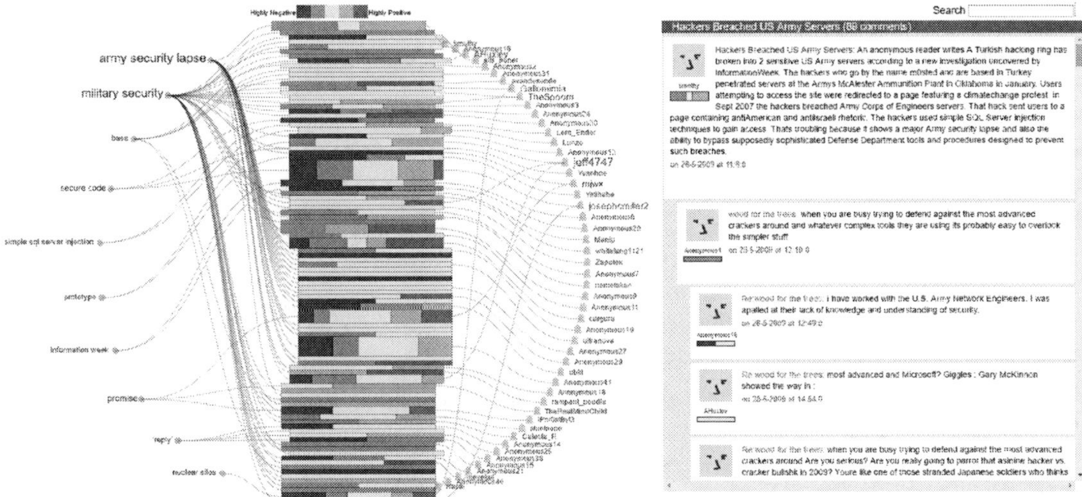

Figure 1: The ConVis interface: The Thread Overview visually represents the whole conversation encoding the thread structure and how the sentiment is ex-pressed for each comment(middle); The topics and authors are arranged circularly around the Thread Overview; and the Conversation View presents the detailed comments in a scrollable list (right).

challenges, open questions, and ideas for future work in the research area of multimedia summarization for online conversations.

2 Multimedia Summarization of Online Conversations

2.1 Our Approach

To generate multimedia summary for online conversation, our primary approach was to apply human-centered design methodologies from the InfoVis literature (Munzner, 2009; Sedlmair et al., 2012) to identify the type of information that needs to be extracted from the conversation as well as to inform the design of the visual encodings and interaction techniques.

Following this approach, we proposed a system that creates a multimedia summary and supports users in exploring a single asynchronous conversation (Hoque and Carenini, 2014, 2015). The underlying topic modeling approach groups the sentences of a blog conversation into a set of topical segments. Then, representative key phrases are assigned to each of these segments (labeling). We adopt a novel topic modeling approach that captures finer level conversation structure in the form of a graph called Fragment Quotation Graph (FQG) (Joty et al., 2013b). All the distinct fragments (both new and quoted) within a conversation are extracted as the nodes of the FQG. Then

the edges are created to represent the replying relationship between fragments. If a comment does not contain any quotation, then its fragments are linked to the fragments of the comment to which it replies, capturing the original 'reply-to' relation.

The FQG is exploited in both topic segmentation and labeling. In segmentation, each path of the FQG is considered as a separate conversation that is independently segmented (Morris and Hirst, 1991). Then, all the resulting segmentation decisions are consolidated in a final segmentation for the whole conversation. After that, topic labeling generates keyphrases to describe each topic segment in the conversation. A novel graph based ranking model is applied that intuitively boosts the rank of keyphrases that appear in the initial sentences of the segment, and/or also appear in text fragments that are central in the FQG (see (Joty et al., 2013b) for details).

While developing the system, we started with a user requirement analysis for the domain of blog conversations to derive a set of design principles. Based on these principles, we designed an overview+detail interface, named ConVis that provides a visual overview of a conversation by presenting topics, authors and the thread structure of a conversation (see Figure 1). Furthermore, it provides various interaction techniques such as brushing and highlighting based on multiple facets to support the user in exploring and navigating the conversation.

We performed an informal user evaluation, which provides anecdotal evidence about the effectiveness of ConVis as well as directions for further design. The participants' feedback from the evaluation suggests that ConVis can help the user to identify the topics and opinions expressed in the conversation; supporting the user in finding comments of interest, even if they are buried near the end of the thread. The informal evaluation also reveals that in few cases the extracted topics and opinions are incorrect and/or may not match the mental model and information needs of the user.

In subsequent work, we focused on supporting readers in exploring a collection of conversations related to a given query (Hoque and Carenini, 2016). Exploring topics of interest that are potentially discussed over multiple conversations is a challenging problem, as the volume and complexity of the data increases. To address this challenge, we devised a novel hierarchical topic modeling technique that organizes the topics within a set of conversations into multiple levels, based on their semantic similarity. For this purpose, we extended the topic modeling approach for a single conversation to generate a topic hierarchy from multiple conversations by considering the specific features of conversations. We then designed a visual interface, named MultiConVis that presents the topic hierarchy along with other conversational data, as shown Figure 2. The user can explore the data, starting from a possibly large set of conversations, then narrowing it down to the subset of conversations, and eventually drilling-down to the set of comments belonging to a single conversation.

We evaluated MultiConVis through both case studies with domain experts and a formal user study with regular blog readers. Our case studies demonstrate that the system can be useful in a variety of contexts of use, while the formal user study provides evidence that the MultiConVis interface supports the user's tasks more effectively than traditional interfaces. In particular, all our participants, both in the case studies and in the user study, appear to benefit from the topic hierarchy as well as the high-level overview of the conversations. The user study also shows that the MultiConVis interface is significantly more useful than the traditional interface, enabling the user to find insightful comments from thousands of com-ments, even when they were scattered across multiple conversations, often buried down near the end of the threads. More importantly, MultiConVis was preferred by the majority of the participants over the traditional interface, suggesting the potential value of our approach for combining NLP and InfoVis.

2.2 Applications

Since our visual text analytics systems have been made publicly available, they have been applied and tailored for a variety of domain problems, both in our own work as well as in other research projects. For example, we conducted a design study in the domain of community question answering (CQA) forums, where our generic solutions for combining NLP and InfoVis were simplified and tailored to support information seeking tasks for a user population possibly having low visualization expertise (Hoque et al., 2017). In addition to our work, several other researchers have applied or partially adopted the data abstractions and visual encodings of MultiConVis and ConVis in a variety of domains, ranging from news comments (Riccardi et al., 2015), to online health forums (Kwon et al., 2015), to educational forums (Fu et al., 2017). We now analyze these recent works and discuss similarities and differences with our systems.

News comments: SENSEI[1] is a research project that was funded by the European Union and was conducted in collaboration with four leading universities and two industry partners in Europe. The main goal of this project was to develop summarization and analytics technology to help users make sense of human conversation streams from diverse media channels, ranging from comments generated for news articles to customer-support conversations in call centers.

After the research work on developing ConVis was published and the tool was made publicly available, the SENSEI project researchers expressed their interest in adopting our system. Their primary objective was to evaluate their text summarization and analytics technology by visualizing the results with ConVis, with the final goal of detecting end-user improvements in task performance and productivity.

In their version of the interface[2], they kept the main features of ConVis, namely the topics, au-

---

[1] www.sensei-conversation.eu

[2] A video demo of their version of the interface is available

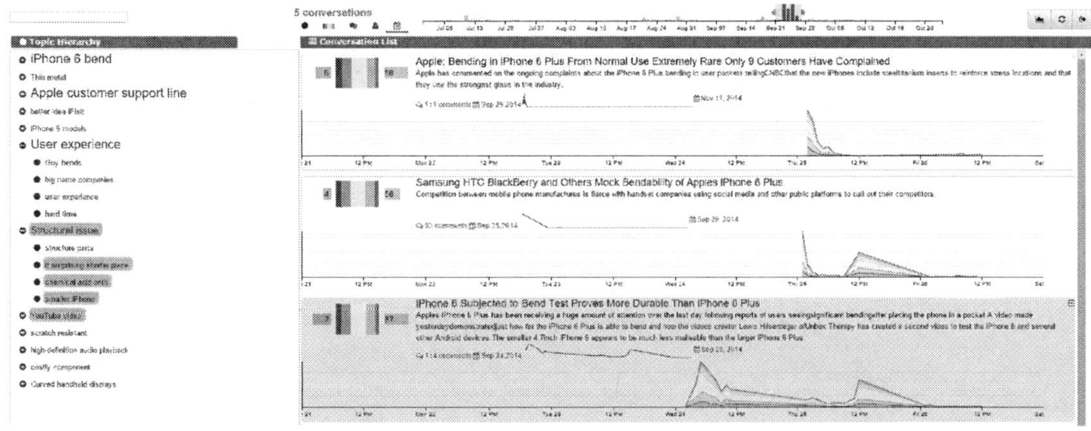

Figure 2: The MultiConVis interface. Here, the user filtered out some conversations from the list using the Timeline located at the top, and then hovered on a conversation item (highlighted row in the right). As a consequence, the related topics from the Topic Hierarchy were highlighted (left).

thors, and thread overview; and then added some new features to show text analytics results specific to their application, as shown in Figure 3 (Riccardi et al., 2015). In particular, within the thread overview, for each comment they encoded how much this comment agrees or disagrees with the original article, instead of showing the sentiment distribution of that comment. Another interactive feature they introduced was that clicking on an author element results in showing the predicted mood of that author (using five different mode types, i.e., amused, satisfied, sad, indignant, and disappointed). Furthermore, they added a summary view that shows a textual summary of the whole conversation in addition to the detailed comments. Finally, they introduced some new interactive features, such as zooming and filtering to deal with conversations that are very long with several hundreds of comments.

Online health forums: Kwon et al. developed VisOHC (Kwon et al., 2015), a visual analytics system designed for administrators of online health communities (OHCs). In this paper, they discuss similarities and differences between VisOHC and ConVis. For instance, similar to the thread overview in ConVis, they represented the comments of a conversation using a sequence of rectangles and used the color encoding within those rectangles to represent sentiment (see Figure 4). However, they encoded additional data in order to support the specific domain goals and tasks of OHC administrators. For instance, they

used a scatter plot to encode the similarities between discussion threads and a histogram view to encode various statistical measures regarding the selected threads, as shown in Figure 4.

Mamykina et al. analyzed how users in online health communities collectively make sense of the vast amount of information and opinions within an online diabetes forum, called TuDiabetes (Mamykina et al., 2015). Their study found that members of TuDiabetes often value a multiplicity of opinions rather than consensus. From their study, they concluded that in order to facilitate the collective sensemaking of such diversity of opinions, a visual text analytics tool like ConVis could be very effective. They also mentioned that in addition to topic modeling and sentiment analysis, some other text analysis methods related to their health forum under study, such as detection of agreement and topic shift in conversation, should be devised and incorporated into tools like ConVis.

Educational forums: More recently, Fu et al. presented iForum, an interactive visual analytics system for helping instructors in understanding the temporal patterns of student activities and discussion topics in a MOOC forum (Fu et al., 2017). They mentioned that while the design of iForum has been inspired by tools such as ConVis, they have tailored their interface to the domain-specific problems of MOOC forums. For instance, like ConVis, their system provides an overview of topics and discussion threads, however, they focused more on temporal trends of an entire forum, as op-

at www.youtube.com/watch?v=XIMP0cuiZIQ

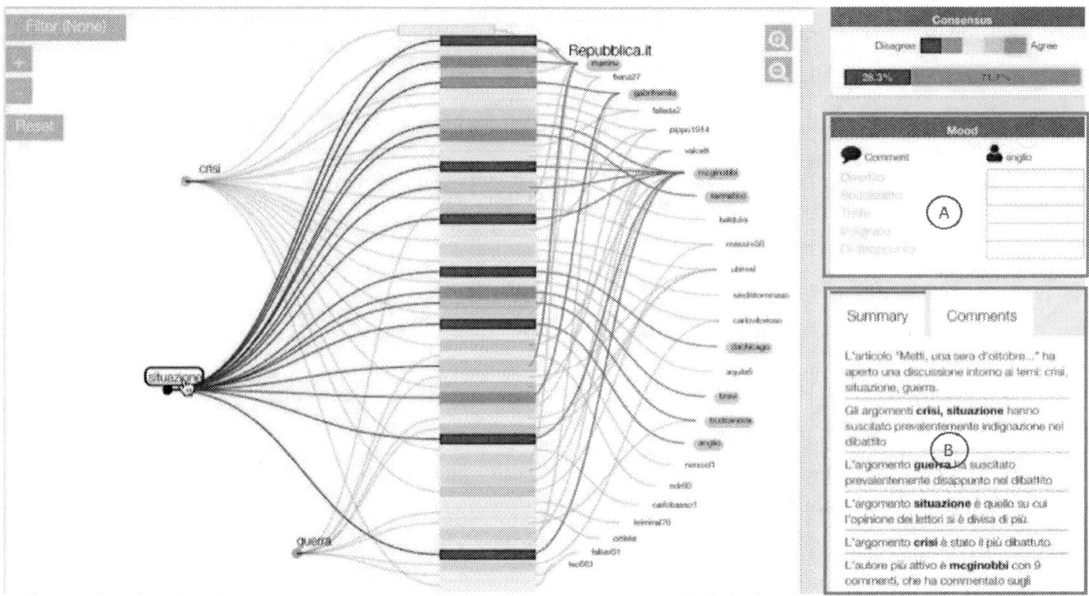

Figure 3: A screenshot of the modified ConVis interface used in the SENSEI project. The interface shows the results of some additional text analysis methods, namely the degree of agreement/disagreement between a comment and the original article (within the thread overview), the predicted mood of the corresponding author (A), and the textual summary of the conversation (B) (Riccardi et al., 2015).

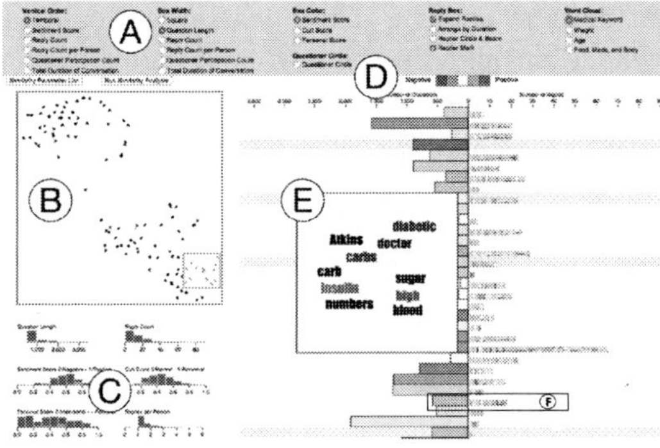

Figure 4: VisOHC visually represents the comments of a conversation using a sequence of rectangles (F), where color within each rectangle represents sentiment expressed in a comment. Additionally it shows a scatter plot (B), and a histogram view (C) (The figure is adapted from (Kwon et al., 2015)).

posed to an individual conversation or a set of conversations related to a specific query.

3 Challenges and Future Directions

While our approach to combining NLP and Info-Vis to generate multimedia summaries has made some significant progress in supporting the exploration and analysis of online conversations, it also raises further challenges, open questions, and ideas for future work. Here we discuss the key challenges and opportunities for future research.

How can we provide more high-level summary to users? In our current systems, we used the results from topic modeling which can be viewed as crud summary of conversations, because each topic is simply summarized by a phrase label and the labels are not combined in a coherent discourse. Based on the tasks of real users we identified the need for higher level summarization. For instance, users may benefit from a more high-level abstract human-like summary of conversations, where the content extracted from the conversations is organized in a sequence of coherent sentences.

Similarly, during our evaluations some users found the current sentiment analysis insufficient in revealing whether a comment is supporting/opposing a preceding one. It seems that opinion seeking tasks (e.g., 'why people were supporting or opposing an opinion?') would require the reader to know the argumentation flow within the conversation, namely the rhetorical structure of each comment (Joty et al., 2013a) and how these structures are linked to each other.

An early work (Yee and Hearst, 2005) attempted to organize the comments using a treemap like layout, where the parent comment is placed on top as a text block and the space below the parent node is divided between supporting and opposing statements. We plan to follow this idea in ConVis, but incorporating a higher level discourse relation analysis of the conversations along with the detection of controversial topics (Allen et al., 2014).

How can we scale up our systems for big data? As social media conversational data is growing in size and complexity at an unprecedented rate, new challenges have emerged from both the computational and the visualization perspectives. In particular, we need to address the following aspects of big data, while designing visual text analytics for online conversations.

Volume: Most of the existing visualizations are inadequate to handle very large amounts of raw conversational data. For example, ConVis scales with conversations with hundreds of comments; however, it is unable to deal with a very long conversation consisting of more than a thousand comments. To tackle the scalability issue, we will investigate computational methods for filtering and aggregating comments, as well as devise interactive visualization techniques such as zooming to progressively disclose the data from a high-level overview to low-level details.

Velocity: The systems that we have developed do not process streaming conversations. Yet in many real-world scenarios, conversational data is constantly produced at a high rate, which poses enormous challenges for mining and visualization methods. For instance, immediately after a product is released a business analyst may want to analyze text streams in social media to identify problems or issues, such as whether customers are complaining about a feature of the product. In these cases, timely analysis of the streaming text can be critical for the company's reputation. For this purpose, we aim to investigate how to efficiently mine and summarize streaming conversations (tre, 2017) and how to visualize the extracted information in real time to the user (Keim et al., 2013).

How can we leverage text summarization and visualization techniques to develop advanced storytelling tools for online conversations? Data storytelling has become increasingly popular among InfoVis practitioners such as journalists, who may want to create a visualization from social media conversations and integrate it into their narratives to convey critical insights. Unfortunately, even sophisticated visualization tools like Tableau [3] offer only limited support for authoring data stories, requiring users to manually create textual annotations and organize the sequence of visualizations. More importantly, they do not provide methods for processing the unstructured or semi-structured data generated in online conversations.

In this context, we aim to investigate how to leverage NLP and InfoVis techniques for online conversations to create effective semi-automatic authoring tools for data storytelling. More specifically, we need to devise methods for generating and organizing the summary content from online conversations and choosing the sequence in which such content is delivered to users. To this end, a starting point could be to investigate current research on narrative visualization (Segel and Heer, 2010; Hullman and Diakopoulos, 2011).

How can we support the user in tailoring our systems to a specify conversational genre, a specific domain, or tasks? In the previous section, we already discussed how our current visual text analytics systems have been applied and tailored to various domains. However, in these systems, the user does not have flexibility in terms of the choice of the datasets and the available interaction techniques. Therefore, it may take a significant amount of programming effort to re-design the interface for a specific conversational domain. For example, when we tailored our system to a community question answering forum with a specific user population in mind, we had to spend a considerable amount of time modifying the existing code in order to re-design the interface for the new conversational genre.

In this context, can we enable a large number of users - not just those who have strong programming skills to author visual interfaces for exploring conversations in a new domain? To answer this question, we need to research how to construct an interactive environment that supports custom visualization design for different domains without requiring the user to write any code. Such interactive environment would allow the user to have more control over the data to be represented and the interactive techniques to be supported.

---

[3] www.tableau.com

To this end, we will investigate current research on general purpose visual authoring tools such as Lyra (Satyanarayan and Heer, 2014) and IVisDesigner (Ren et al., 2014), which provide custom visualization authoring environments, to understand how we can build a similar tool, but specifically for conversational data.

How can the system adapt to a diverse range of users? A critical challenge of introducing a new visualization is that the effectiveness of visualization techniques can be impacted by different user characteristics, such as visualization expertise, cognitive abilities, and personality traits (Conati et al., 2014). Unfortunately, most previous work has focused on finding individual differences for simple visualizations only, such as bar and radar graphs (Toker et al., 2012). It is still unknown how individual differences might impact the reading ability of multimedia summary that requires coordinations between text and visualization. In this regard, we need to examine what aspects of a multimedia output are impacted by user characteristics and how to dynamically adapt the system to such characteristics.

4 Conclusions

Multimedia summarization of online conversations is a promising approach for supporting the exploration of online conversations. In this paper, we present our current work on generating multimedia summaries combining text and visualization. We also discuss how our research has influenced the subsequent work in this research space. We believe that by addressing the critical challenges and research questions posed in the paper, we will able to support users in understanding online conversations more efficiently and effectively.

References

2017. TREC real-time summarization track (accessed June 05, 2017). http://trecrts.github.io/.

Kelsey Allen, Giuseppe Carenini, and Raymond T Ng. 2014. Detecting disagreement in conversations using pseudo-monologic rhetorical structure. In *Proceedings of the Empirical Methods on Natural Language Processing (EMNLP)*.

Giuseppe Carenini, Gabriel Murray, and Raymond Ng. 2011. *Methods for Mining and Summarizing Text Conversations*. Morgan Claypool.

C. Conati, G. Carenini, E. Hoque, B. Steichen, and D. Toker. 2014. Evaluating the impact of user characteristics and different layouts on an interactive visualization for decision making. *Computer Graphics Forum (Proceedings of EuroVis)* 33(3):371–380.

Siwei Fu, Jian Zhao, Weiwei Cui, and Huamin Qu. 2017. Visual analysis of MOOC forums with iForum. *IEEE Transactions on Visualization and Computer Graphics (Prooceedings of VAST)* 23(1):201–210.

Enamul Hoque and Giuseppe Carenini. 2014. ConVis: A visual text analytic system for exploring blog conversations. *Computer Graphics Forum (Proceedings EuroVis)* 33(3):221–230.

Enamul Hoque and Giuseppe Carenini. 2015. ConVisIT: Interactive topic modeling for exploring asynchronous online conversations. In *Proceedings ACM conference on Intelligent User Interfaces (IUI)*. pages 169–180.

Enamul Hoque and Giuseppe Carenini. 2016. MultiConVis: A visual text analytics system for exploring a collection of online conversations. In *Proceedings of the ACM Conference on Intelligent User Interfaces (IUI)*. pages 96–107.

Enamul Hoque, Shafiq Joty, Màrquez Lluís, and Giuseppe Carenini. 2017. CQAVis: Visual text analytics for community question answering. In *Proceedings of the ACM conference on Intelligent User Interfaces (IUI)*. pages 161–172.

Jessica Hullman and Nick Diakopoulos. 2011. Visualization rhetoric: Framing effects in narrative visualization. *IEEE Transactions on Visualization and Computer Graphics (Proceedings of InfoVis)* 17(12):2231–2240.

Quentin Jones, Gilad Ravid, and Sheizaf Rafaeli. 2004. Information overload and the message dynamics of online interaction spaces: A theoretical model and empirical exploration. *Information Systems Research* 15(2):194–210.

Shafiq Joty, Giuseppe Carenini, Raymond Ng, and Yashar Mehdad. 2013a. Combining intra-and multi-sentential rhetorical parsing for document-level discourse analysis. In *Proceedings of the Annual Meeting on Association for Computational Linguistics*.

Shafiq Joty, Giuseppe Carenini, and Raymond T Ng. 2013b. Topic segmentation and labeling in asynchronous conversations. *Journal of Artificial Intelligence Research* 47:521–573.

Daniel A Keim, Miloš Krstajic, Christian Rohrdantz, and Tobias Schreck. 2013. Real-time visual analytics of text data streams. *IEEE Computer* 46(7):47–55.

Bernard Kerr. 2003. Thread arcs: An email thread visualization. In *IEEE Symposium on Information Visualization*. pages 211–218.

Bum Kwon, Sung-Hee Kim, Sukwon Lee, Jaegul Choo, and Ji Yi Jina Huh. 2015. Visohc: Designing visual analytics for online health communities. *IEEE Transactions on Visualization and Computer Graphics* .

Lena Mamykina, Drashko Nakikj, and Noemie Elhadad. 2015. Collective sensemaking in online health forums. In *Proceedings of the ACM Conference on Human Factors in Computing Systems (CHI)*. pages 3217–3226.

Jane Morris and Graeme Hirst. 1991. Lexical cohesion computed by thesaural relations as an indicator of the structure of text. *Computational Linguistics* 17(1):21–48.

Tamara Munzner. 2009. A nested model for visualization design and validation. *Transactions on Visualization and Computer Graphics (Proocedings of InfoVis)* 15(6):921–928.

Victor Pascual-Cid and Andreas Kaltenbrunner. 2009. Exploring asynchronous online discussions through hierarchical visualisation. In *IEEE Conference on Information Visualization*. pages 191–196.

Donghao Ren, Tobias Höllerer, and Xiaoru Yuan. 2014. iVisDesigner: Expressive interactive design of information visualizations. *IEEE Transactions on Visualization and Computer Graphics (Proceedings of InfoVis)* 20(12):2092–2101.

Giuseppe Riccardi, A R Celli Balamurali, Favre Benoit Fabio, Ferrante Carmelo, Adam Funk, Rob Gaizauskas, and Vincenzo Lanzolla. 2015. Report on the summarization views of the sensei prototype. In *Technical report*.

Arvind Satyanarayan and Jeffrey Heer. 2014. Lyra: An interactive visualization design environment 33(3):351–360.

Michael Sedlmair, Miriah Meyer, and Tamara Munzner. 2012. Design study methodology: reflections from the trenches and the stacks. *IEEE Transactions on Visualization and Computer Graphics* 18(12):2431–2440.

Edward Segel and Jeffrey Heer. 2010. Narrative visualization: Telling stories with data. *IEEE Transactions on Visualization and Computer Graphics* 16(6):1139–1148.

Maite Taboada, Julian Brooke, Milan Tofiloski, Kimberly Voll, and Manfred Stede. 2011. Lexicon-based methods for sentiment analysis. *Computational Linguistics* 37(2):267–307.

Dereck Toker, Cristina Conati, Giuseppe Carenini, and Mona Haraty. 2012. Towards adaptive information visualization: on the influence of user characteristics. In *International Conference on User Modeling, Adaptation, and Personalization*. Springer, pages 274–285.

Gina Danielle Venolia and Carman Neustaedter. 2003. Understanding sequence and reply relationships within email conversations: a mixed-model visualization. In *Proceedings of the ACM Conference on Human Factors in Computing Systems (CHI)*. pages 361–368.

Martin Wattenberg and David Millen. 2003. Conversation thumbnails for large-scale discussions. In *Extended Abstract Proceedings of the ACM Conference on Human Factors in Computing Systems (CHI)*. pages 742–743.

Ka-Ping Yee and Marti Hearst. 2005. Content-centered discussion mapping. *Online Deliberation 2005/DIAC-2005* .

Low-Resource Neural Headline Generation

Ottokar Tilk and **Tanel Alumäe**
Department of Software Science, School of Information Technologies,
Tallinn University of Technology, Estonia
`ottokar.tilk@ttu.ee, tanel.alumae@ttu.ee`

Abstract

Recent neural headline generation models have shown great results, but are generally trained on very large datasets. We focus our efforts on improving headline quality on smaller datasets by the means of pre-training. We propose new methods that enable pre-training all the parameters of the model and utilize all available text, resulting in improvements by up to 32.4% relative in perplexity and 2.84 points in ROUGE.

1 Introduction

Neural headline generation (NHG) is the process of automatically generating a headline based on the text of the document using artificial neural networks.

Headline generation is a subtask of text summarization. While a summary may cover multiple documents, generally uses similar style to the summarized document, and consists of multiple sentences, headline, in contrast, covers a single document, is often written in a different style (Headlinese (Mårdh, 1980)), and is much shorter (frequently limited to a single sentence).

Due to shortness and specific style, condensing the the document into a headline often requires the ability to paraphrase which makes this task a good fit for abstractive summarization approaches where neural networks based attentive encoder-decoder (Bahdanau et al., 2015) type of models have recently shown impressive results (e.g., Rush et al. (2015); Nallapati et al. (2016)).

While state-of-the art results have been obtained by training NHG models on large datasets like Gigaword, access to such resources is often not possible, especially when it comes to low-resource languages. In this work we focus on maximizing performance on smaller datasets with different pre-training methods.

One of the reasons to expect pre-training to be an effective way to improve performance on small datasets, is that NHG models are generally trained to generate headlines based on just a few first sentences of the documents (Rush et al., 2015; Shen et al., 2016; Chopra et al., 2016; Nallapati et al., 2016). This leaves the rest of the text unutilized, which can be alleviated by pre-training subsets of the model on full documents. Additionally, the decoder component of NHG models can be regarded as a language model (LM) whose predictions are biased by the external information from the encoder. As a LM it sees only headlines during training, which is a small fraction of text compared to the documents. Supplementing the training data of the decoder with documents via pre-training might enable it to learn more about words and language structure.

Although, some of the previous work has used pre-training before (Nallapati et al., 2016; Alifimoff, 2015), it is not fully explored how much pre-training helps and what is the optimal way to do it. Another problem is, that in previous work only a subset of parameters (usually just embeddings) is pre-trained leaving the rest of the parameters randomly initialized.

The main contributions of this paper are: LM pre-training for fully initializing the encoder and decoder (sections 2.1 and 2.2); combining LM pre-training with distant supervision (Mintz et al., 2009) pre-training using filtered sentences of the documents as noisy targets (i.e. predicting one sentence given the rest) to maximally utilize the entire available dataset and pre-train all the paramters of the NHG model (section 2.3); and analysis of the effect of pre-training different components of the NHG model (section 3.3).

20

Proceedings of the Workshop on New Frontiers in Summarization, pages 20–26
Copenhagen, Denmark, September 7, 2017. ©2017 Association for Computational Linguistics

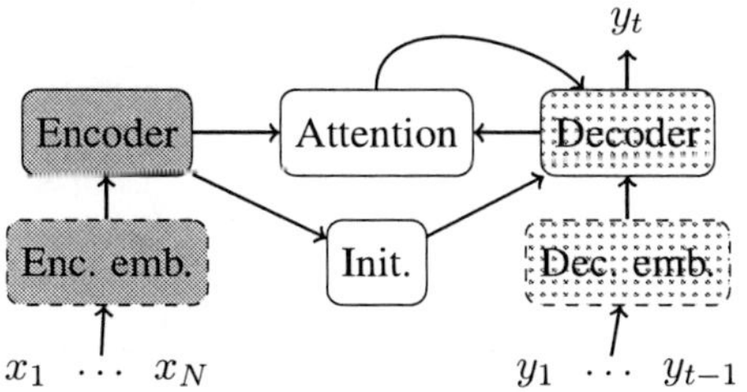

Figure 1: A high level description of the NHG model. The model predicts the next headline word y_t given the words in the document $x_1 \ldots x_N$ and already generated headline words $y_1 \ldots y_{t-1}$.

2 Method

The model that we use follows the architecture described by Bahdanau et al. (2015). Although originally created for neural machine translation, this architecture has been successfully used for NHG (e.g., by Shen et al. (2016); Nallapati et al. (2016) and in a simplified form by Chopra et al. (2016)).

The NHG model consists of: a bidirectional (Schuster and Paliwal, 1997) encoder with gated recurrent units (GRU) (Cho et al., 2014); a uni-directional GRU decoder; and an attention mechanism and a decoder initialization layer that connect the encoder and decoder (Bahdanau et al., 2015).

During headline generation, the encoder reads and encodes the words of the document. Initialized by the encoder, the decoder then starts generating the headline one word at a time, attending to relevant parts in the document using the attention mechanism (Figure 1). During training the parameters are optimized to maximize the probabilities of reference headlines.

While generally at the start of training either the parameters of all the components are randomly initialized or only pre-trained embeddings (with dashed outline in Figure 1) are used (Nallapati et al., 2016; Paulus et al., 2017; Gulcehre et al., 2016), we propose pre-training methods for more extensive initialization.

2.1 Encoder Pre-Training

When training a NHG model, most approaches generally use a limited number of first sentences or tokens of the document. For example Rush et al. (2015); Shen et al. (2016); Chopra et al. (2016) use only the first sentence of the document and Nallapati et al. (2016) use up to 2 first sentences. While efficient (training is faster and takes less memory

as the input sequences are shorter) and effective (the most informative content tends to be at the beginning of the document (Nallapati et al., 2016)), this leaves the rest of the sentences in the document unused. Better understanding of words and their context can be learned if all sentences are used, especially on small training sets.

To utilize the entire training set, we pre-train the encoder on all the sentences of the training set documents. Since the encoder consists of two recurrent components – a forward and backward GRU – we pre-train them separately. First we add a softmax output layer to the forward GRU and train it on the sentences to predict the next word given the previous ones (i.e. we train it as a LM). After convergence on the validation set sentences, we take the embedding weights of the forward GRU and use them as fixed parameters for the backward GRU. Then we train the backwards GRU following the same procedure as with the forward GRU, with the exception of processing the sentences in a reverse order. When both models are fully trained, we remove the softmax output layers and initialize the encoder of the NHG model with the embeddings and GRU parameters of the trained LMs (highlighted with gray background in Figure 1).

2.2 Decoder Pre-Training

Pre-training the decoder as a LM seems natural, since it is essentially a conditional LM. During NHG model training the decoder is fed only headline words, which is relatively little data compared to the document contents. To improve the quality of the headlines it is essential to have high quality embeddings that are a good semantic representation of the input words and to have a well trained recurrent and output layer to predict sensible words that make up coherent sentences. When it comes to statistical models, the simplest way to improve the quality of the parameters is to train the model on more data, but it also has to be the right kind of data (Moore and Lewis, 2010).

To increase the amount of suitable training data for the decoder we use LM pre-training on filtered sentences of the training set documents. For filtering we use the XenC tool by Rousseau (2013) with the cross-entropy difference filtering (Moore and Lewis, 2010). In our case the in-domain data is training set headlines, out-domain data is the sentences from training set documents, and the best cut-off point is evaluated on validation set headlines. The careful selection of sentences is mostly motivated by preventing the pre-trained decoder from deviating too much from Headlinese, but it also reduces training time.

Before pre-training we initialize the input and output embeddings of the LM for words that are common in both encoder and decoder vocabulary with the corresponding pre-trained encoder embeddings. We train the LM on the selected sentences until perplexity on the validation set headlines stops improving and then use it to initialize the decoder parameters of the NHG model (highlighted with dotted background in Figure 1).

A similar approach, without data selection and embedding initialization, has also been used by Alifimoff (2015).

2.3 Distant Supervision Pre-Training

Approaches described in sections 2.1 and 2.2 enable full pre-training of the encoder and decoder, but this still leaves the connecting parameters (with white background in Figure 1) untrained.

As results in language modelling suggest, surrounding sentences contain useful information to predict words in the current sentence (Wang and Cho, 2016). This implies that other sentences contain informative sections that the attention mechanism can learn to attend to and general context that the initialization component can learn to extract.

To utilize this phenomenon, we propose using carefully picked sentences from the documents as pseudo-headlines and pre-train the NHG model to generate these given the rest of sentences in the document. Our pseudo-headline picking strategy consists of choosing sentences that occur within 100 first tokens of the document and were retained during cross-entropy filtering in section 2.2. Picking sentences from the beginning of the document should give us the most informative sentences, and cross-entropy filtering keeps sentences that most closely resemble headlines.

The pre-training procedure starts with initializing the encoder and decoder with LM pre-trained parameters (sections 2.1 and 2.2). After that, we continue training the attention and initialization parameters until perplexity on validation set headlines converges. We then use the trained parameters to initialize all parameters of the NHG model.

Distant supervision has been also used for multi-document summarization by Bravo-Marquez and Manriquez (2012).

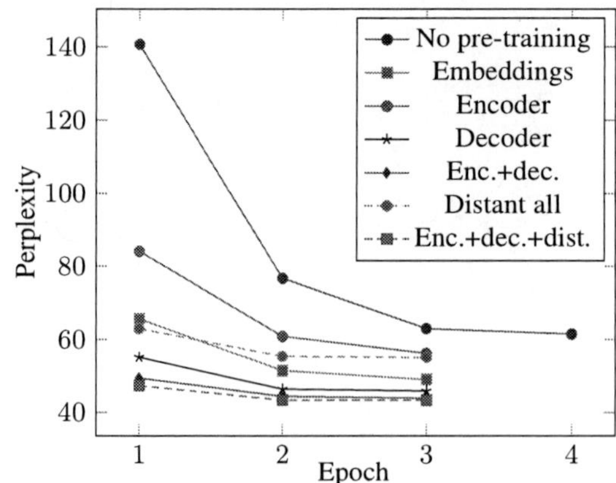

Figure 2: Validation set (EN) perplexities of the NHG model with different pre-training methods.

Model	PPL (EN)	PPL (ET)
No pre-training	65.1 ±1.0	25.9 ±0.4
Embeddings	51.8 ±0.7	20.7 ±0.3
Encoder (2.1)	59.3 ±0.9	23.5 ±0.4
Decoder (2.2)	48.3 ±0.7	18.8 ±0.3
Enc.+dec.	46.2 ±0.7	17.7 ±0.3
Distant all	58.6 ±0.9	21.3 ±0.3
Enc.+dec.+dist. (2.3)	**45.8 ±0.7**	**17.5 ±0.3**

Table 1: Perplexities on the test set with a 95% confidence interval (Klakow and Peters, 2002). All pre-trained models are significantly better than the *No pre-training* baseline.

3 Experiments

We evaluate the proposed pre-training methods in terms of ROUGE and perplexity on two relatively small datasets (English and Estonian).

3.1 Training Details

All our models use hidden layer sizes of 256 and the weights are initialized according to Glorot and Bengio (2010). The vocabularies consist of up to 50000 most frequent training set words that occur at least 3 times. The model is implemented in Theano (Bergstra et al., 2010; Bastien et al., 2012) and trained on GPUs using mini-batches of size 128. During training the weights are updated with Adam (Kingma and Ba, 2014) (parameters: α=0.001, β_1=0.9, β_2=0.999, ϵ=10^{-8} and λ=$1 - 10^{-8}$) and L_2-norm of the gradient is kept within a threshold of 5.0 (Pascanu et al., 2013). During headline generation we use beam search with beam size 5.

Model	EN				ET			
	$R1_R$	$R1_P$	RL_R	RL_P	$R1_R$	$R1_P$	RL_R	RL_P
No pre-training	20.36	33.51	17.68	29.03	26.44	34.23	25.31	32.74
Embeddings	21.09	33.36	18.23	28.72	28.42	35.94	27.02	34.16
Encoder (2.1)	21.25	34.1	18.45	29.5	**29.28**	**37.04**	**27.88**	**35.24**
Decoder (2.2)	20.11	31.1	17.43	26.87	25.12	32.6	23.89	30.99
Enc.+dec.	20.72	33.93	18.04	29.43	27.18	34.58	25.79	32.78
Distant all	20.32	31.54	17.59	27.25	26.17	34.49	24.96	32.87
Enc.+dec.+dist. (2.3)	**21.34**	**34.81**	**18.53**	**30.14**	27.74	35.46	26.35	33.67

Table 2: Recall and precision of ROUGE-1 and ROUGE-L on the test sets. Best scores in bold. Results with statistically significant differences (95% confidence) compared to *No pre-training* underlined.

3.2 Datasets

We use the CNN/Daily Mail dataset (Hermann et al., 2015)[1] for experiments on English (EN). The number of headline-document pairs is 287227, 13368 and 11490 in training, validation and test set correspondingly. The preprocessing consists of tokenization, lowercasing, replacing numeric characters with #, and removing irrelevant parts (editor notes, timestamps etc.) from the beginning of the document with heuristic rules.

For Estonian (ET) experiments we use a similarly sized (341607, 18979 and 18977 training, validation and test split) dataset that also consist of news from two sources. During preprocessing, compound words are split, words are truecased and numbers are written out as words. We used Estnltk (Orasmaa et al., 2016) stemmer for ROUGE evaluations.

3.3 Results and Analysis

Models are evaluated in terms of perplexity (PPL) and full length ROUGE (Lin, 2004). In addition to pre-training methods described in sections 2.1-2.3, we also test: initializing only the embeddings using parameters from the LM pre-trained encoder and decoder (*Embeddings*); initializing the encoder and decoder, but leaving connecting parameters randomized (*Enc.+dec.*); pre-training the whole model from random initialization with distant supervision only (*Distant all*); and a baseline that is not pre-trained at all (*No pre-training*).

All pre-training methods gave significant improvements in PPL (Table 1). The best method (*Enc.+dec.+dist.*) improved the test set PPL by 29.6-32.4% relative. Pre-trained NHG models also converged faster during training (Figure 2)

[1]http://cs.nyu.edu/~kcho/DMQA/

and most of them beat the final PPL of the baseline already after the first epoch. General trend is that pre-training a larger amount of parameters and the parameters closer to the outputs of the NHG model improves the PPL more. *Distant all* is an exception to that observation as it used much less training data (same as baseline) than other methods.

For ROUGE evaluations, we report ROUGE-1 and ROUGE-L (Table 2). In contrast with PPL evaluations, some pre-training methods either don't improve significantly or even worsen ROUGE measures. Another difference compared to PPL evaluations is that for ROUGE, pre-training parameters that reside further from outputs (embeddings and encoder) seems more beneficial. This might imply that a better document representation is more important to stay on topic during beam search while it is less important during PPL evaluation where predicting next target headline word with high confidence is rewarded and the process is aided by previous target headline words that are fed to the decoder as inputs. It is also possible, that a well trained decoder becomes too reliant on expecting correct words as inputs making it sensitive to errors during generation which would somewhat explain why *Enc.+dec.* performs worse than *Encoder* alone. This hypothesis can be checked in further work by experimenting with methods like scheduled sampling (Bengio et al., 2015) that should increase the robustness to mistakes during generation. Pre-training all parameters on all available text (*Enc.+dec.+dist.*) still gives the best result on English and quite decent results on Estonian. Best models improve ROUGE by 0.85-2.84 points.

Some examples of the generated headlines on the CNN/Daily Mail dataset are shown in Table 3.

Document	a democratic congressman is at the head of a group of representatives trying to help undocumented immigrants avoid deportations with what they have called the family defender toolkit . the informational pamphlet includes a bilingual card - that some are calling a get out of deportation free card - that lists reasons a person should not be deported under expanded .
Reference headline	congressman is developing a get out of deportation toolkit to help undocumented immigrants if they are detained
No pre-training	congressman calls for undocumented immigrants
Embeddings	congressman calls for help from immigrants trying to help immigrants avoiding deportation
Encoder (2.1)	republican congressman calls for immigrants trying to avoid deportation
Decoder (2.2)	congressman who tried to stop deportations of immigrants
Enc.+Dec.	immigration congressman at the head of the head of the group who tries to avoid deportation
Distant all	congressman calls for deportation to immigrants who stay in the country
Enc.+dec.+dist. (2.3)	congressman tries to help undocumented immigrants avoid deportation
Document	a chihuahua and a bearded dragon showed off their interspecies friendship when they embarked upon a game of tag together . videoed in their front room , the dog named foxxy cleopatra and the reptile called ryuu can be seen chasing after one another around a coffee table . standing perfectly still while looking in the other direction , the bearded dragon initially appears disinterested as the chihuahua jumps around excitedly .
Reference headline	you re it!
No pre-training	is this the creepiest crawly?
Embeddings	meet the poodle!
Encoder (2.1)	it's a knockout!
Decoder (2.2)	the bearded dragon lizard: the bearded dragon lizard spotted in the middle of the street
Enc.+Dec.	oh, this is a lion!
Distant all	meet the dragon dragon: meet the dragon dragon
Enc.+dec.+dist. (2.3)	is this the world's youngest lion?

Table 3: Examples of generated headlines on CNN/Daily Mail dataset.

4 Conclusions

We proposed three new NHG model pre-training methods that in combination enable utilizing the entire dataset and initializing all parameters of the NHG model. We also evaluated and analyzed pre-training methods and their combinations in terms of perplexity (PPL) and ROUGE. The results revealed that better PPL doesn't necessarily translate to better ROUGE – PPL tends to benefit from pre-training parameters that are closer to outputs, but for ROUGE it is generally the opposite. Also, PPL benefited from pre-training more parameters while for ROUGE it was not always the case. Pre-training in general proved to be useful – our best results improved PPL by 29.6-32.4% relative and ROUGE measures by 0.85-2.84 points compared to a NHG model without pre-training.

Current work focused on maximally utilizing available headlined corpora. One interesting future direction would be to additionally utilize potentially much more abundant corpora of documents without headlines (also proposed by Shen et al. (2016)) for pre-training. Another open question is the relationship between the dataset size and the effect of pre-training.

Acknowledgments

We would like to thank NVIDIA for the donated GPU, the anonymous reviewers for their valuable comments, and Kyunghyun Cho for the help with the CNN/Daily Mail dataset.

References

Alex Alifimoff. 2015. Abstractive sentence summarization with attentive deep recurrent neural networks.

Dzmitry Bahdanau, Kyunghyun Cho, and Yoshua Bengio. 2015. Neural machine translation by jointly learning to align and translate. *ICLR2015, arXiv:1409.0473*.

Frédéric Bastien, Pascal Lamblin, Razvan Pascanu, James Bergstra, Ian J. Goodfellow, Arnaud Bergeron, Nicolas Bouchard, and Yoshua Bengio. 2012. Theano: new features and speed improvements. In *Deep Learning and Unsupervised Feature Learning NIPS 2012 Workshop*.

Samy Bengio, Oriol Vinyals, Navdeep Jaitly, and Noam Shazeer. 2015. Scheduled sampling for sequence prediction with recurrent neural networks. In *Advances in Neural Information Processing Systems*, pages 1171–1179.

James Bergstra, Olivier Breuleux, Frédéric Bastien, Pascal Lamblin, Razvan Pascanu, Guillaume Desjardins, Joseph Turian, David Warde-Farley, and Yoshua Bengio. 2010. Theano: a CPU and GPU math expression compiler. In *Proceedings of the Python for Scientific Computing Conference (SciPy)*. Oral Presentation.

Felipe Bravo-Marquez and Manuel Manriquez. 2012. A zipf-like distant supervision approach for multi-document summarization using wikinews articles. In *International Symposium on String Processing and Information Retrieval*, pages 143–154. Springer.

Kyunghyun Cho, Bart van Merrienboer, Caglar Gulcehre, Dzmitry Bahdanau, Fethi Bougares, Holger Schwenk, and Yoshua Bengio. 2014. Learning phrase representations using rnn encoder–decoder for statistical machine translation. In *Proceedings of the 2014 Conference on Empirical Methods in Natural Language Processing (EMNLP)*, pages 1724–1734. Association for Computational Linguistics.

Sumit Chopra, Michael Auli, and M. Alexander Rush. 2016. Abstractive sentence summarization with attentive recurrent neural networks. In *Proceedings of the 2016 Conference of the North American Chapter of the Association for Computational Linguistics: Human Language Technologies*, pages 93–98. Association for Computational Linguistics.

Xavier Glorot and Yoshua Bengio. 2010. Understanding the difficulty of training deep feedforward neural networks. In *International conference on artificial intelligence and statistics*, pages 249–256.

Caglar Gulcehre, Sungjin Ahn, Ramesh Nallapati, Bowen Zhou, and Yoshua Bengio. 2016. Pointing the unknown words. In *Proceedings of the 54th Annual Meeting of the Association for Computational Linguistics (Volume 1: Long Papers)*, pages 140–149. Association for Computational Linguistics.

Karl Moritz Hermann, Tomáš Kočiský, Edward Grefenstette, Lasse Espeholt, Will Kay, Mustafa Suleyman, and Phil Blunsom. 2015. Teaching machines to read and comprehend. In *Advances in Neural Information Processing Systems (NIPS)*.

Diederik Kingma and Jimmy Ba. 2014. Adam: A method for stochastic optimization. *arXiv preprint arXiv:1412.6980*.

Dietrich Klakow and Jochen Peters. 2002. Testing the correlation of word error rate and perplexity. *Speech Communication*, 38(1):19–28.

Chin-Yew Lin. 2004. *Text Summarization Branches Out*, chapter ROUGE: A Package for Automatic Evaluation of Summaries.

Ingrid Mårdh. 1980. *Headlinese: On the grammar of English front page headlines*, volume 58. Liberläromedel/Gleerup.

Mike Mintz, Steven Bills, Rion Snow, and Daniel Jurafsky. 2009. Distant supervision for relation extraction without labeled data. In *Proceedings of the Joint Conference of the 47th Annual Meeting of the ACL and the 4th International Joint Conference on Natural Language Processing of the AFNLP*, pages 1003–1011. Association for Computational Linguistics.

C. Robert Moore and William Lewis. 2010. Intelligent selection of language model training data. In *Proceedings of the ACL 2010 Conference Short Papers*, pages 220–224. Association for Computational Linguistics.

Ramesh Nallapati, Bowen Zhou, Cicero dos Santos, Caglar Gulcehre, and Bing Xiang. 2016. Abstractive text summarization using sequence-to-sequence rnns and beyond. In *Proceedings of The 20th SIGNLL Conference on Computational Natural Language Learning*, pages 280–290. Association for Computational Linguistics.

Siim Orasmaa, Timo Petmanson, Alexander Tkachenko, Sven Laur, and Heiki-Jaan Kaalep. 2016. Estnltk - nlp toolkit for estonian. In *Proceedings of the Tenth International Conference on Language Resources and Evaluation (LREC 2016)*, Paris, France. European Language Resources Association (ELRA).

Razvan Pascanu, Tomas Mikolov, and Yoshua Bengio. 2013. On the difficulty of training recurrent neural networks. *Proceedings of the 30th International Conference on Machine Learning (ICML 2013)*.

Romain Paulus, Caiming Xiong, and Richard Socher. 2017. A deep reinforced model for abstractive summarization. *arXiv preprint arXiv:1705.04304*.

Anthony Rousseau. 2013. Xenc: An open-source tool for data selection in natural language processing. *The Prague Bulletin of Mathematical Linguistics*, (100):73–82.

M. Alexander Rush, Sumit Chopra, and Jason Weston. 2015. A neural attention model for abstractive sentence summarization. In *Proceedings of the 2015 Conference on Empirical Methods in Natural Language Processing*, pages 379–389. Association for Computational Linguistics.

Mike Schuster and Kuldip K Paliwal. 1997. Bidirectional recurrent neural networks. *IEEE Transactions on Signal Processing*, 45(11):2673–2681.

Shiqi Shen, Yu Zhao, Zhiyuan Liu, Maosong Sun, et al. 2016. Neural headline generation with sentence-wise optimization. *arXiv preprint arXiv:1604.01904*.

Tian Wang and Kyunghyun Cho. 2016. Larger-context language modelling with recurrent neural network. In *Proceedings of the 54th Annual Meeting of the Association for Computational Linguistics (Volume 1: Long Papers)*, pages 1319–1329. Association for Computational Linguistics.

Towards Improving Abstractive Summarization
via Entailment Generation

Ramakanth Pasunuru   **Han Guo**   **Mohit Bansal**
UNC Chapel Hill
{ram@cs.unc.edu, hanguo@unc.edu, mbansal@cs.unc.edu}

Abstract

Abstractive summarization, the task of rewriting and compressing a document into a short summary, has achieved considerable success with neural sequence-to-sequence models. However, these models can still benefit from stronger natural language inference skills, since a correct summary is logically entailed by the input document, i.e., it should not contain any contradictory or unrelated information. We incorporate such knowledge into an abstractive summarization model via multi-task learning, where we share its decoder parameters with those of an entailment generation model. We achieve promising initial improvements based on multiple metrics and datasets (including a test-only setting). The domain mismatch between the entailment (captions) and summarization (news) datasets suggests that the model is learning some domain-agnostic inference skills.

1 Introduction

Abstractive summarization, the task of rewriting a document into a short summary is a significantly more challenging (and natural) task than extractive summarization, which only involves choosing which sentence from the original document to keep or discard in the output summary. Neural sequence-to-sequence models have led to substantial improvements on this task of abstractive summarization, via machine translation inspired encoder-aligner-decoder approaches, further enhanced via convolutional encoders, pointer-copy mechanisms, and hierarchical attention (Rush et al., 2015; Nallapati et al., 2016; See et al., 2017).

Despite these promising recent improvements,

Input Document: *may is a pivotal month for moving and storage companies .*
Ground-truth Summary: *moving companies hit bumps in economic road*
Baseline Summary: *a month to move storage companies*
Multi-task Summary: *pivotal month for storage firms*

Figure 1: Motivating output example from our summarization+entailment multi-task model.

there is still scope in better teaching summarization models about the general natural language inference skill of logical entailment generation. This is because the task of abstractive summarization involves two subtasks: salient (important) event detection as well as logical compression, i.e., the summary should not contain any information that is contradictory or unrelated to the original document. Current methods have to learn both these skills from the same dataset and a single model. Therefore, there is benefit in learning the latter ability of logical compression via external knowledge from a separate entailment generation task, that will specifically teach the model how to rewrite and compress a sentence such that it logically follows from the original input.

To achieve this, we employ the recent paradigm of sequence-to-sequence multi-task learning (Luong et al., 2016). We share the decoder parameters of the summarization model with those of the entailment-generation model, so as to generate summaries that are good at both extracting important facts from as well as being logically entailed by the input document. Fig. 1 shows such an (actual) output example from our model, where it successfully learns both salient information extraction as well as entailment, unlike the strong baseline model.

Empirically, we report promising initial improvements over some solid baselines based on several metrics, and on multiple datasets: Gigaword and also a test-only setting of DUC. Impor-

Proceedings of the Workshop on New Frontiers in Summarization, pages 27–32
Copenhagen, Denmark, September 7, 2017. ©2017 Association for Computational Linguistics

tantly, these improvements are achieved despite the fact that the domain of the entailment dataset (image captions) is substantially different from the domain of the summarization datasets (general news), which suggests that the model is learning certain domain-independent inference skills. Our next steps to this workshop paper include incorporating stronger pointer-based models and employing the new multi-domain entailment corpus (Williams et al., 2017).

2   Related Work

Earlier summarization work focused more towards extractive (and compression) based summarization, i.e., selecting which sentences to keep vs discard, and also compressing based on choosing grammatically correct sub-sentences having the most important pieces of information (Jing, 2000; Knight and Marcu, 2002; Clarke and Lapata, 2008; Filippova et al., 2015). Bigger datasets and neural models have allowed the addressing of the complex reasoning involved in abstractive summarization, i.e., rewriting and compressing the input document into a new summary. Several advances have been made in this direction using machine translation inspired encoder-aligner-decoder models, convolution-based encoders, switching pointer and copy mechanisms, and hierarchical attention models (Rush et al., 2015; Nallapati et al., 2016; See et al., 2017).

Recognizing textual entailment (RTE) is the classification task of predicting whether the relationship between a premise and hypothesis sentence is that of entailment (i.e., logically follows), contradiction, or independence (Dagan et al., 2006). The SNLI corpus Bowman et al. (2015) allows training accurate end-to-end neural networks for this task. Some previous work (Mehdad et al., 2013; Gupta et al., 2014) has explored the use of textual entailment recognition for redundancy detection in summarization. They label relationships between sentences, so as to select the most informative and non-redundant sentences for summarization, via sentence connectivity and graph-based optimization and fusion. Our focus, on the other hand, is entailment generation and not recognition, i.e., to teach summarization models the general natural language inference skill of generating a compressed sentence that logically entails the original longer sentence, so as to produce more effective short summaries. We achieve this via multi-task learning with entailment generation.

Multi-task learning involves sharing parameters between related tasks, whereby each task benefits from extra information in the training signals of the related tasks, and also improves its generalization performance. Luong et al. (2016) showed improvements on translation, captioning, and parsing in a shared multi-task setting. Recently, Pasunuru and Bansal (2017) extend this idea to video captioning with two related tasks: video completion and entailment generation. We demonstrate that abstractive text summarization models can also be improved by sharing parameters with an entailment generation task.

3   Models

First, we discuss our baseline model which is similar to the machine translation encoder-aligner-decoder model of Luong et al. (2015), and presented by Chopra et al. (2016). Next, we introduce our multi-task learning approach of sharing the parameters between abstractive summarization and entailment generation models.

3.1   Baseline Model

Our baseline model is a strong, multi-layered encoder-attention-decoder model with bilinear attention, similar to Luong et al. (2015) and following the details in Chopra et al. (2016). Here, we encode the source document with a two-layered LSTM-RNN and generate the summary using another two-layered LSTM-RNN decoder. The word probability distribution at time step t of the decoder is defined as follows:

$$p(w_t|w_{<t}, c_t, s_t) = softmax(W_s g(c_t, s_t)) \quad (1)$$

where g is a non-linear function and c_t and s_t are the context vector and LSTM-RNN decoder hidden state at time step t, respectively. The context vector $c_t = \sum \alpha_{t,i} h_i$ is a weighted combination of encoder hidden states h_i, where the attention weights are learned through the bilinear attention mechanism proposed in Luong et al. (2015). For the rest of the paper, we use same notations.

We also use the same model architecture for the entailment generation task, i.e., a sequence-to-sequence model encoding the premise and decoding the entailed hypothesis, via bilinear attention between them.

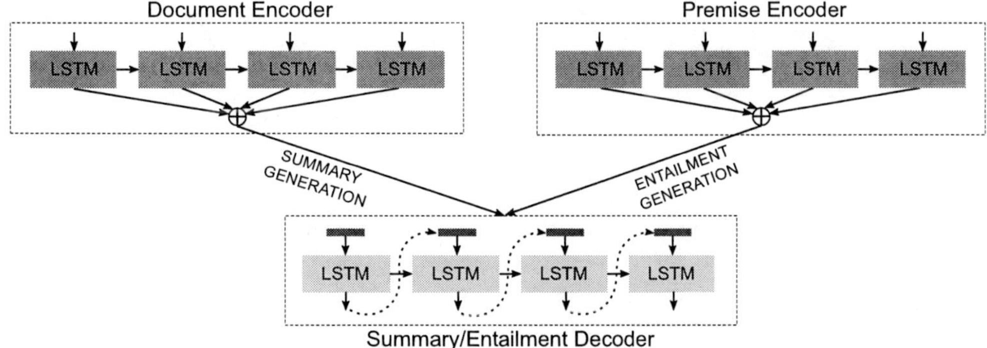

Figure 2: Multi-task learning of the summarization task (left) with the entailment generation task (right).

3.2 Multi-Task Learning

Multi-task learning helps in sharing knowledge between related tasks across domains (Luong et al., 2015). In this work, we show improvements on the task of abstractive summarization by sharing its parameters with the task of entailment generation. Since a summary is entailed by the input document, sharing parameters with the entailment generation task improves the logically-directed aspect of the summarization model, while maintaining the salient information extraction aspect.

In our multi-task setup, we share the decoder parameters of both the tasks (along with the word embeddings), as shown in Fig. 2, and we optimize the two loss functions (one for summarization and another for entailment generation) in alternate mini-batches of training. Let α_s be the number of mini-batches of training for summarization after which it is switched to train α_e number of mini-batches for entailment generation. Then, the mixing ratio is defined as $\frac{\alpha_s}{\alpha_s+\alpha_e} : \frac{\alpha_e}{\alpha_s+\alpha_e}$.

4 Experimental Setup

4.1 Datasets

Gigaword Corpus We use the exact annotated Gigaword corpus provided by Rush et al. (2015). The dataset has approximately 3.8 million training pairs. We use $10,000$ pairs as validation set and the exact test sample provided by Rush et al. (2015) as our test set. We use the first sentence of the article as the source with vocabulary size of $119,505$ and article headline as target with vocabulary size of $68,885$.

DUC Test Corpus The DUC corpus[1] comes in two variants: DUC-2003 corpus consists of

624 documents and DUC-2004 corpus consists of 500 documents. Each document in these datasets has four human annotated summaries. For experiments on this corpus, we directly used the Gigaword-trained model and tested on the DUC-2004 corpus. This is similar to the setups of Nallapati et al. (2016) and Chopra et al. (2016) (whereas the Rush et al. (2015) setup tunes on the DUC-2003 corpus).

SNLI corpus For the task of entailment generation, we use the Standford Natural Language Inference (SNLI) corpus (Bowman et al., 2015), where we only use the entailment-labeled pairs and regroup the splits to have a zero overlap train-test split and have a multi-reference test set, as suggested by Pasunuru and Bansal (2017). Out of $190,113$ entailments pairs, we use $145,822$ unique premise pairs for training, and the rest of them are equally divided into dev and test sets.

4.2 Evaluation

Following previous work (Nallapati et al., 2016; Chopra et al., 2016; Rush et al., 2015), we use the full-length F1 variant of Rouge (Lin, 2004) for the Gigaword results, and the 75-bytes length limited Recall variant of Rouge for DUC. Additionally, we also report other standard language generation metrics (as motivated recently by See et al. (2017)): METEOR (Denkowski and Lavie, 2014), BLEU-4 (Papineni et al., 2002), and CIDEr-D (Vedantam et al., 2015), based on the MS-COCO evaluation script (Chen et al., 2015).

4.3 Training Details

We use the following simple settings for all the models, unless otherwise specified. We unroll the encoder RNN's to a maximum of 50 time steps and decoder RNN's to a maximum of 30 time steps.

---

[1] http://duc.nist.gov/duc2004/tasks.html

Models	ROUGE-1	ROUGE-2	ROUGE-L	METEOR	BLEU-4	CIDEr-D
PREVIOUS WORK						
ABS+ (Rush et al., 2015)	29.76	11.88	26.96	-	-	-
RAS-Elman (Chopra et al., 2016)	33.78	15.97	31.15	-	-	-
words-lvt2k-1sent (Nallapati et al., 2016)	32.67	15.59	30.64	-	-	-
OUR MODELS						
Baseline	31.75	14.71	29.91	14.54	10.31	128.22
Multi-Task with Entailment Generation	32.75	15.35	30.82	15.25	11.09	130.44

Table 1: Summarization results on Gigaword. Rouge scores are full length F-1, following previous work.

We use RNN hidden state dimension of 512 and word embedding dimension of 256. We do not initialize our word embeddings with any pre-trained models, i.e., we learn them from scratch. We use the Adam (Kingma and Ba, 2015) optimizer with a learning rate of 0.001. During training, to handle the large vocabulary, we use the sampled loss trick of Jean et al. (2014). We always tune hyperparameters on the validation set of the corresponding dataset, where applicable. For multi-task learning, we tried a few mixing ratios and found 1 : 0.05 to work better, i.e., 100 mini-batches of summarization with 5 mini-batches of entailment generation task in alternate training rounds.

5 Results and Analysis

5.1 Summarization Results: Gigaword

Baseline Results and Previous Work Our baseline is a strong encoder-attention-decoder model based on Luong et al. (2015) and presented by Chopra et al. (2016). As shown in Table 1, it is reasonably close to some of the state-of-the-art (comparable) results in previous work, though making this baseline further strong (e.g., based on pointer-copy mechanism) is our next step.

Multi-Task Results We show promising initial multi-task improvements on top of our baseline, based on several metrics. This suggests that the entailment generation model is teaching the summarization model some skills about how to choose a logical subset of the events in the full input document. This is especially promising given that the domain of the entailment dataset (image captions) is very different from the domain of the summarization datasets (news), suggesting that the model might be learning some domain-agnostic inference skills.

5.2 Summarization Results: DUC

Here, we directly use the Gigaword-trained model to test on the DUC-2004 dataset (see tuning discussion in Sec. 4.1). In Table 2, we again see that

Models	R-1	R-2	R-L
Rush et al. (2015)	28.18	8.49	23.81
Chopra et al. (2016)	28.97	8.26	24.06
Nallapati et al. (2016)	28.35	9.46	24.59
Baseline	27.74	8.82	24.45
Multi-Task	28.17	9.22	24.84

Table 2: Summarization test results on DUC-2004 corpus. Rouge scores are based on 75-byte Recall, following previous work.

Input Document: *results from the second round of the french first-division soccer league -lrb- home teams listed first -rrb- : UNK*
Ground-truth Summary: *french soccer results*
Baseline Summary: *first round results of french league soccer league*
Multi-task Summary: *second round of french soccer league results*

Input Document: *austrian women in leading positions complained about lingering male domination in their society in a meeting tuesday with visiting u.s. first lady hillary rodham clinton .*
Ground-truth Summary: *austrian women complain to mrs. clinton about male domination by roland prinz*
Baseline Summary: *first lady meets with first lady*
Multi-task Summary: *austrian women complained about male domination*

Figure 3: Output examples of our multi-task model in comparison with the baseline.

our Luong et al. (2015) baseline model achieves competitive performance with previous work, esp. on Rouge-2 and Rouge-L. Next, we show promising multi-task improvements over this baseline of around 0.4% across all metrics, despite being a test-only setting and also with the mismatch between the summarization and entailment domains.

5.3 Analysis Examples

Figure 3 shows some additional interesting output examples of our multi-task model and how it generates summaries that are better at being logically entailed by the input document, whereas the baseline model contains some crucial contradictory or unrelated information.

6   Conclusion and Next Steps

We presented a multi-task learning approach to incorporate entailment generation knowledge into summarization models. We demonstrated promising initial improvements based on multiple datasets and metrics, even when the entailment knowledge was extracted from a domain different from the summarization domain.

Our next steps to this workshop paper include: (1) stronger summarization baselines, e.g., using pointer copy mechanism (See et al., 2017; Nallapati et al., 2016), and also adding this capability to the entailment generation model; (2) results on CNN/Daily Mail corpora (Nallapati et al., 2016); (3) incorporating entailment knowledge from other news-style domains such as the new Multi-NLI corpus (Williams et al., 2017), and (4) demonstrating mutual improvements on the entailment generation task.

Acknowledgments

We thank the anonymous reviewers for their helpful comments. This work was supported by a Google Faculty Research Award, an IBM Faculty Award, a Bloomberg Data Science Research Grant, and NVidia GPU awards.

References

Samuel R Bowman, Gabor Angeli, Christopher Potts, and Christopher D Manning. 2015. A large annotated corpus for learning natural language inference. In *EMNLP*.

Xinlei Chen, Hao Fang, Tsung-Yi Lin, Ramakrishna Vedantam, Saurabh Gupta, Piotr Dollár, and C Lawrence Zitnick. 2015. Microsoft coco captions: Data collection and evaluation server. *arXiv preprint arXiv:1504.00325*.

Sumit Chopra, Michael Auli, and Alexander M Rush. 2016. Abstractive sentence summarization with attentive recurrent neural networks. In *HLT-NAACL*.

James Clarke and Mirella Lapata. 2008. Global inference for sentence compression: An integer linear programming approach. *Journal of Artificial Intelligence Research*, 31:399–429.

Ido Dagan, Oren Glickman, and Bernardo Magnini. 2006. The pascal recognising textual entailment challenge. In *Machine learning challenges. evaluating predictive uncertainty, visual object classification, and recognising tectual entailment*, pages 177–190. Springer.

Michael Denkowski and Alon Lavie. 2014. Meteor universal: Language specific translation evaluation for any target language. In *EACL*.

Katja Filippova, Enrique Alfonseca, Carlos A Colmenares, Lukasz Kaiser, and Oriol Vinyals. 2015. Sentence compression by deletion with lstms. In *EMNLP*, pages 360–368.

Anand Gupta, Manpreet Kaur, Adarsh Singh, Aseem Goel, and Shachar Mirkin. 2014. Text summarization through entailment-based minimum vertex cover. *Lexical and Computational Semantics (* SEM 2014)*, page 75.

Sébastien Jean, Kyunghyun Cho, Roland Memisevic, and Yoshua Bengio. 2014. On using very large target vocabulary for neural machine translation. *CoRR*.

Hongyan Jing. 2000. Sentence reduction for automatic text summarization. In *ANLP*.

Diederik Kingma and Jimmy Ba. 2015. Adam: A method for stochastic optimization. In *ICLR*.

Kevin Knight and Daniel Marcu. 2002. Summarization beyond sentence extraction: A probabilistic approach to sentence compression. *Artificial Intelligence*, 139(1):91–107.

Chin-Yew Lin. 2004. ROUGE: A package for automatic evaluation of summaries. In *Text Summarization Branches Out: Proceedings of the ACL-04 workshop*, volume 8.

Minh-Thang Luong, Quoc V. Le, Ilya Sutskever, Oriol Vinyals, and Lukasz Kaiser. 2016. Multi-task sequence to sequence learning. In *ICLR*.

Minh-Thang Luong, Hieu Pham, and Christopher D. Manning. 2015. Effective approaches to attention-based neural machine translation. In *EMNLP*, pages 1412–1421.

Yashar Mehdad, Giuseppe Carenini, Frank W Tompa, and Raymond T Ng. 2013. Abstractive meeting summarization with entailment and fusion. In *Proc. of the 14th European Workshop on Natural Language Generation*, pages 136–146.

Ramesh Nallapati, Bowen Zhou, Caglar Gulcehre, Bing Xiang, et al. 2016. Abstractive text summarization using sequence-to-sequence rnns and beyond. In *CoNLL*.

Kishore Papineni, Salim Roukos, Todd Ward, and Wei-Jing Zhu. 2002. BLEU: a method for automatic evaluation of machine translation. In *ACL*, pages 311–318.

Ramakanth Pasunuru and Mohit Bansal. 2017. Multi-task video captioning with video and entailment generation. In *ACL*.

Alexander M Rush, Sumit Chopra, and Jason Weston. 2015. A neural attention model for abstractive sentence summarization. In *CoRR*.

Abigail See, Peter J Liu, and Christopher D Manning. 2017. Get to the point: Summarization with pointer-generator networks. In *ACL*.

Ramakrishna Vedantam, C Lawrence Zitnick, and Devi Parikh. 2015. CIDEr: Consensus-based image description evaluation. In *CVPR*, pages 4566–4575.

Adina Williams, Nikita Nangia, and Samuel R Bowman. 2017. A broad-coverage challenge corpus for sentence understanding through inference. *arXiv preprint arXiv:1704.05426*.

Coarse-to-Fine Attention Models for Document Summarization

Jeffrey Ling and **Alexander M. Rush**
Harvard University
{jling@college, srush@seas}.harvard.edu

Abstract

Sequence-to-sequence models with attention have been successful for a variety of NLP problems, but their speed does not scale well for tasks with long source sequences such as document summarization. We propose a novel coarse-to-fine attention model that hierarchically reads a document, using coarse attention to select top-level chunks of text and fine attention to read the words of the chosen chunks. While the computation for training standard attention models scales linearly with source sequence length, our method scales with the number of top-level chunks and can handle much longer sequences. Empirically, we find that while coarse-to-fine attention models lag behind state-of-the-art baselines, our method achieves the desired behavior of sparsely attending to subsets of the document for generation.

1 Introduction

The sequence-to-sequence architecture of Sutskever et al. (2014), also known as the encoder-decoder architecture, is now the gold standard for many NLP tasks, including machine translation (Sutskever et al., 2014; Bahdanau et al., 2015), question answering (Hermann et al., 2015), dialogue (Li et al., 2016), caption generation (Xu et al., 2015), and in particular summarization (Rush et al., 2015).

A popular variant of sequence-to-sequence models are *attention* models (Bahdanau et al., 2015). By keeping an encoded representation of each part of the input, we "attend" to the relevant part each time we produce an output from the decoder. In practice, this means computing attention weights for all encoder hidden states, then taking the weighted average as our new context vector.

While successful, existing sequence-to-sequence methods are computationally limited by the length of source and target sequences. For a problem such as document summarization, a source sequence of length N (where N could potentially be very large) requires $O(N)$ model computations to encode. However, it makes sense intuitively that not every word of the source will be necessary for generating a summary, and so we would like to reduce the amount of computation performed on the source.

Therefore, in order to scale attention models for this problem, we aim to prune down the length of the source sequence in an intelligent way. Instead of naively attending to all the words of the source at once, our solution is to use a two-layer hierarchical attention. For document summarization, this means dividing the document into chunks of text, sparsely attending to one or a few chunks at a time using hard attention, then applying the usual full attention over those chunks – we call this method *coarse-to-fine attention*. Through experiments, we find that while coarse-to-fine attention does not perform as well as standard attention, it does show the desired behavior of sparsely reading the source sequence.

We structure the rest of the paper as follows. In Section 2, we introduce related work on summarization and neural attention. In Section 3, we review the encoder-decoder framework, and in Section 4 introduce our models. In Section 5, we describe our experimental setup, and in Section 6 show results. Finally, we conclude in Section 7.

2 Related Work

In summarization, neural attention models were first applied by Rush et al. (2015) to do headline

33

Proceedings of the Workshop on New Frontiers in Summarization, pages 33–42
Copenhagen, Denmark, September 7, 2017. ©2017 Association for Computational Linguistics

generation, i.e. produce a title for a news article given only the first sentence. Nallapati et al. (2016) and See et al. (2017) apply attention models to summarize full documents, achieving state-of-the-art results on the CNN/Dailymail dataset. All of these models, however, suffer from the inherent complexity of attention over the full document. Indeed, See et al. (2017) report that a single model takes over 3 days to train.

Many techniques have been proposed in the literature to efficiently handle the problem of large inputs to deep neural networks. One particular framework is that of "conditional computation", as coined by Bengio et al. (2013) — the idea is to only compute a subset of a network's units for a given input by gating different parts of the network.

Several methods, some stochastic and some deterministic, have been explored in the vein of conditional computation. In this work, we will focus on stochastic methods, although deterministic methods are worth considering as future work (Rae et al., 2016; Shazeer et al., 2017; Miller et al., 2016; Martins and Astudillo, 2016).

On the stochastic front, Xu et al. (2015) demonstrate the effectiveness of "hard" attention. While standard "soft" attention averages the representations of where the model attends to, hard attention discretely selects a single location. Hard attention has been successfully applied in various computer vision tasks (Mnih et al., 2014; Ba et al., 2015), but so far has limited usage in NLP. We will apply hard attention to the document summarization task by sparsifying our reading of the source text.

3 Background

We begin by describing the standard sequence-to-sequence attention model, also known as encoder-decoder models.

In the encoder-decoder architecture, an *encoder* recurrent neural network (RNN) reads the source sequence as input to produce the *context*, and a *decoder* RNN generates the output sequence using the context as input.

Formally, suppose we have a vocabulary $\mathcal{V}$. A given input sequence $w_1, \ldots, w_n \in \mathcal{V}$ is transformed into a sequence of vectors $\mathbf{x}_1, \ldots, \mathbf{x}_n \in \mathbb{R}^{d_{in}}$ through a word embedding matrix $\mathbf{E} \in \mathbb{R}^{|\mathcal{V}| \times d_{in}}$ as $\mathbf{x}_t = \mathbf{E}w_t$.

The encoder RNN is given by a parameterizable function f_{enc} and a hidden state $\mathbf{h}_t \in \mathbb{R}^{d_{hid}}$ at each time step t with $\mathbf{h}_t = f_{enc}(\mathbf{x}_t, \mathbf{h}_{t-1})$. In our models, we use the long-short term memory (LSTM) network (Hochreiter and Schmidhuber, 1997).

The decoder is another RNN f_{dec} that generates output words $y_t \in \mathcal{V}$. It keeps hidden state $\mathbf{h}_t^{dec} \in \mathbb{R}^{d_{hid}}$ as $\mathbf{h}_t^{dec} = f_{dec}(y_t, \mathbf{h}_{t-1}^{dec})$ similar to the encoder RNN. A context vector is produced at each time step using an attention function a that takes the encoded hidden states $[\mathbf{h}_1, \ldots, \mathbf{h}_n]$ and the current decoder hidden state $\mathbf{h}_t^{dec}$ and produces the context $\mathbf{c}_t \in \mathbb{R}^{d_{ctx}}$: $\mathbf{c}_t = a([\mathbf{h}_1, \ldots, \mathbf{h}_n], \mathbf{h}_t^{dec})$. As in Luong et al. (2015), we feed the context vector at time $t-1$ back into the decoder RNN at time t, i.e. $\mathbf{h}_t^{dec} = f_{dec}([y_t, \mathbf{c}_{t-1}], \mathbf{h}_{t-1}^{dec})$.

Finally, a linear projection and softmax (the generator) produces a distribution over output words $y_t \in \mathcal{V}$:

$$p(y_t | y_{t-1}, \ldots, y_1, [\mathbf{h}_1, \ldots, \mathbf{h}_n]) =$$
$$\mathrm{softmax}(\mathbf{W}^{out}\mathbf{c}_t + \mathbf{b}^{out})$$

The models are then trained end-to-end to minimize negative log-likelihood loss (NLL).

We note that we have great flexibility in how our attention function $a(\cdot)$ combines the encoder context and the current decoder hidden state. In the next section, we describe our models for $a(\cdot)$.

4 Models

We describe a few instantiations for the attention function $a(\cdot)$: **standard attention**, **hierarchical attention**, and **coarse-to-fine attention**.

4.1 Standard Attention

In Bahdanau et al. (2015), the function $a(\cdot)$ is implemented with an *attention network*. We compute attention weights for each encoder hidden state h_i as follows:

$$\beta_{t,i} = \mathbf{h}_i^{\top} \mathbf{W}^{attn} \mathbf{h}_t^{dec} \quad \forall i = 1, \ldots, n \quad (1)$$
$$\boldsymbol{\alpha}_t = \mathrm{softmax}(\boldsymbol{\beta}_t) \quad (2)$$
$$\widetilde{\mathbf{c}}_t = \sum_{i=1}^{n} \alpha_{t,i} \mathbf{h}_i \quad (3)$$

Attention allows us to select the most relevant words of the source (by assigning higher attention weights) when generating words at each time step.

Our final context vector is then $\mathbf{c}_t = \tanh(\mathbf{W}^2[\widetilde{\mathbf{c}}_t, \mathbf{h}_t^{dec}])$ for $\mathbf{W}^2 \in \mathbb{R}^{2d_{hid} \times d_{ctx}}$ a learned matrix.

Going forward, we call this instantiation of the attention function STANDARD.

4.2 Hierarchical Attention

The attention network of STANDARD is computationally expensive for long sequences — for each hidden state of the decoder, we need to compare it to every hidden state of the encoder in order to determine where to attend to. This seems unnecessary for a problem such as document summarization; intuitively, we only need to attend to a few important chunks of text at a time. Therefore, we propose a hierarchical method of attending to the document — by segmenting the document into large top-level chunks of text, we first attend to these chunks, then to the words within the chunks.

To accomplish this hierarchical attention, we construct encodings of the document at both levels. Suppose we have chunks $s_1, \ldots, s_m$ with words $w_{i,1}, \ldots, w_{i,n_i}$ in chunk s_i. For the top-level representations, we use a simple encoding model (e.g. bag of words or convolutions) on each s_i to obtain hidden states $\mathbf{h}_i^s \in \mathbb{R}^{d_{sent}}$ (see Section 5 for details). For the word representations, we run an LSTM encoder separately on the words of each chunk; specifically, we apply an RNN on s_i to get hidden states $\mathbf{h}_{i,j}$ for $i = 1, \ldots, m$ and $j = 1, \ldots, n_i$ where $\mathbf{h}_{i,j} = \mathrm{RNN}(\mathbf{h}_{i,j-1}, w_{i,j})$.

Using the top-level representations $\mathbf{h}_i^s$ and the word representations $\mathbf{h}_{i,j}$, we compute coarse attention weights $\alpha_1^s, \ldots, \alpha_m^s$ for the top-level chunks in the same way as STANDARD, and similarly compute fine attention weights $\alpha_{i,1}^w, \ldots, \alpha_{i,n_i}^w$ for each i. We then compute the final soft attention on word $w_{i,j}$ as $\alpha_{i,j} = \alpha_i^s \cdot \alpha_{i,j}^w$ (note this ensures that the weights normalize to 1 over the whole document). Finally, we proceed exactly as in standard attention by computing the weighted average over hidden states $\mathbf{h}_{i,j}$ to produce the context, i.e. $\widetilde{\mathbf{c}} = \sum_{i,j} \alpha_{i,j} \mathbf{h}_{i,j}$.

We label this attention method HIER. Next, we consider the hard attention version of this model to achieve sparsity in our network.

4.3 Coarse-to-Fine Attention

With the previous models STANDARD and HIER, we are required to compute hidden states over all words and top-level chunks in the document, so that if we have M chunks and N words per chunk, the computational complexity is $O(MN)$ for each attention step.

However, if we are able to perform conditional computation and only read M^+ of the chunks at a time, we can reduce the attention complexity to $O(M + M^+N)$, where we choose the chunks to attend to in $O(M)$ and read the selected chunks in $O(M^+N)$. Note that this expression ignores the total the number of words of the document, and the bottleneck becomes the length of each chunk of text.

In our model, we will apply stochastic sampling to the top-level attention distribution in the spirit of hard attention (Xu et al., 2015; Mnih et al., 2014; Ba et al., 2015) while keeping the lower-level attention as is. We call our method *coarse-to-fine attention*[1].

Specifically, using the top-level attention distribution $\alpha_1^s, \ldots, \alpha_m^s$, we select a single chunk s_i by sampling this distribution. We then set the context vector as $\sum_{j=1}^{n_i} \alpha_{i,j}^w \mathbf{h}_{i,j}$, where we use the word attention weights for the chosen chunk s_i. Note that this is equivalent to converting the top-level distribution α_i^s to a one-hot encoding based on the hard sample, then writing $\alpha_{i,j} = \alpha_i^s \cdot \alpha_{i,j}^w$ as in HIER. At test time, we take the max α_i^s for a one-hot encoding instead of sampling. We label this coarse-to-fine method C2F.

Because the hard attention model loses the property of being end-to-end differentiable, we use reinforcement learning to train our network. Specifically, we use the REINFORCE algorithm (Williams, 1992), also formalized by Schulman et al. (2015) in the stochastic computation graph framework. Layers before the hard attention node receive backpropagated policy gradient $\frac{\partial \mathcal{L}}{\partial \theta} = r \cdot \frac{\partial \log p(\alpha|\theta)}{\partial \theta}$, where r is some reward and $p(\alpha|\theta)$ is the attention distribution that we sample from.

Rewards and variance reduction We can think of our decoder RNN as a reinforcement learning agent where the state is the LSTM decoder state at time t and actions are the hard attention decisions. Since samples from α_t at time t of the RNN decoder can also affect future rewards, the total influenced reward is $\sum_{s=t}^{T} r_s$ at time t, where $r_t = \log p(y_t|y_1, \ldots, y_{t-1}, \mathbf{x})$ is the single step reward. Inspired by the discount factor from RL, we slightly modify the total reward: instead of simply taking the sum, we can scale later rewards with a discount factor γ, giving total reward $\sum_{s=t}^{T} \gamma^{s-t} r_s$ for the stochastic hard attention node a_t. We found

---

[1]The term coarse-to-fine attention has previously been introduced in the literature (Mei et al., 2016). However, their idea is different: they use coarse attention to reweight the fine attention computed over the entire input. This idea has also been called hierarchical attention (Nallapati et al., 2016).

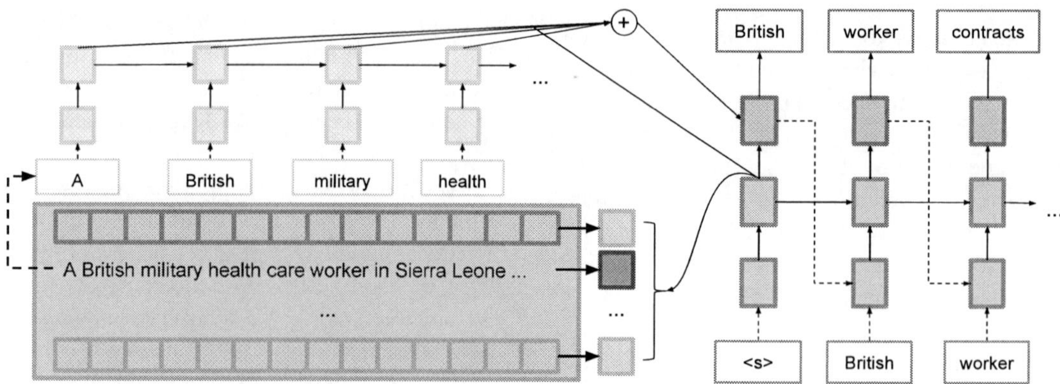

Figure 1: Model architecture for sequence-to-sequence with coarse-to-fine attention. The left side is the encoder that reads the document, and the right side is the decoder that produces the output sequence. On the encoder side, the top-level hidden states are used for the coarse attention weights, while the word-level hidden states are used for the fine attention weights. The context vector is then produced by a weighted average of the word-level states. In HIER, we average over the coarse attention weights, thus requiring computation of all word-level hidden states. In C2F, we make a hard decision for which chunk of text to use, and so we only need to compute word-level hidden states for one chunk.

that adding a discount factor helps in practice (we use $\gamma = 0.5$).

Training on the reward directly tends to have high variance, and so we subtract a baseline reward to help reduce variance as per Weaver and Tao (2001). To calculate these baselines, we store a constant b_t for each decoder time step t. We follow Xu et al. (2015) and keep an exponentially moving average of the reward for each time step t as $b_t \leftarrow b_t + \beta(r_t - b_t)$ where r_t is the average minibatch reward and β a learning rate (set to 0.1).

In addition to including a baseline, we also scale the rewards by a tuned hyperparameter λ — we found that scaling helped to stabilize training. We empirically set λ to 0.3. Therefore, our final reward at time t can be written as

$$\lambda \sum_{s=t}^{T} \gamma^{s-t}(r_s - b_s) \qquad (4)$$

ALTERNATE training   Xu et al. (2015) explain that training hard attention with REINFORCE has very high variance, even when including a baseline. Thus, for every minibatch of training, they randomly use soft attention instead of hard attention with some probability (they use 0.5). The backpropagated gradient is then the standard soft attention gradient instead of the REINFORCE gradient. When we use this training method in our results, we label it as +ALTERNATE.

Multiple samples   From our initial experiments with C2F, we found that taking a single sample

was not very effective. However, we discovered that sampling multiple times from the attention distribution α^s improves performance.

To be precise, we fix a number k_{mul} for the number of times we sample from α^s. Then, we sample based on the multinomial distribution $\mu \sim \mathrm{Mult}(k_{mul}, \{\alpha_i\}_{i=1}^{m})$ to produce the new top-level attention vector $\widetilde{\alpha}^s$, with $\widetilde{\alpha}_i^s = \mu_i / k_{mul}$. In our results, we label this as +MULTI.

Intuitively, k_{mul} is the number of top-level chunks we select to produce the context. With higher k_{mul}, the hard attention model more closely approximates the soft attention model, and hence should lead to better performance. This, however, incurs a cost in computational complexity.

5   Experiments

5.1   Data

Experiments were performed on a version of the CNN/Dailymail dataset from Hermann et al. (2015). Each data point is a news document accompanied by up to 4 "highlights", and we take the first of these as our target summary. Note that our dataset differs from related work (Nallapati et al., 2016; See et al., 2017) which take all the highlights as the summary, as we were less interested in target side length and more in correctly locating sparse attention in the source.

Train, validation, and test splits are provided with the original dataset along with document tokenization and sentence splitting. We do additional preprocessing by replacing all numbers with # and appending end of sentence tokens </s> to each sentence. We limit our vocabulary size to the 50000 most frequent words, replacing the rest with <unk> tokens.

5.2 Implementation Details

To ease minibatch training on the hierarchical models, we arrange the first 400 words of the document into a 10 by 40 image and take each row to be a top-level chunk. For HIER, we also experiment with shapes of 5 by 80 and 2 by 200 (denoted 5x80, 2x200 resp.). These should more closely approximate STANDARD as the shape approaches a single sequence.

In addition, we pad short documents to the maximum length with a special padding word and allow the model to attend to it. However, we zero out word embeddings for the padding states and also zero out their corresponding LSTM states. We found in practice that very little of the attention ended up on the corresponding states.

5.3 Models

Baselines We consider a few baseline models. A strong and simple baseline is the first sentence of the document, which we denote FIRST.

We also consider the integer linear programming (ILP) based document summarizer of Durrett et al. (2016). We apply the code [2] directly on the test set without retraining the system. We provide the necessary preprocessing using the Berkeley coreference system[3]. We call this baseline ILP.

Our models We ran experiments with the models STANDARD, HIER, and C2F as described above.

For the coarse attention representations $\mathbf{h}_i^s$ of HIER and C2F, we experiment with convolutional and bag of words encodings. We use convolutions for the top-level representations by default, where we follow Kim (2014) and perform a convolution over each window of words in the chunk using 600 filters of kernel width 6. We use max-over-time pooling to obtain a fixed-dimensional top-level representation in $\mathbb{R}^{d_f}$ where $d_f = 600$ is the number of filters. For bag of words, we simply take the top-level representation as the sum of

the chunk's word embeddings (for a separate embedding matrix), and we write BOW when we use this encoding. For BOW models, we fix the word embeddings on the encoder side (in other models, they are fine tuned).

As an addition to any top-level representation method, we can include *positional embeddings*. In general, we expect the order of text in the document to matter for summarization — for example, the first few sentences are usually important. We therefore include the option to concatenate a 25-dimensional embedding of the chunk's position to the representation. When we use positional embeddings, we write +POS.

For C2F, we include options +MULTI for $k_{mul} > 1$, +PRETRAIN for starting with a model pretrained with soft attention for 1 epoch, and +ALTERNATE for sampling between hard and soft attention with probability 0.5.

5.4 Training

We train with minibatch stochastic gradient descent (SGD) with batch size 20 for 20 epochs, renormalizing gradients below norm 5. We initialize the learning rate to 0.1 for the top-level encoder and 1 for the rest of the model, and begin decaying it by a factor of 0.5 each epoch after the validation perplexity stops decreasing.

We use 2 layer LSTMs with 500 hidden units, and we initialize word embeddings with 300-dimensional word2vec embeddings (Mikolov and Dean, 2013). We initialize all other parameters as uniform in the interval $[-0.1, 0.1]$. For convolutional layers, we use a kernel width of 6 and 600 filters. Positional embeddings have dimension 25. We use dropout (Srivastava et al., 2014) between stacked LSTM hidden states and before the final word generator layer to regularize (with dropout probability 0.3). At test time, we run beam search to produce the summary with a beam size of 5.

Our models are implemented using Torch based on a past version of the OpenNMT system[4] (Klein et al., 2017). We ran our experiments on a 12GB Geforce GTX Titan X GPU. The models take between 2-2.5 hours to train per epoch.

5.5 Evaluation

We report metrics for perplexity and ROUGE balanced F-scores (Lin, 2004) on the test set.

---

[2]https://github.com/gregdurrett/berkeley-doc-summarizer
[3]https://github.com/gregdurrett/berkeley-entity

[4]http://opennmt.net

With multiple gold summaries in the CNN/Dailymail highlights, we take the max ROUGE score over the gold summaries for a predicted summary, as our models are trained to produce a single sentence. The final metric is then the average over all test data points.[5]

Note that because we are training the model to output a single highlight, our numbers are not comparable with Nallapati et al. (2016) or See et al. (2017).

6 Results

Table 1 shows summarization results. We see that our soft attention models comfortably beat the baselines, while hard attention lags behind.

The ILP model ROUGE scores are surprisingly low. We attribute this to the fact that our models usually produce a single sentence as the summary, while the ILP system can produce multiple. ILP therefore has comparatively high ROUGE recall while suffering in precision.

Unfortunately, the STANDARD sequence-to-sequence baseline proves to be difficult to beat. HIER performs surprisingly poorly, even though the hierarchical assumption seems like a natural one to make. We believe that the assumption that we can factor the attention distribution into learned coarse and fine factors may in fact be too strong. Because the training signal is back-propagated to the word-level LSTM via the coarse attention, the training algorithm cannot directly compare word attention weights as in STANDARD. Thus, the model does not learn how to attend to the most relevant top-level chunks, instead averaging the attention as a backoff (see 6.1). Additionally, the shapes 5x80 and 2x200 perform slightly better, indicating that the model prefers to have fewer sequences to attend to.

C2F results are significantly worse than soft attention results. As has been previously observed (Zaremba and Sutskever, 2015), training with reinforcement learning is inherently more difficult than standard maximum likelihood, as the signal from rewards tends to have high variance (even with variance reduction techniques). Thus, it may be too difficult to train the encoder (which forms a large part of the model) using such a noisy gradient. Even with soft attention pretraining (+PRETRAIN) and alternating training

---

[5]We run the ROUGE 1.5.5 script with flags -m -n 2 -a -f B.

(+ALTERNATE), C2F fails to reach HIER performance.

While taking a single sample performs quite poorly, we see that taking more than one sample gives a significant boost to scores (+MULTI2, +MULTI3). There seem to be diminishing returns as we take more samples.

Finally, we note that positional embeddings (+POS) give a nontrivial boost to scores and causes the attention to prefer the front of the document. The exception, C2F + POS, is due to the fact that the attention collapses to always highlight the first top-level chunk.

We show predicted summaries from each model in Figure 2. We note that the ILP system, which extracts sentences first, produces long summaries. In contrast, the generated summaries tend to be quite succinct, and most are the result of copying or paraphrasing specific sentences.

Source: isis supporters have vowed to murder twitter staff because they believe the site 's policy of shutting down their extremist pages is a ' virtual war ' . </s> a mocked - up image of the site 's founder jack dorsey in <unk> was posted yesterday alongside a diatribe written in arabic , which claimed twitter employees ' necks are ' a target for the soldiers of the caliphate ' . </s> addressing mr dorsey personally , it claimed twitter was taking sides in a ' media war ' which allowed ' slaughter ' , adding : ' your virtual war on us will cause a real war on you . </s> diatribe : an image of twitter founder jack dorsey in <unk> was posted alongside a rant in arabic </s> ...

GOLD: diatribe in arabic posted anonymously yesterday and shared online
FIRST: isis supporters have vowed to murder twitter staff because they believe the site 's policy of shutting down their extremist pages is a ' virtual war ' .
ILP: ISIS supporters have vowed to murder Twitter staff because they believe the site 's policy of shutting down their extremist pages is a ' virtual war ' . Twitter was taking sides . Islamic State militants have swept through huge tracts of Syria and Iraq , murdering thousands of people .

STANDARD: image of jack dorsey 's founder jack dorsey posted on twitter
HIER: the message was posted in arabic and posted on twitter
HIER BOW: the message was posted on twitter and posted on twitter
HIER +POS: dorsey in <unk> was posted yesterday alongside a diatribe in arabic
C2F: ' lone war ' is a ' virtual war ' image of the islamic state
C2F +MULTI2: isis supporters say site 's policy of shutting down is a ' propaganda war '
C2F +POS +MULTI2: twitter users say they believe site 's policy of closure is a ' media war '

Figure 2: Predicted summaries for each model. The source document is truncated for clarity.

6.1 Analysis

Sharpness of Attention We are interested in measuring the ability of our models to focus on a single top-level chunk using attention. Quantitatively, we measure the entropy of the coarse attention on the validation set in Table 2. Intu-

Model	PPL	ROUGE-1	ROUGE-2	ROUGE-L
FIRST	-	32.3	15.5	27.4
ILP	-	29.1	16.0	26.5
STANDARD	13.9	34.7	18.8	32.3
HIER	16.0	33.3	17.5	31.0
HIER BOW	16.3	33.0	17.4	30.7
HIER +POS	15.4	34.2	18.3	31.8
HIER 5x80	15.0	33.9	18.0	31.5
HIER 2x200	14.5	33.9	18.1	31.6
C2F	32.8	28.2	12.9	26.2
C2F +POS	37.8	28.3	12.5	26.1
C2F +MULTI2	25.5	30.0	14.4	27.9
C2F +POS +MULTI2	21.9	31.2	15.3	29.0
C2F +MULTI3	22.9	30.4	14.9	28.3
C2F +PRETRAIN	26.3	29.7	14.2	27.5
C2F +ALTERNATE	23.6	31.1	15.4	28.8

Table 1: Summarization results for CNN/Dailymail (first highlight as target) on perplexity (PPL) and ROUGE metrics.

Model	Entropy
STANDARD	1.31
HIER	2.14
C2F	0.15
C2F +MULTI2	0.59
C2F +POS +MULTI2	0.46

Table 2: Entropy over coarse attention, averaged over all attention distributions in the validation set. For reference, uniform attention in our case gives entropy ≈ 2.30.

itively, higher entropy means the attention is more spread out, while lower entropy means the attention is concentrated.

We compute the entropy numbers by averaging over all generated words in the validation set. Because each document has been split into 10 chunks, perfectly uniform entropy would be ≈ 2.30.

We note that the entropy of C2F is very low (before taking the argmax at test time). This is exactly what we had hoped for — we will see that the model in fact learns to focus on only a few top-level chunks of the document over the course of generation. If we have multiple samples with +MULTI2, the model is allowed to use 2 chunks at a time, which relaxes the entropy slightly.

We also observe that the HIER entropy is very high and almost uniform. The model appears to be averaging the encoder hidden states across chunks, indicating that the training failed to find the same optimum as in STANDARD. We discuss this further in the next section.

Attention Heatmaps For the document in Figure 2, we visualize the coarse attention distributions produced by each model in Figure 3.

In each figure, the rows are the top-level chunks of each document (40 words per row), and the columns are the summary words produced by the model. The intensity of each box for a given column represents the strength of the attention weight on that row. For STANDARD, the heatmap is produced by summing the word-level attention weights in each row.

In HIER, we observe that the attention becomes washed out (in accord with its high entropy) and is essentially averaging all of the encoder hidden states. This is surprising because in theory, HIER should be able to replicate the same attention distribution as STANDARD.

If we examine the word-level attention (not pictured here), we find that the model focuses on stop words (e.g. punctuation marks, </s>) in the encoder. We posit this may be due to the LSTM "saving" information at these words, and so the soft attention model can best retrieve the information by averaging over these hidden states. Alternatively, the model may be ignoring the encoder and generating only from the decoder language model.

In C2F, we see that we get very sharp attention on some rows as we had hoped. Unfortunately, the model has trouble deciding where to attend to, oscillating between the first and second-to-last rows. We partially alleviate this problem by allowing the model to attend to multiple rows in hard attention. Indeed, with +MULTI2 +POS, the model actually produces a very coherent output by focusing attention near the beginning. We believe that the improved result for this example is not only due to more flexibility in where to attend, but a better

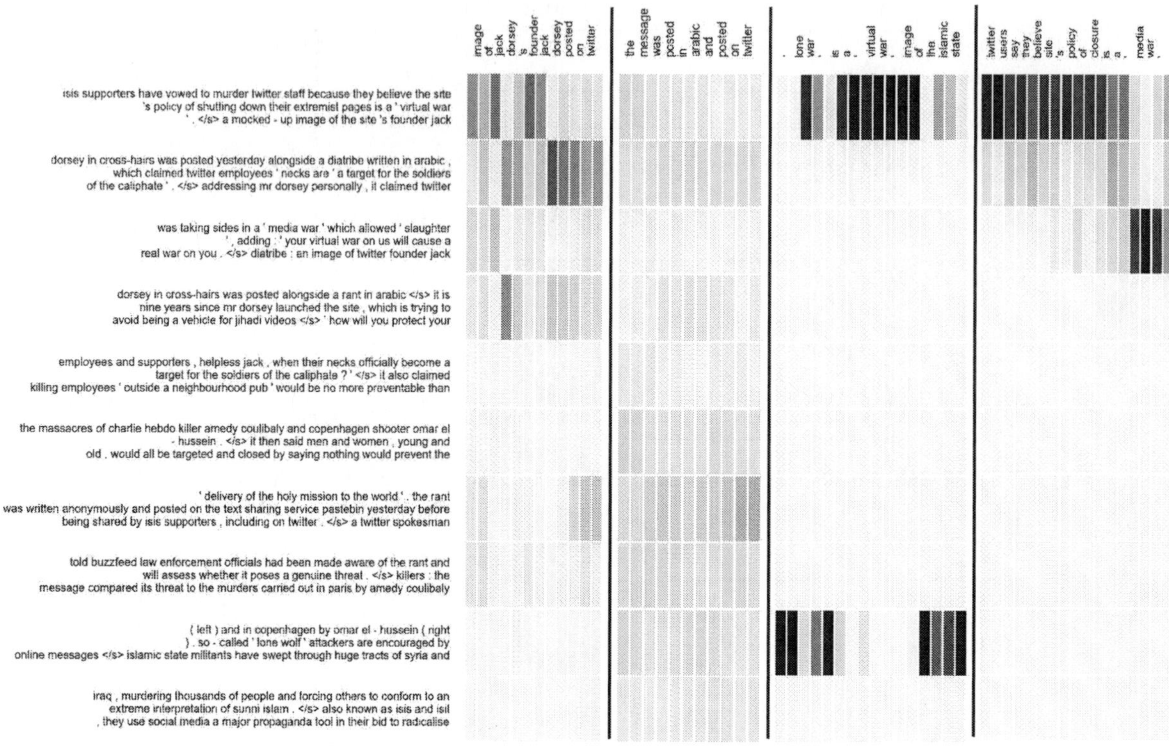

Figure 3: Sentence attention visualizations for different models. From left to right: (1) STANDARD, (2) HIER, (3) C2F, (4) C2F +MULTI2 +POS.

encoding model due to the training process.

7 Conclusion

In this work, we experiment with a novel coarse-to-fine attention model on the CNN/Dailymail dataset. We find that both versions of our model, HIER and C2F, fail to beat the standard sequence-to-sequence model on metrics, but C2F has the desired property of sharp attention on a small subset of the source. Therefore, coarse-to-fine attention shows promise for scaling up existing models to larger inputs.

Further experimentation is needed to improve these attention models to state of the art. In particular, we need to better understand (1) the reason for the subpar performance and high entropy of hierarchical attention, (2) how to control the variance training of reinforcement learning, and (3) how to balance the tradeoff between stronger models and attention sparsity over long source sequences. We would also like to investigate alternatives to reinforcement learning for implementing sparse attention, e.g. sparsemax (Martins and Astudillo, 2016) and key-value memory networks

(Miller et al., 2016) (preliminary investigations with sparsemax were not extremely promising, but we leave this to future work). Resolving these issues can allow attention models to become more scalable, especially in computationally intensive tasks such as document summarization.

References

Jimmy Ba, Volodymyr Mnih, and Koray Kavukcuoglu. 2015. Multiple Object Recognition with Visual Attention. *Proceedings of the International Conference on Learning Representations (ICLR)* .

Dzmitry Bahdanau, Kyunghyun Cho, and Yoshua Bengio. 2015. Neural Machine Translation By Jointly Learning To Align and Translate. *ICLR* .

Yoshua Bengio, Nicholas Léonard, and Aaron C Courville. 2013. Estimating or Propagating Gradients Through Stochastic Neurons for Conditional Computation. *CoRR abs/1308.3*.

Greg Durrett, Taylor Berg-Kirkpatrick, and Dan Klein. 2016. Learning-Based Single-Document Summarization with Compression and Anaphoricity Constraints. *Proceedings of the 54th Annual Meeting of the Association for Computational Linguistics (Volume 1: Long Papers)* pages 1998–2008.

KM Hermann, T Kocisky, and E Grefenstette. 2015. Teaching machines to read and comprehend. *Advances in Neural Information Processing Systems* pages 1–9.

Sepp Hochreiter and Jürgen Schmidhuber. 1997. Long short-term memory. *Neural computation* 9(8):1735–1780.

Yoon Kim. 2014. Convolutional Neural Networks for Sentence Classification. *Proceedings of the 2014 Conference on Empirical Methods in Natural Language Processing (EMNLP 2014)* pages 1746–1751.

Guillaume Klein, Yoon Kim, Yuntian Deng, Jean Senellart, and Alexander M. Rush. 2017. OpenNMT: Open-Source Toolkit for Neural Machine Translation .

Jiwei Li, Michel Galley, Chris Brockett, Jianfeng Gao, and Bill Dolan. 2016. A Persona-Based Neural Conversation Model. *arXiv preprint arXiv:1603.06155* .

Chin-Yew Lin. 2004. Rouge: A package for automatic evaluation of summaries. In *Text summarization branches out: Proceedings of the ACL-04 workshop*. Barcelona, Spain, volume 8.

Minh-Thang Luong, Hieu Pham, and Christopher D. Manning. 2015. Effective Approaches to Attention-based Neural Machine Translation. *Emnlp* (September):11.

André F. T. Martins and Ramón Fernandez Astudillo. 2016. From Softmax to Sparsemax: A Sparse Model of Attention and Multi-Label Classification. *Proceedings of The 33rd International Conference on Machine Learning* pages 1614–1623.

Hongyuan Mei, Mohit Bansal, and Matthew R. Walter. 2016. What to talk about and how? Selective Generation using LSTMs with Coarse-to-Fine Alignment. *Proceedings of NAACL-HLT* pages 1–11.

Tomas Mikolov and Jeffrey Dean. 2013. Distributed representations of words and phrases and their compositionality. *Advances in Neural Information Processing Systems* .

Alexander Miller, Adam Fisch, Jesse Dodge, Amir-Hossein Karimi, Antoine Bordes, and Jason Weston. 2016. Key-Value Memory Networks for Directly Reading Documents. *Proceedings of the 2016 Conference on Empirical Methods in Natural Language Processing (EMNLP-16)* abs/1606.0:1400–1409.

Volodymyr Mnih, Nicolas Heess, Alex Graves, and koray Kavukcuoglu. 2014. Recurrent models of visual attention. *Advances in Neural Information Processing Systems* pages 2204—-2212.

Ramesh Nallapati, Bowen Zhou, Cicero Nogueira dos Santos, Caglar Gulcehre, and Bing Xiang. 2016. Abstractive Text Summarization Using Sequence-to-Sequence RNNs and Beyond. *Proceedings of CoNLL* abs/1602.0:280–290.

Jack Rae, Jonathan J Hunt, Ivo Danihelka, Timothy Harley, Andrew W Senior, Gregory Wayne, Alex Graves, and Tim Lillicrap. 2016. Scaling Memory-Augmented Neural Networks with Sparse Reads and Writes. In D D Lee, M Sugiyama, U V Luxburg, I Guyon, and R Garnett, editors, *Advances in Neural Information Processing Systems 29*, Curran Associates, Inc., pages 3621–3629.

Alexander M Rush, Sumit Chopra, and Jason Weston. 2015. A Neural Attention Model for Abstractive Sentence Summarization. *In Proceedings of the Conference on Empirical Methods in Natural Language Processing (EMNLP)* .

John Schulman, Nicolas Heess, Theophane Weber, and Pieter Abbeel. 2015. Gradient Estimation Using Stochastic Computation Graphs. *NIPS* pages 1–13.

Abigail See, Peter J. Liu, and Christopher D. Manning. 2017. Get To The Point: Summarization with Pointer-Generator Networks .

Noam Shazeer, Azalia Mirhoseini, Krzysztof Maziarz, Andy Davis, Quoc Le, Geoffrey Hinton, and Jeff Dean. 2017. Outrageously Large Neural Networks: the Sparsely-Gated Mixture-of-Experts Layer. *Proceedings of the International Conference on Learning Representations (ICLR)* .

Nitish Srivastava, Geoffrey Hinton, Alex Krizhevsky, Ilya Sutskever, and Ruslan Salakhutdinov. 2014. Dropout: A Simple Way to Prevent Neural Networks from Overfitting. *Journal of Machine Learning Research* 15:1929–1958.

Ilya Sutskever, Oriol Vinyals, and Quoc V Le. 2014. Sequence to sequence learning with neural networks. In *Advances in neural information processing systems*. pages 3104–3112.

Lex Weaver and Nigel Tao. 2001. The optimal reward baseline for gradient-based reinforcement learning. *Proceedings of the Seventeenth conference on Uncertainty in artificial intelligence* pages 538–545.

Ronald J Williams. 1992. Simple statistical gradient-following algorithms for connectionist reinforcement learning. *Machine learning* 8(3-4):229–256.

Kelvin Xu, Jimmy Ba, Ryan Kiros, Kyunghyun Cho, Aaron C Courville, Ruslan Salakhutdinov, Richard S Zemel, and Yoshua Bengio. 2015. Show, Attend and Tell: Neural Image Caption Generation with Visual Attention. *ICML* 14:77—-81.

Wojciech Zaremba and Ilya Sutskever. 2015. Reinforcement Learning Neural Turing Machines. *CoRR* abs/1505.0.

Automatic Community Creation
for Abstractive Spoken Conversation Summarization

Karan Singla[1,2], Evgeny A. Stepanov[2], Ali Orkan Bayer[2],
Giuseppe Carenini[3], Giuseppe Riccardi[2]

[1]SAIL, University of Southern California, Los Angeles, CA, USA

[2]Signals and Interactive Systems Lab, DISI, University of Trento, Trento, Italy

[3]Department of Computer Science, University of British Columbia, Vancouver, Canada

`singlak@usc.edu`, `carenini@cs.ubc.ca`

`{evgeny.stepanov,aliorkan.bayer,giuseppe.riccardi}@unitn.it`

Abstract

Summarization of spoken conversations is a challenging task, since it requires deep understanding of dialogs. Abstractive summarization techniques rely on linking the summary sentences to sets of original conversation sentences, i.e. communities. Unfortunately, such linking information is rarely available or requires trained annotators. We propose and experiment automatic community creation using cosine similarity on different levels of representation: raw text, WordNet SynSet IDs, and word embeddings. We show that the abstractive summarization systems with automatic communities significantly outperform previously published results on both English and Italian corpora.

1 Introduction

Spoken conversation summarization is an important task, since speech is the primary medium of human-human communication. Vast amounts of spoken conversation data are produced daily in call-centers. Due to this overwhelming number of conversations, call-centers can only evaluate a small percentage of the incoming calls (Stepanov et al., 2015). Automatic methods of conversation summarization have a potential to increase the capacity of the call-centers to analyze and assess their work.

Earlier works on conversation summarization have mainly focused on extractive techniques. However, as pointed out in (Murray et al., 2010) and (Oya et al., 2014), abstractive summaries are preferred to extractive ones by human judges. The possible reason for this is that extractive techniques are not well suited for the conversation summarization, since there are style differences between spoken conversations and human-authored summaries. Abstractive conversation summarization systems, on the other hand, are mainly based on the extraction of lexical information (Mehdad et al., 2013; Oya et al., 2014). The authors cluster conversation sentences/utterances into communities to identify most relevant ones and aggregate them using word-graph models.

The graph paths are ranked to yield abstract sentences – a template. And these templates are selected for population with entities extracted from a conversation. Thus the abstractive summarization systems are limited to these templates generated by supervised data sources. The template selection strategy in these systems leverages on the manual links between summary and conversation sentences. Unfortunately, such manual links are rarely available.

In this paper we evaluate a set of heuristics for automatic linking of summary and conversations sentences, i.e. 'community' creation. The heuristics rely on the similarity between the two, and we experiment with the cosine similarity computation on different levels of representation – raw text, text after replacing the verbs with their Word-Net SynSet IDs, and the similarity computed using distributed word embeddings. The heuristics are evaluated within the template-based abstractive summarization system of Oya et al. (2014). We extend this system to Italian using required NLP tools. However, the approach transparently extends to other languages with available Word-Net, minimal supervised summarization corpus and running text. Heuristics are evaluated and compared on AMI meeting corpus and Italian LUNA Human-Human conversation corpus.

The overall description of the system with the more detailed description of the heuristics is provided in Section 2. In Section 3 we describe the corpora, evaluation methodology and the commu-

43

Proceedings of the Workshop on New Frontiers in Summarization, pages 43–47

Copenhagen, Denmark, September 7, 2017. ©2017 Association for Computational Linguistics

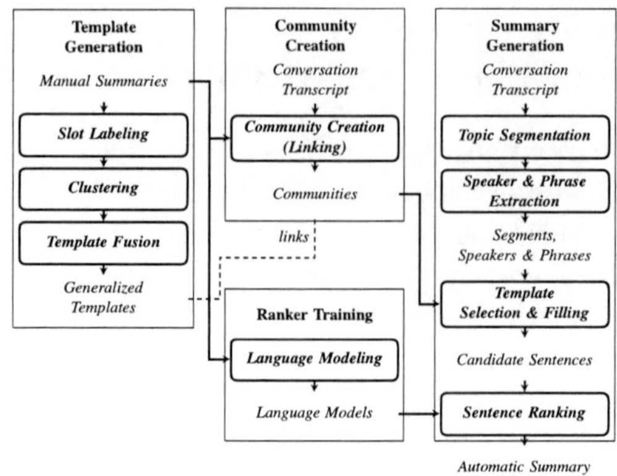

Figure 1: Abstractive summarization pipeline.

nity creation experiments. Section 4 provides concluding remarks and future directions.

2 Methodology

In this section we describe the conversation summarization pipeline that is partitioned into community creation, template generation, ranker training, and summary generation components. The whole pipeline is depicted in Figure 1.

2.1 Template Generation

Template Generation follows the approach of (Oya et al., 2014) and, starting from human-authored summaries, produces abstract templates applying slot labeling, summary clustering and template fusion steps. The information required for the template generation are part-of-speech (POS) tags, noun and verb phrase chunks, and root verbs from dependency parsing.

For English, we use Illinois Chunker (Punyakanok and Roth, 2001) to identify noun phrases and extract part-of-speech tags; and the the tool of (De Marneffe et al., 2006) for generating dependency parses. For Italian, on the other hand, we use TextPro 2.0 (Pianta et al., 2008) to perform all the Natural Language Processing tasks.

In the slot labeling step, noun phrases from human-authored summaries are replaced by WordNet (Fellbaum, 1998) SynSet IDs of the head nouns (right most for English). For a word, SynSet ID of the most frequent sense is selected with respect to the POS-tag. To get hypernyms for Italian we use MultiWordNet (Pianta et al., 2002).

The clustering of the abstract templates generated in the previous step is performed using the WordNet hierarchy of the root verb of a sentence.

The similarity between verbs is computed with respect to the shortest path that connects the senses in the hypernym taxonomy of WordNet. The template graphs, created using this similarity, are then clustered using the Normalized Cuts method (Shi and Malik, 2000).

The clustered templates are further generalized using a word graph algorithm extended to templates in (Oya et al., 2014). The paths in the word graph are ranked using language models trained on the abstract templates and the top 10 are selected as a template for the cluster.

2.2 Community Creation

In the AMI Corpus, sentences in human-authored summaries are manually linked to a set of the sentences/utterances in the meeting transcripts, referred to as communities. It is hypothesized that a community sentence covers a single topic and conveys vital information about the conversation segment. For the automatic community creation we explore four heuristics.

- *H1* (baseline): take the whole conversation as a community for each sentence;
- *H2*: The 4 closest turns with respect to cosine similarity between a summary and a conversation sentence.
- *H3*: The 4 closest turns with respect to cosine similarity after replacing the verbs with WordNet SynSet ID.
- *H4*: The 4 closest turns with respect to cosine similarity of averaged word embedding vectors obtained using word2vec for a turn.(Mikolov et al., 2013).

The number of sentences selected for a community is set to 4, since it is the average size of the manual community in the AMI corpus.

We use word2vec tool (Mikolov et al., 2013) for learning distributed word embeddings. For English, we obtained pre-trained word embeddings trained on a part of Google News data set (about 3 billion words)[1]. The model contains 300-dimensional vectors for 3 million words and phrases. For Italian, we use the word2vec to train word embeddings on the Europarl Italian corpus (Koehn, 2005)[2]. We empirically choose 300, 5, and 5 for the embedding size, window length, and word count threshold, respectively.

---

[1] https://github.com/mmihaltz/word2vec-GoogleNews-vectors
[2] http://www.statmt.org/europarl/

2.3 Summary Generation

The first step in summary generation is the segmentation of conversations into topics using a lexical cohesion-based domain-independent discourse segmenter – LCSeg (Galley et al., 2003). The purpose of this step is to cover all the conversation topics. Next, all possible slot 'fillers' are extracted from the topic segments and are ranked with respect to their frequency in the conversation.

An abstract template for a segment is selected with respect to the average cosine similarity of the segment and the community linked to that template. The selected template slots are filled with the 'fillers' extracted earlier.

2.4 Sentence Ranking

Since the system produces many sentences that might repeat the same information, the final set of automatic sentences is selected from these filled templates with respect to the ranking using the token and part-of-speech tag 3-gram language models. In this paper, different from (Oya et al., 2014), the sentence ranking is based solely on the n-gram language models trained on the tokens and part-of-speech tags from the human-authored summaries.

3 Experiments and Results

We evaluate the automatic community creation heuristics on the AMI meeting corpus (Carletta et al., 2006) and Italian and English LUNA Human-Human corpora (Dinarelli et al., 2009).

3.1 Data Sets

The two corpora used for the evaluation of the heuristics are AMI and LUNA. The AMI meeting corpus (Carletta et al., 2006) is a collection of 139 meeting records where groups of people are engaged in a 'roleplay' as a team and each speaker assumes a certain role in a team (e.g. project manager (PM)). Following (Oya et al., 2014), we removed 20 dialogs used by the authors for development, and use the remaining dialogs for the three-fold cross-validation.

The LUNA Human-Human corpus (Dinarelli et al., 2009) consists of 572 call-center dialogs where a client and an agent are engaged in a problem solving task over the phone. The 200 Italian LUNA dialogs have been annotated with summaries by 5 native speakers (5 summaries per dialog). For the Call Centre Conversation Summarization (CCCS) shared task (Favre et al., 2015)

a set of 100 dialogs was manually translated to English. The conversations are equally split into training and testing sets as 100/100 for Italian, and 50/50 for English.

3.2 Evaluation

ROUGE-2 metric (Lin, 2004) is used for the evaluation. The metric considers bigram-level precision, recall and F-measure between a set of reference and hypothesis summaries. For AMI corpus, following (Oya et al., 2014), we report ROUGE-2 F-measures on 3-fold cross-validation. For LUNA Corpus, on the other hand, we have used the modified version of ROUGE 1.5.5 toolkit from the CCCS Shared Task (Favre et al., 2015), which was adapted to deal with a conversation-dependent length limit of 7%. Unlike the AMI Corpus, the official reported results for the CCCS Shared Task were recall; thus, for LUNA Corpus the reported values are ROUGE-2 recall.

For statistical significance testing, we use a paired bootstrap resampling method proposed in (Koehn, 2004). We create new virtual test sets of 15 conversations with random re-sampling 100 times. For each set, we compute the ROUGE-2 score and compare the system performances using paired t-test with $p = 0.05$.

3.3 Results

In this section we report on the results of the abstractive summarization system using the community creation heuristics described in Section 2.

Following the Call-Center Conversation Summarization Shared Task at MultiLing 2015 (Favre et al., 2015), for LUNA Corpus (Dinarelli et al., 2009) we compare performances to three extractive baselines: (1) the longest turn in the conversation up to the length limit (7% of a conversation) (*Baseline-L*), (2) the longest turn in the first 25% of the conversation up to the length limit (*Baseline-LB*) (Trione, 2014), and (3) Maximal Marginal Relevance (*MMR*) (Carbonell and Goldstein, 1998) with $\lambda = 0.7$. For AMI corpus, on the other hand, we compare performances to the abstractive systems reported in (Oya et al., 2014).

The performances of the heuristics on AMI corpus are given in Table 1. In the table we also report the performances of the previously published summarization systems that make use of the manual communities – (Oya et al., 2014) and (Mehdad et al., 2013); and our run of the system of (Oya et al., 2014). With manual communities we have

Model	ROUGE-2
Mehdad et al. (2013)	0.040
Oya et al. (2014) (15 seg.)	0.068
Manual Communities	0.072
(H2) Top 4 turns: token	0.076
(H3) Top 4 turns: SynSetID	0.077
(H4) Top 4 turns: Av. WE	**0.079**

Table 1: Average ROUGE-2 F-measures on 3-fold cross-validation for the abstractive summarization systems on AMI corpus.

Model	EN	IT
Extractive Systems		
Baseline-L	0.015	0.015
Baseline-LB	0.023	0.027
MMR	0.024	0.020
Abstractive Systems		
(H1) Whole Conversation	0.019	0.018
(H2) Top 4 turns: token	0.039	0.021
(H3) Top 4 turns: SynSetID	0.041	0.025
(H4) Top 4 turns: Av. WE	**0.051**	**0.029**

Table 2: ROUGE-2 recall with 7% summary length limit for the extractive baselines (Favre et al., 2015) and abstractive summarization systems with the community creation heuristics on LUNA corpus.

obtained average F-measure of 0.072. From the table, we can observe that all the systems with automatic community creation heuristics and the simplified sentence ranking described in Section 2 outperform the systems with manual communities. Among the heuristics, average word embedding-based cosine similarity metric performs the best with average F-measure of 0.079. All the systems with automatic community creation heuristics (*H2*, *H3*, *H4*) perform significantly better than the system with manual communities.

For Italian, the extractive baseline that selects the longest utterance from the first quarter of a conversation, is the strong baseline with ROUGE-2 recall of 0.027. It is not surprising, since the longest turn from the beginning of the conversation is usually a problem description, which appears in human-authored summaries. In the CCCS Shared Task, none of the submitted systems was able to outperform it. The system with a word embedding-based automatic community creation heuristic, however, achieves recall of 0.029, significantly outperforming it.

Using word embeddings allow us to exploit monolingual data, which helps to avoid the problem of data sparsity encountered using WordNet, which allows for better communities on out-of-domain data set and better coverage. This fact can account for the wider gap in performance between using H2 – H4 heuristics.

For the 100 English LUNA dialogs, we observe the same pattern as for Italian dialogs and AMI corpus: the best performance is observed for the similarity using word embeddings (0.051). However, for English LUNA, the best extractive baseline is weaker, as *H2* and *H3* heuristics are able to outperform it.

The additional observation is that the performance for English is generally higher. Moreover, word embeddings provide larger boost on English LUNA. Whether this is due to the properties of Italian or the differences in the amount and domain of data used for training word embeddings is a question we plan to address in the future. We also observe that English WordNet gives a better lexical coverage than the Multilingual WordNet used for Italian. Thus, it becomes important to explore methods which does not rely on WordNet, as now the Italian system may be suffering from the data sparsity problem due to it.

Overall, the heuristics with word embedding vectors perform the best on both corpora and across-languages. Consequently, we conclude that automatic community creation with word embedding for similarity computation is a good technique for the abstractive summarization of spoken conversations.

4 Conclusion

In this paper we have presented automatic community creation heuristics for abstractive spoken conversation summarization. The heuristics are based on the cosine similarity between conversation and summary sentences. The similarity is computed as different levels: raw text, text after verbs are replaces with WordNet SynSet IDs and average word embedding similarity. The heuristics are evaluated on AMI meeting corpus and LUNA human-human conversation corpus. The community creation heuristic based on cosine similarity using word embedding vectors outperforms all the other heuristics on both corpora, as well as it outperforms the previously published results.

We have observed that the systems generally perform better on English; and the performance differences among heuristics is less for Italian. The Italian word embedding were trained on Europarl, that is much smaller in size than the data that was used to train English embeddings. In the future we plan to address these issues and train embeddings on a larger more diverse corpus.

References

Jaime Carbonell and Jade Goldstein. 1998. The use of mmr, diversity-based reranking for reordering documents and producing summaries. In *Proc. of the 21st Annual International ACM SIGIR Conference on Research and Development in Information Retrieval*. ACM, pages 335–336.

Jean Carletta, Simone Ashby, Sebastien Bourban, Mike Flynn, Mael Guillemot, Thomas Hain, Jaroslav Kadlec, Vasilis Karaiskos, Wessel Kraaij, Melissa Kronenthal, et al. 2006. The ami meeting corpus: A pre-announcement. In *Machine Learning for Multimodal Interaction*, Springer, pages 28–39.

Marie-Catherine De Marneffe, Bill MacCartney, Christopher D Manning, et al. 2006. Generating typed dependency parses from phrase structure parses. In *Proceedings of LREC*. pages 449–454.

Marco Dinarelli, Silvia Quarteroni, Sara Tonelli, Alessandro Moschitti, and Giuseppe Riccardi. 2009. Annotating spoken dialogs: from speech segments to dialog acts and frame semantics. In *Proc. of EACL Workshop on the Semantic Representation of Spoken Language*. Athens, Greece, pages 34–41.

Benoit Favre, Evgeny A. Stepanov, Jérémy Trione, Frédéric Béchet, and Giuseppe Riccardi. 2015. Call centre conversation summarization: A pilot task at MultiLing 2015. In *The 16th Annual SIGdial Meeting on Discourse and Dialogue (SIGDIAL)*. ACL, Prague, Czech Republic, pages 232–236.

Christiane Fellbaum. 1998. *WordNet*. Wiley Online Library.

Michel Galley, Kathleen McKeown, Eric Fosler-Lussier, and Hongyan Jing. 2003. Discourse segmentation of multi-party conversation. In *Proc. of the 41st Annual Meeting of the Association for Computational Linguistics (ACL)*. ACL, pages 562–569.

Philipp Koehn. 2004. Statistical significance tests for machine translation evaluation. In *EMNLP*. Citeseer, pages 388–395.

Philipp Koehn. 2005. Europarl: A parallel corpus for statistical machine translation. In *Machine Translation Summit X*.

Chin-Yew Lin. 2004. Rouge: A package for automatic evaluation of summaries. In *Text Summarization Branches out: Proc. of the ACL-04 Workshop*. volume 8.

Yashar Mehdad, Giuseppe Carenini, Frank W. Tompa, and Raymond T. Ng. 2013. Abstractive meeting summarization with entailment and fusion. In *Proc. of European Natural Language Generation Workshop (ENLG)*. pages 136–146.

Tomas Mikolov, Kai Chen, Greg Corrado, and Jeffrey Dean. 2013. Efficient estimation of word representations in vector space. *arXiv preprint arXiv:1301.3781* .

Gabriel Murray, Giuseppe Carenini, and Raymond Ng. 2010. Generating and validating abstracts of meeting conversations: a user study. In *Proceedings of the 6th International Natural Language Generation Conference*. Association for Computational Linguistics, pages 105–113.

Tatsuro Oya, Yashar Mehdad, Giuseppe Carenini, and Raymond Ng. 2014. A template-based abstractive meeting summarization: Leveraging summary and source text relationships. In *Proc. of the 8th International Natural Language Generation Conference (INLG 2014)*. pages 45–53.

Emanuele Pianta, Luisa Bentivogli, and Christian Girardi. 2002. Multiwordnet: developing an aligned multilingual database. In *Proceedings of the first international conference on global WordNet*. volume 152, pages 55–63.

Emanuele Pianta, Christian Girardi, and Roberto Zanoli. 2008. The textpro tool suite. In *Proc. of LREC*. ELRA.

Vasin Punyakanok and Dan Roth. 2001. The use of classifiers in sequential inference. *arXiv preprint cs/0111003* .

Jianbo Shi and Jitendra Malik. 2000. Normalized cuts and image segmentation. *Pattern Analysis and Machine Intelligence, IEEE Transactions on* 22(8):888–905.

Evgeny A. Stepanov, Benoit Favre, Firoj Alam, Shammur Absar Chowdhury, Karan Singla, Jérémy Trione, Frédéric Béchet, and Giuseppe Riccardi. 2015. Automatic summarization of call-center conversations. In *IEEE Workshop on Automatic Speech Recognition and Understanding (ASRU) - Demo Papers*. IEEE, Scottsdale, Arizona, USA.

Jérémy Trione. 2014. Méthodes par extraction pour le résumé automatique de conversations parlées provenant de centres d'appels. In *16éme Rencontre des ètudiants Chercheurs en Informatique pour le Traitement Automatique des Langues (RECITAL)*. pages 104–111.

Combining Graph Degeneracy and Submodularity for Unsupervised Extractive Summarization

Antoine J.-P. Tixier, Polykarpos Meladianos, Michalis Vazirgiannis
Data Science and Mining Team (DaSciM)
École Polytechnique
Palaiseau, France

Abstract

We present a fully unsupervised, extractive text summarization system that leverages a submodularity framework introduced by past research. The framework allows summaries to be generated in a greedy way while preserving near-optimal performance guarantees. Our main contribution is the novel coverage reward term of the objective function optimized by the greedy algorithm. This component builds on the graph-of-words representation of text and the k-core decomposition algorithm to assign meaningful scores to words. We evaluate our approach on the AMI and ICSI meeting speech corpora, and on the DUC2001 news corpus. We reach state-of-the-art performance on all datasets. Results indicate that our method is particularly well-suited to the meeting domain.

1 Introduction

We present an extractive text summarization system and test it on automatic meeting speech transcriptions and news articles. Summarizing spontaneous multiparty meeting speech text is a difficult task fraught with many unique challenges (McKeown et al., 2005). Rather than the well-formed grammatical sentences found in traditional documents, the input data consist of *utterances*, or fragments of speech transcripts. Information is diluted across utterances due to speakers frequently hesitating and interrupting each other, and noise abounds in the form of disfluencies (often expressed with filler words such as "um", "uh-huh", etc.) and unrelated chit-chat. Since human transcriptions are very costly, the only transcriptions available in practice are often Automatic Speech Recognition (ASR) output. Recognition errors introduce much additional noise, making the task of summarization even more difficult. In this paper, we use ASR output as our sole input, and do not make use of additional data such as prosodic features (Murray et al., 2005).

2 Background

2.1 Graph-of-words representation

A graph-of-words represents a piece of text as a network whose nodes are unique terms in the document, and whose edges encode some kind of term-term relationship information. Unlike the traditional vector space model that assumes term independence, a graph-of-words is an information-rich structure, and enables many powerful tools from graph theory to be applied to NLP tasks. The most famous example is probably the use of PageRank for unsupervised keyword extraction and document summarization (Mihalcea and Tarau, 2004).

More recent unsupervised NLP studies based on graphs reached state-of-the-art performance on a variety of tasks such as multi-sentence compression, information retrieval, real-time sub-event detection from text streams, keyword extraction, and real-time topic detection (Filippova, 2010; Rousseau and Vazirgiannis, 2013; Meladianos et al., 2015; Tixier et al., 2016a; Meladianos et al., 2017).

While several variants of the graph-of-words representation exist, with different levels of sophistication and many graph building and graph mining parameters (Tixier et al., 2016b), we stick here to the traditional configuration of (Mihalcea and Tarau, 2004), which simply records co-occurrence statistics. In this setting, as illustrated in Figure 1, an undirected edge is drawn between two nodes if the unigrams they represent co-occur

48

Proceedings of the Workshop on New Frontiers in Summarization, pages 48–58
Copenhagen, Denmark, September 7, 2017. ©2017 Association for Computational Linguistics

within a window of fixed size W that is slided over the full text from start to finish, overspanning sentences. In addition, edges are assigned integer weights matching co-occurrence counts. This approach follows the *Distributional Hypothesis* (Harris, 1954), in that it assumes the existence and strength of the dependence between textual units to be solely determined by the frequency with which they share local contexts of occurrence.

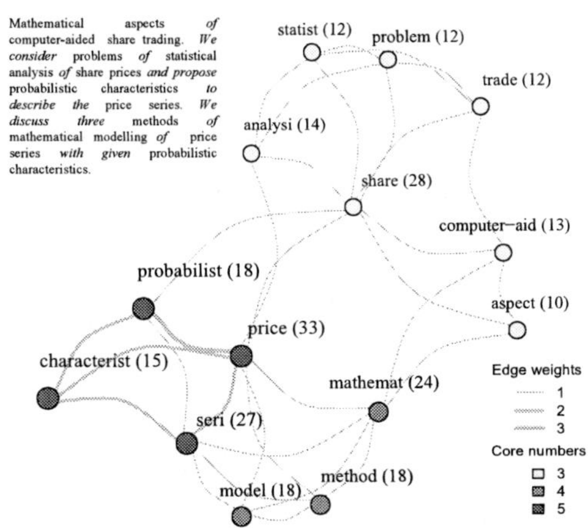

Figure 1: Undirected, weighted graph-of-words example. $W = 8$ and overspans sentences. Stemmed words, weighted k-core decomposition. Numbers inside parentheses are CoreRank scores. For clarity, non-(nouns and adjectives) in *italic* have been removed.

2.2 Graph degeneracy

Within the rest of this subsection, we will consider $G(V, E)$ to be an undirected, weighted graph with $n = |V|$ nodes and $m = |E|$ edges. The concept of graph degeneracy was introduced by (Seidman, 1983) and first applied to the study of cohesion in social networks. It is inherently related to the k-core decomposition technique.

k-core. A core of order k (or k-core) of G is a maximal connected subgraph of G in which every vertex v has at least degree k. The degree of v is the sum of the weights of its incident edges. Note that here, since edge weights are integers (co-occurrence counts), node degrees, and thus, the k's, are also integers.

The **k-core decomposition** of G is the set of all its cores from 0 or 1 (G itself, respectively in the disconnected/connected case) to k_{max} (its main core). As shown in Figure 2, it forms a hierarchy of nested subgraphs whose cohesiveness and size respectively increase and decrease with k.

The higher-level cores can be viewed as a *filtered version* of the graph that excludes noise (actually, the main core of a graph is a coarse approximation of its densest subgraph). This property of the core decomposition is highly valuable when dealing with graphs constructed from noisy text. The **core number** of a node is the highest order of a core that contains this node. As detailed in Algorithm 1, the k-core decomposition is obtained by implementing a pruning process that iteratively removes the lowest degree nodes from the graph.

Algorithm 1 k-core decomposition

Input: Undirected graph $G = (V, E)$
Output: Core numbers $c(v), \forall v \in V$
1: $\quad i \leftarrow 0$
2: $\quad$**while** $|V| > 0$ **do**
3: $\qquad$**while** $\exists v : degree(v) \leq i$ **do**
4: $\qquad\quad c(v) \leftarrow i$
5: $\qquad\quad V \leftarrow V \setminus \{v\}$
6: $\qquad\quad E \leftarrow E \setminus \{(u, v) | u \in V\}$
7: $\qquad$**end while**
8: $\qquad i \leftarrow i + 1$
9: **end while**

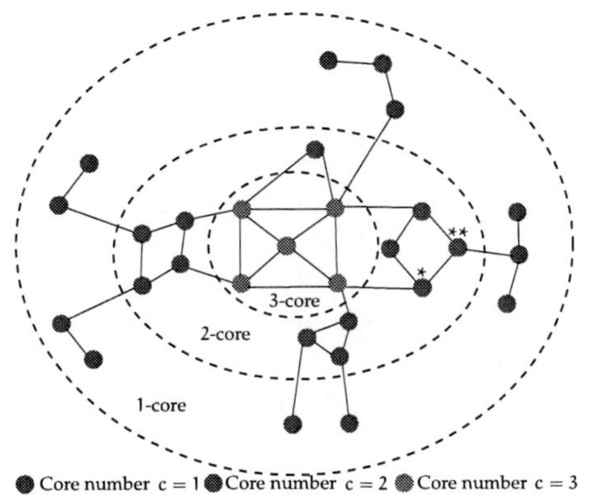

Figure 2: k-core decomposition of a graph and illustration of the value added by CoreRank. While nodes $\star$ and $\star\star$ have the same core number (=2), node $\star$ has a greater CoreRank score (3+2+2=7 vs 2+2+1=5), which better reflects its more central position in the graph.

Time complexity. While linear algorithms are available to compute the core decomposition of unweighted graphs (Batagelj and Zaversnik, 2003), it is slightly more expensive to obtain in the weighted case (our setting here), and requires $\mathcal{O}(m \log(n))$ (Batagelj and Zaveršnik, 2002). Finally, building a graph-of-words is linear: $\mathcal{O}(nW)$. Overall though, the whole pipeline remains very affordable, given that word co-occurrence networks constructed from single documents rarely feature more than hundreds of nodes. In fact, when dealing with single, short pieces of text, the k-core decomposition is fast enough to be used in real-time settings (Meladianos et al., 2017).

2.3 Submodularity and extractive summarization

Just like their convex counterparts in the continuous case, submodular functions share unique properties that make them conveniently optimizable. For this reason, they are are popular and have been applied to a variety of real-world problems, such as viral marketing (Kempe et al., 2003), sensor placement (Krause et al., 2008), and document summarization (Lin and Bilmes, 2011). In what follows, we briefly introduce the concept of submodularity and outline how it spontaneously comes into play when dealing with extractive summarization. For clarity and consistency, we provide explanations within the context of document summarization (without loss of generality).

Submodularity. A set function $F : 2^V \to \mathbb{R}$ where $V = \{v_1, ..., v_n\}$ is said to be *submodular* if it satisfies the property of *diminishing returns* (Krause and Golovin, 2012):

$$\forall A \subseteq B \subseteq V \setminus v, F(A \cup v) - F(A) \geq F(B \cup v) - F(B) \tag{1}$$

If F measures summary quality, *diminishing returns* means that the gain of adding a new sentence to a given summary should be greater than the gain of adding the same sentence to a larger summary containing the smaller one.

Monotonocity. Trivially, a set function is *monotone non-decreasing* if:

$$\forall A \subseteq B, F(A) \leq F(B) \tag{2}$$

Which means that the quality of a summary can only increase or stay the same as it grows in size, i.e., as we add sentences to it.

Budgeted maximization. The task of extractive summarization can be viewed as the selection, under a budget constraint, of the subset of sentences that best represents the entire set (i.e., the document). This problem translates to a combinatorial optimization task:

$$\arg\max_{S \subseteq V} F(S) \mid \sum_{v \in S} c_v \leq B \tag{3}$$

Where S is a subset of the full set of sentences V (i.e., a summary), $c_v \geq 0$ is the cost of sentence v, and B is the budget. Finally, F is a summary quality scoring set function, mapping 2^V (the finite ensemble of all subsets of V, i.e., of all possible summaries), to $\mathbb{R}$. In other words, F assigns a single numeric score to a given summary.

While finding an exact solution for Equation 3 is NP-hard, it was proven that under a cardinality constraint (unit costs), a greedy algorithm can approach it with factor $(e - 1)/e \approx 0.63$ in the worst case (Nemhauser et al., 1978). However, for this guarantee to hold, F has to be submodular and monotone non-decreasing.

More recently, (Lin and Bilmes, 2010) proposed a modified greedy algorithm whose solution is guaranteed to be at least $1 - 1/\sqrt{e} \approx 0.39$ as good as the best one, under a general budget constraint (not necessarily unit costs). Empirically, the approximation factor was shown to be close to 90%. The constraints on F remain unchanged. More precisely, the algorithm of (Lin and Bilmes, 2010) iteratively selects the sentence that maximizes the ratio of objective function gain to scaled cost:

$$\frac{F(G \cup v) - F(G)}{c_v^r} \tag{4}$$

Where G is the current summary, c_v is the cost of sentence v (e.g., number of words, bytes...), and $r > 0$, the scaling factor, adjusts for the fact that the objective function F and the cost of a sentence might be expressed in different units and thus not be directly comparable.

Objective function. The choice of F is what matters here. Naturally, F should capture the desirable properties in a summary, which have traditionally been formalized in the literature as *relevance* and *non-redundancy*.

A well-known function capturing both aspects is Maximum Marginal Relevance (MMR) (Carbonell and Goldstein, 1998). Unfortunately, MMR *penalizes* for redundancy, which makes it non-monotone. Therefore, it cannot benefit from the near-optimality guarantees. To address this issue, (Lin and Bilmes, 2011) proposed to *positively reward* diversity, with objective function:

$$F(S) = C(S) + \lambda D(S) \tag{5}$$

Where C and D respectively reward coverage and diversity, and $\lambda \geq 0$ is a trade-off parameter. $\lambda D(S)$ can be viewed as a regularization term. We used an objective function of the form described by Equation 5 in our system. In the next subsection, we present and motivate our choices for C

and D.

3 Proposed system

Our system can be broken down into the four modules shown in Figure 3, which we detail in what follows.

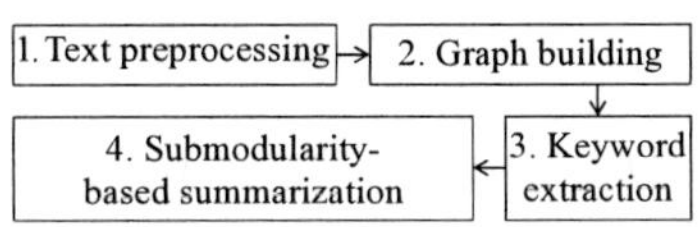

Figure 3: Overarching system process flow

3.1 Text preprocessing

The fully unsupervised nature of our system gives it the advantage of being applicable to different languages (and different types of textual input) with only minimal changes in the preprocessing steps. A necessary first step is thus to detect the language of the input text. So far, our model supports English and French, although our experiments were ran for the English language only.

• **Meeting speech**: utterances shorter than 0.85 second are then pruned out, words are lowercased and stemmed, and specific flags introduced by the ASR system (e.g., indicating inaudible sounds, such as "{vocalsound}" in English) are removed. Punctuation is also discarded. Custom stopwords and fillerwords for meeting speech, learned from the development sets of the AMI and ICSI corpora[1], are also discarded. French stopwords and fillerwords were learned from a database of French speech curated from various sources[2]. The surviving words are considered as node candidates for the next phase, without any part-of-speech-based filtering. Note that the absence of requirement for a POS tagger makes our system even more flexible.

• **Traditional documents**: standard stopwords are removed (e.g., SMART stopwords[3] for the English language), punctuation is removed, and words are lowercased and stemmed.

In parallel, a copy of the original untouched utterances/sentences is created. It is from this set that the algorithm will select from to generate the summary at step 4. In the meeting domain only, in order to improve readability, the last 3 words

of each utterance are eliminated if they are filler words, and repeated consecutive unigrams (e.g. "remote remote"), and bigrams (e.g. "remote control remote control") are collapsed to single terms ("remote", "remote control"). Note that these extra cleaning steps were performed for our system as well as all the baselines.

3.2 Graph-building

A word co-occurrence network, as defined in Subsection 2.1, is built. The size of the sliding window was tuned on the development sets of each dataset, as will be explained in Subsection 4.4.

3.3 Keyword extraction and scoring

We used the *Density* and *CoreRank* heuristics introduced by (Tixier et al., 2016a). In brief, these techniques are based on the assumption, verified empirically, that *spreading influence* is a better "keywordedness" metric than random walk-based ones, such as PageRank. Influential spreaders are those nodes in the graph that can reach a large portion of the other nodes in the network at minimum time and cost. Research has shown (Kitsak et al., 2010) that the spreading influence of a node is better captured by its core number, because unlike the eigenvector centrality or PageRank measures, which only capture individual *prestige*, graph degeneracy also takes into account the extent to which a node is part of a dense, cohesive part of the graph. Such positional information is highly valuable in determining the ability of the node to propagate information throughout the network.

More precisely, the "Density" and "CoreRank" techniques were shown by (Tixier et al., 2016a) to reach state-of-the-art unsupervised keyword extraction performance on medium and large documents, respectively. Both methods decompose the word co-occurrence network of a given piece of text with the weighted k-core algorithm.

• "Density" then computes the density of each k-core subgraph and selects the optimal cut-off k_{best} in the hierarchy as the elbow in the *density* vs. k curve. It finally returns the members of the k_{best}-core of the graph as keywords. The assumption is that it is valuable to descend the hierarchy of cores as long as the desirable density properties are maintained, but once they are lost (as identified by the elbow), it is time to stop.

• The second method, "CoreRank", assigns to each node a score computed as the sum of the

---

[1] most frequent words followed by manual inspection

[2] available at `https://github.com/Tixierae/EMNLP2017_NewSum`

[3] `http://jmlr.org/papers/volume5/lewis04a/all-smart-stop-list/english.stop`

core numbers of its neighbors (see Figure 1), and retains the top $p\%$ nodes as keywords (we used $p = 0.15$). As illustrated in Figure 2, by decreasing granularity from the subgraph to the node level, CoreRank generates a ranking of nodes that better captures their structural position in the graph. Also, stabilizing scores across node neighborhoods increases even more the inherent noise robustness property of graph degeneracy, which is particularly desirable when dealing with noisy text such as automatic speech transcriptions.

We encourage the reader to refer to the original paper for more information about the Density and CoreRank heuristics.

3.4 Extractive summarization

An objective function of the form presented in Equation 5 and the modified greedy algorithm of (Lin and Bilmes, 2010) are finally used to compose summaries by selecting from the original utterances with coverage and diversity functions as detailed next.

- *Coverage function.* We chose a concept-based coverage function. Such functions fulfill the monotonicity and submodularity requirements (Lin and Bilmes, 2011). More precisely, we compute the coverage of a candidate summary S as the weighted sum of the scores of the keywords it contains:

$$C(S) = \sum_{i \in S} n_i w_i \qquad (6)$$

Where n_i is the number of times keyword i appears in S, and w_i is the score of keyword i. Non-keywords are not taken into account. Therefore, a summary not containing any keyword gets a null score. Remember that the keywords and their scores are given by the "Density" and "CoreRank" techniques, respectively for the AMI and ICSI corpora.

Note that (Riedhammer et al., 2008a) also used a concept-based relevance measure. However, the way we define, and the mechanism by which we extract and assign scores to concepts radically differ. Our degeneracy-based methods natively assign weights to all the words in the graph, and then extract keywords based on those weights, while (Riedhammer et al., 2008a) consider all n-grams and then use a basic frequency-based weighting scheme. Our work is also related to (Lin et al., 2009), but unlike us, the authors use a sentence semantic graph and a different objective function.

- *Diversity reward function.* We encourage diversity by taking into account the proportion of keywords covered by a candidate summary, irrespective of the scores of the keywords:

$$D(S) = N_{keywords \in S} / N_{keywords} \qquad (7)$$

Where $N_{keywords \in S}$ is the number of (unique) keywords contained in the summary, and $N_{keywords}$ is the total number of keywords extracted for the meeting. Promoting non-redundancy is important as our coverage term does not inherently penalizes for redundancy, unlike for instance (Gillick et al., 2009).

4 Experimental setup

4.1 Datasets

We tested our approach on ASR output and regular text. The lists of meetings/documents IDs we used for development and testing are available on the project online repository[4].

4.1.1 Meeting speech transcriptions

We used two standard datasets very popular in the field of meeting speech summarization, the AMI and ICSI corpora.

- The **AMI corpus** (McCowan et al., 2005) comprises ASR transcripts for 137 meetings where 4 participants play a role within a fictive company. Average duration is 30 minutes (843 utterances, 6758 words, unprocessed). Each meeting is associated with a human-written abstractive summary of 300 words on average, and with a human-composed extractive summary (140 utterances on average). We used the same test set as in (Riedhammer et al., 2008b), featuring 20 meetings.

- The **ICSI corpus** (Janin et al., 2003) is a collection of 57 real life meetings involving between 2 and 6 participants. The average duration, 56 minutes, is much longer than for the AMI meetings, which reflects in the average size of the ASR transcriptions (1454 utterances, 15211 words, unprocessed). For consistency with previous work, we selected the standard test set of 6 meetings. For each meeting of this test set, 3 human abstractive and 3 human extractive summaries are available, of respective average sizes 390 words and 133 utterances.

---

[4] `https://github.com/Tixierae/EMNLP2017_NewSum` (`name_lists.txt`)

Note that for both the AMI and ICSI corpora, the ASR word error rate is quite high: it approaches 37%. For each corpus, we constructed a development set of 15 meetings randomly selected from the training set in order to perform parameter tuning.

4.1.2 Traditional documents

We also tested our approach on the **DUC2001** corpus[5]. This collection comprises 304 newswire/newspaper articles of average size 800 words. Each document is associated with a human-written abstractive summary of about 100 words. After removing the 13 articles that did not have an abstract and/or a body, whose bodies were shorter than 200 words, and whose abstracts contained less than 10 words, we generated a small development set of 15 randomly selected articles for parameter tuning. We then used the remaining documents as the test set, removing the ones whose size differed too much from the size of the articles in the development set (by at least 2 standard deviations, i.e. exceeded 46 sentences in size, see Fig 4). This left us with a test set of 207 documents.

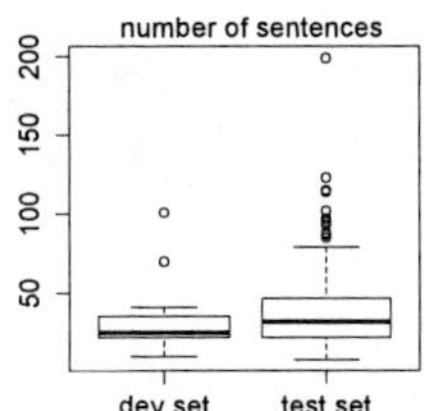

Figure 4: Size of the DUC2001 documents in development and test sets.

4.2 Evaluation

To align with previous efforts, the extractive summaries generated by our system and the baselines (that will be presented subsequently) were compared against the human *abstractive* summaries. We used the ROUGE-1 evaluation metric (Lin, 2004). ROUGE, based on n-gram overlap, is the standard way of evaluating performance in the field of textual summarization. In particular, ROUGE-1, which works at the unigram level, was shown to significantly correlate with human evaluations. While it has been suggested than correlation may be weaker in the meeting domain (Liu and Liu, 2008), we stuck to ROUGE because

of the lack of a clear substitute, and for consistency with the literature, as a very large majority of studies previously published in the domain use ROUGE.

For each dataset, and for a given summarization method, ROUGE scores were computed for each meeting in the test set and then averaged to obtain an overall score for the method (macro-averaging). For the ICSI corpus, 3 human abstractive summaries are available for each meeting in the test set, so an average score was first computed.

4.3 Baseline systems

We benchmarked the performance of our system against six different baselines, presented below. The first two baselines were included based on the best practice recommendation of (Riedhammer et al., 2008b), in order to ease cross-comparison with other studies.

Random. This system randomly selects elements from the full list of utterances/sentences until the budget is violated. Since this approach is stochastic, ROUGE scores were averaged across 30 runs.

Longest greedy. Here, the longest utterance/sentence is selected at each step until the size constraint is satisfied.

TextRank (Mihalcea and Tarau, 2004). An undirected complete graph is built where nodes are utterances/sentences and edges are weighted according to the normalized content overlap of their endpoints. Finally, weighted PageRank is applied and the highest ranked nodes are selected for inclusion in the summary. We used a publicly available Python implementation[6].

ClusterRank (Garg et al., 2009). *AMI & ICSI only.* ClusterRank is an extension of TextRank tailored to meeting summarization. Utterances are first clustered based on their position in the transcript and their TF-IDF cosine similarity. Then, a complete graph is built from the clusters, with normalized cosine similarity edge weights. Finally, each utterance is assigned a score based on the weighted PageRank score of the node it belongs to and its cosine similarity with the node centroid. The utterances associated with the highest scores are then added to the summary, if they differ enough from it. Since the authors did not make their code publicly available, we wrote our own implementation in Python[7]. We set the win-

[5] http://www-nlpir.nist.gov/projects/duc/ guidelines/2001.html

[6] https://github.com/summanlp/textrank
[7] available on the project repository.

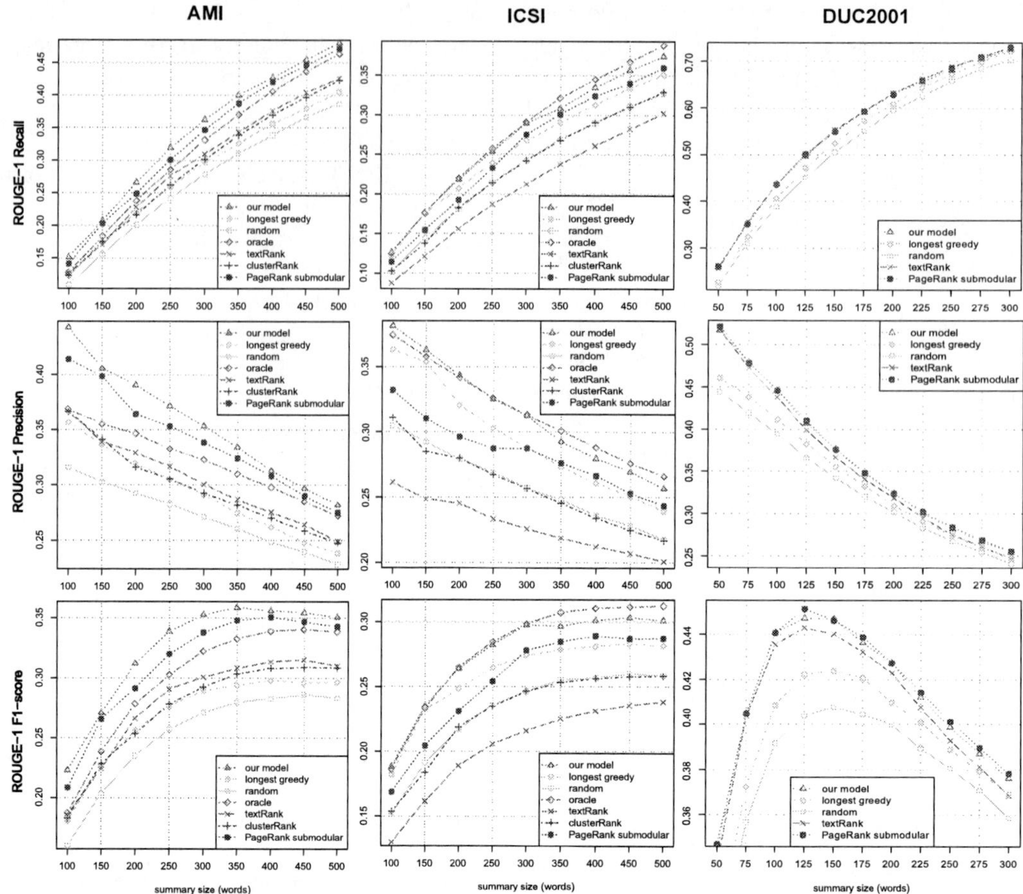

Figure 5: ROUGE-1 score comparisons for various budgets, on the 3 datasets used in this study.

dow threshold parameter to 3 like in the original paper, but increased the similarity threshold from 0.4 to 0.6 because 0.4 returned too many clusters.

PageRank submodular (PRsub). This baseline is exactly the same as our system, the only difference being that keyword scores are obtained through weighted PageRank rather than via a degeneracy-based technique (Density or CoreRank).

Oracle. *AMI & ICSI only*. This last baseline randomly selects utterances from the human extractive summaries until the budget has been reached. Again, we average ROUGE scores over 30 runs to account for the randomness of the procedure. Note that this approach assumes the human extractive summaries to be the best possible ones, which is arguable.

4.4 Parameter tuning

• λ and r. Recall that the main tuning parameters of our method and the PageRank submodular baseline (PRsub) are λ, which controls the trade-off between the coverage and the diversity terms C and D of our objective function, and r, the scaling factor, which makes the gain in objective function value and utterance cost comparable (see Equation 4). To tune these parameters, we conducted a grid search on the development set of each corpus, retaining the parameter combination maximizing the average ROUGE-1 F1-score, for summaries of fixed size equal to 300 and 100 words, respectively for the AMI & ICSI and the DUC2001 corpora. More precisely, our grid had axes $[0, 7]$ and $[0, 2]$ for λ and r respectively, with steps of 0.1 in each case. The best λ and r for each dataset are summarized in Table 1.

• W and heuristic. Still on the development sets of each collection, we also experimented with two window sizes for building the word co-occurrence network (6 and 12), and for our model, whether we should use the Density or CoreRank technique. The best window size was 12 on the AMI and ICSI corpora, and 6 on DUC2001. The Density method

54

turned out to be best on the AMI corpus, while CoreRank yielded better results on the ICSI and DUC2001 corpora.

The reason why is not entirely clear. (Tixier et al., 2016a) initially found that with respect to keyword extraction, Density was better suited to medium-size documents ($\sim$ 400 words) while CoreRank was superior on longer documents ($\sim$ 1,300 words), because the latter is working at a finer granularity level (node level instead of subgraph level), and thus enjoys more flexibility. However, the AMI corpus comprises much bigger pieces of text (2,200 words on average, after pre-processing). Therefore, we could have expected the CoreRank heuristic to give better results on this dataset also. We hypothesize that the difference in task might explain why this is not the case. Indeed, in keyword extraction, we are interested in *selecting* keywords for direct comparison with the gold standard, whereas in summarization, we are only interested in *scoring* keywords, as an intermediary step towards sentence scoring and selection. Therefore, in summarization, working at the subgraph level and extracting larger numbers of keywords is not directly equivalent to sacrificing precision, since the less relevant keywords will have minimal impact on the sentence selection process due to their low scores.

System	AMI	ICSI	DUC2001
Our model	$(2, 0.9)$	$(5, 0.3)$	$(0.6, 0.1)$
PRsub	$(4.7, 0.5)$	$(4, 0.6)$	$(1.6, 0.2)$

Table 1: Optimal parameter values (λ, r) for our system and the submodular baseline.

As shown in Table 1, the λ values are all non-zero (and quite high), indicating that including a regularization term favoring diversity in our objective function is necessary. Moreover, the significantly greater values reached by λ on the AMI & ICSI datasets show that ensuring diversity is even more important when dealing with meeting transcripts, most probably because there is much more redundancy in spontaneous, noisy utterances than in sentences belonging to properly written news article, and also because more (sub)topics are discussed during meetings.

5 Results

5.1 Quantitative results

We consider the cost of an utterance/a sentence to be the number of words it contains, and the budget to be the maximum size allowed for a summary, measured in number of words. For each meeting/document in the test sets, we generated extractive summaries with budgets ranging from 100 to 500 words (AMI & ICSI corpora) and from 50 to 300 words (DUC2001 collection), with steps of 50 in each case.

Results for all datasets and all budgets are shown in Figure 5, while Tables 2, 3, and 4 provide detailed comparisons for the budget corresponding to the best performance achieved by a non-oracle system, respectively on the AMI, ICSI, and DUC2001 datasets. We tested for statistical significance in macro-averaged F1 scores using the non-parametric version of the t-test, the Mann-Whitney U test[8].

System	Recall	Precision	F-1 score
Our model	39.98	33.40	35.88*
PRsub	38.73	32.41	34.80
Oracle	37.02	30.99	33.27
TextRank	34.33	28.66	30.82
ClusterRank	33.87	28.18	30.35
Longest greedy	32.61	27.47	29.41
Random	31.06	26.05	27.95

Table 2: Macro-averaged ROUGE-1 scores on the AMI test set (20 meetings) for summaries of 350 words. *Statistically significant difference ($p < 0.03$) w.r.t. all baselines except PRsub.

System	Recall	Precision	F-1 score
Oracle	36.64	27.59	31.16
Our model	35.60	26.94	30.34*
PRsub	33.97	25.28	28.70
Longest greedy	33.37	25.06	28.33
Random	31.06	22.83	26.02
ClusterRank	31.00	22.48	25.78
TextRank	28.19	20.71	23.57

Table 3: Macro-averaged ROUGE scores on the ICSI test set (6 meetings) for summaries of 450 words. *Statistically significant difference ($p < 0.05$) w.r.t. all baselines except the oracle and PRsub.

System	Recall	Precision	F-1 score
PRsub	50.17	41.08	45.13
Our model	49.69	40.71	44.71*
TextRank	50.00	39.92	44.29
Longest greedy	47.22	38.29	42.25
Random	45.13	36.61	40.39

Table 4: Macro-averaged ROUGE scores on the DUC2001 test set (207 documents) for summaries of 125 words. *Statistically significant difference ($p < 0.03$) w.r.t. the Longest greedy and Random baselines.

• **Meeting domain**. Our approach significantly outperforms all baselines on the AMI corpus (including the oracle) and all systems on the ICSI corpus (except the oracle), both in terms of precision and recall. Also, our system proves con-

[8] https://stat.ethz.ch/R-manual/R-devel/library/stats/html/wilcox.test.html

sistently better throughout the different summary sizes. Until the peak is reached, the margin in F1 score between our model and the competitors even tend to widen as the budget increases.

Performance is weaker for all models on the ICSI corpus because in that case the system summaries have to jointly match 3 human summaries of different sizes (instead of a single summary), which is a much more difficult task.

Best performance is attained for a larger budget on the ICSI corpus (450 vs. 350 words), which can be explained by the fact that the ICSI human summaries tend to be larger than the AMI ones (390 vs 300 words, on average). Finally, remember that the extractive summaries generated by the systems were compared against the *abstractive* summaries freely written by human annotators, using their own words. This makes it impossible for extractive systems to reach perfect scores, because the gold standard contains words that were never used during the meeting, and thus that do not appear in the ASR transcriptions. Overall, our model is very competitive to the oracle, which is notable since the oracle has direct access to the human extractive summaries.

• **Regular documents**. The absolute ROUGE scores and the margins between systems are much greater (resp. smaller) than on the AMI and ICSI corpora, confirming without surprise that summarization is a much easier task when performed on well-written documents than on spontaneous meeting speech transcriptions. Although very close (0.42 difference in F1-score), our method does not reach absolute best performance, which is attained by the submodular baseline with PageRank-based coverage function, for summaries of 125 words (average size of the gold standard summaries is about 100 words). The absence of superiority on this dataset might be explained by the fact that graph degeneracy really adds value when dealing with noisy input, such as automatic speech transcriptions. However, on regular documents, the recognized superiority of degeneracy-based techniques over PageRank (Tixier et al., 2016a; Rousseau and Vazirgiannis, 2015) for keyword extraction does not seem to translate into a significantly better measure of coverage for sentence scoring.

5.2 Qualitative results

Instead of providing a single sample summary at the end of this paper, we deployed our system as an interactive web application[9]. With the interface, the user can generate summaries with our system for all the meetings/documents in the AMI, ICSI, and DUC2001 test sets. Custom files are accepted as well, and links to examples of such files in French and English are provided.

What can be observed in the meeting domain is that while the keywords extracted tend to be very relevant and their scores meaningful, and while the utterances selected by our system tend to have good coverage and relatively low redundancy, the summaries suffer in readability, which can be explained by the fully extractive nature of our approach, and the low quality of the input (37% word error rate). This qualitative aspect of performance is not captured by ROUGE-1 which simply computes unigram overlap statistics.

6 Conclusion

We presented a fully unsupervised system that uses a powerful submodularity framework introduced by past research to generate extractive summaries of textual documents in a greedy way with near-optimal performance guarantees. Our principal contribution is in the coverage term of the objective function that is optimized by the greedy algorithm. This term leverages graph degeneracy applied on word co-occurrence networks to rank words according to their structural position in the graph. Evaluation shows that our system reaches state-of-the-art extractive performance, and is especially well-suited to be used on noisy text, such as ASR output from meetings. Future work should focus on improving the readability of the final summaries. To this purpose, unsupervised graph-based sentence compression and/or natural language generation techniques, like in (Filippova, 2010; Mehdad et al., 2013) seem very promising.

7 Acknowledgments

We are thankful to the three anonymous reviewers for their helpful comments and suggestions, and to Prof. Benoît Favre for his kind help in getting access to the meeting datasets. This research was supported by the OpenPaaS::NG project.

---

[9]`http://bit.ly/2r5jeL0` (works better in Chrome).

References

Vladimir Batagelj and Matjaž Zaveršnik. 2002. Generalized cores. *arXiv preprint cs/0202039* .

Vladimir Batagelj and Matjaz Zaversnik. 2003. An o (m) algorithm for cores decomposition of networks. *arXiv preprint cs/0310049* .

Jaime Carbonell and Jade Goldstein. 1998. The use of mmr, diversity-based reranking for reordering documents and producing summaries. In *Proceedings of the 21st annual international ACM SIGIR conference on Research and development in information retrieval*. ACM, pages 335–336.

Katja Filippova. 2010. Multi-sentence compression: Finding shortest paths in word graphs. In *Proceedings of the 23rd International Conference on Computational Linguistics*. Association for Computational Linguistics, pages 322–330.

Nikhil Garg, Benoit Favre, Korbinian Reidhammer, and Dilek Hakkani Tür. 2009. Clusterrank: a graph based method for meeting summarization. Technical report, Idiap.

Daniel Gillick, Benoit Favre, Dilek Hakkani-Tür, Bernd Bohnet, Yang Liu, and Shasha Xie. 2009. The icsi/utd summarization system at tac 2009. In *TAC*.

Zellig S Harris. 1954. Distributional structure. *Word* 10(2-3):146–162.

Adam Janin, Don Baron, Jane Edwards, Dan Ellis, David Gelbart, Nelson Morgan, Barbara Peskin, Thilo Pfau, Elizabeth Shriberg, Andreas Stolcke, et al. 2003. The icsi meeting corpus. In *Acoustics, Speech, and Signal Processing, 2003. Proceedings.(ICASSP'03). 2003 IEEE International Conference on*. IEEE, volume 1, pages I–364.

David Kempe, Jon Kleinberg, and Éva Tardos. 2003. Maximizing the Spread of Influence through a Social Network. In *Proceedings of the 9th International Conference on Knowledge Discovery and Data Mining*. pages 137–146.

Maksim Kitsak, Lazaros K Gallos, Shlomo Havlin, Fredrik Liljeros, Lev Muchnik, H Eugene Stanley, and Hernán A Makse. 2010. Identification of influential spreaders in complex networks. *Nature Physics* 6(11):888–893.

Andreas Krause and Daniel Golovin. 2012. Submodular function maximization. *Tractability: Practical Approaches to Hard Problems* 3(19):8.

Andreas Krause, Jure Leskovec, Carlos Guestrin, Jeanne VanBriesen, and Christos Faloutsos. 2008. Efficient sensor placement optimization for securing large water distribution networks. *Journal of Water Resources Planning and Management* 134(6):516–526.

Chin-Yew Lin. 2004. Rouge: A package for automatic evaluation of summaries. In *Text summarization branches out: Proceedings of the ACL-04 workshop*. volume 8.

Hui Lin and Jeff Bilmes. 2010. Multi-document summarization via budgeted maximization of submodular functions. In *Human Language Technologies: The 2010 Annual Conference of the North American Chapter of the Association for Computational Linguistics*. Association for Computational Linguistics, pages 912–920.

Hui Lin and Jeff Bilmes. 2011. A Class of Submodular Functions for Document Summarization. In *Proceedings of the 49th Annual Meeting of the Association for Computational Linguistics: Human Language Technologies*. pages 510–520.

Hui Lin, Jeff Bilmes, and Shasha Xie. 2009. Graph-based submodular selection for extractive summarization. In *Automatic Speech Recognition & Understanding, 2009. ASRU 2009. IEEE Workshop on*. IEEE, pages 381–386.

Feifan Liu and Yang Liu. 2008. Correlation between rouge and human evaluation of extractive meeting summaries. In *Proceedings of the 46th annual meeting of the association for computational linguistics on human language technologies: Short papers*. Association for Computational Linguistics, pages 201–204.

Iain McCowan, Jean Carletta, W Kraaij, S Ashby, S Bourban, M Flynn, M Guillemot, T Hain, J Kadlec, V Karaiskos, et al. 2005. The ami meeting corpus. In *Proceedings of the 5th International Conference on Methods and Techniques in Behavioral Research*. volume 88.

Kathleen McKeown, Julia Hirschberg, Michel Galley, and Sameer Maskey. 2005. From text to speech summarization. In *Acoustics, Speech, and Signal Processing, 2005. Proceedings.(ICASSP'05). IEEE International Conference on*. IEEE, volume 5, pages v–997.

Yashar Mehdad, Giuseppe Carenini, Frank W Tompa, and Raymond T Ng. 2013. Abstractive meeting summarization with entailment and fusion. In *Proc. of the 14th European Workshop on Natural Language Generation*. pages 136–146.

Polykarpos Meladianos, Giannis Nikolentzos, François Rousseau, Yannis Stavrakas, and Michalis Vazirgiannis. 2015. Degeneracy-based real-time sub-event detection in twitter stream. In *Ninth International AAAI Conference on Web and Social Media (ICWSM)*.

Polykarpos Meladianos, Antoine J-P Tixier, Giannis Nikolentzos, and Michalis Vazirgiannis. 2017. Real-time keyword extraction from conversations. *EACL 2017* page 462.

Rada Mihalcea and Paul Tarau. 2004. TextRank: bringing order into texts. In *Proceedings of the 2004 Conference on Empirical Methods in Natural Language Processing (EMNLP)*. Association for Computational Linguistics.

Gabriel Murray, Steve Renals, and Jean Carletta. 2005. Extractive summarization of meeting recordings. .

George L Nemhauser, Laurence A Wolsey, and Marshall L Fisher. 1978. An analysis of approximations for maximizing submodular set functionsi. *Mathematical Programming* 14(1):265–294.

Korbinian Riedhammer, Benoit Favre, and Dilek Hakkani-Tur. 2008a. A keyphrase based approach to interactive meeting summarization. In *Spoken Language Technology Workshop, 2008. SLT 2008. IEEE*. IEEE, pages 153–156.

Korbinian Riedhammer, Dan Gillick, Benoit Favre, and Dilek Hakkani-Tür. 2008b. Packing the meeting summarization knapsack. In *Ninth Annual Conference of the International Speech Communication Association*.

François Rousseau and Michalis Vazirgiannis. 2013. Graph-of-word and tw-idf: new approach to ad hoc ir. In *Proceedings of the 22nd ACM international conference on Conference on Information & Knowledge Management (CIKM)*. ACM, pages 59–68.

François Rousseau and Michalis Vazirgiannis. 2015. Main core retention on graph-of-words for single-document keyword extraction. In *European Conference on Information Retrieval*. Springer, pages 382–393.

Stephen B Seidman. 1983. Network structure and minimum degree. *Social networks* 5(3):269–287.

Antoine J-P Tixier, Fragkiskos D Malliaros, and Michalis Vazirgiannis. 2016a. A graph degeneracy-based approach to keyword extraction. In *Proceedings of the Conference on Empirical Methods in Natural Language Processing*.

Antoine J-P Tixier, Konstantinos Skianis, and Michalis Vazirgiannis. 2016b. Gowvis: a web application for graph-of-words-based text visualization and summarization. *ACL 2016* page 151.

TL;DR: Mining Reddit to Learn Automatic Summarization

Michael Völske and **Martin Potthast** and **Shahbaz Syed** and **Benno Stein**
Faculty of Media, Bauhaus-Universität Weimar, Germany
`<firstname>.<lastname>@uni-weimar.de`

Abstract

Recent advances in automatic text summarization have used deep neural networks to generate high-quality abstractive summaries, but the performance of these models strongly depends on large amounts of suitable training data. We propose a new method for mining social media for author-provided summaries, taking advantage of the common practice of appending a "TL;DR" to long posts. A case study using a large Reddit crawl yields the Webis-TLDR-17 corpus, complementing existing corpora primarily from the news genre. Our technique is likely applicable to other social media sites and general web crawls.

1 Introduction

Given a document, automatic summarization is the task of generating a coherent shorter version of the document that conveys its main points. Depending on the use case, the target length of a summary may be chosen relative to that of the input document, or it may be limited. Either way, a summary must be considered "accurate" by a human judge in relation to its length: the shorter a summary has to be, the more it will have to abstract over the input text. Automatic *abstractive* summarization can be considered one of the most challenging variants of automatic summarization (Gambhir and Gupta, 2017). But with recent advancements in the field of deep learning, new ground was broken using various kinds of neural network models (Rush et al., 2015; Hu et al., 2015; Chopra et al., 2016; See et al., 2017).

The performance of these kinds of summarization models strongly depends on large amounts of suitable training data. To the best of our knowledge, the top rows of Table 1 list all English-

Table 1: Top rows: commonly used English-language corpora; bottom row: our contribution.

Corpus	Genre	Training pairs
English Gigaword	News articles	4 million
CNN/Daily Mail	News articles	300,000
DUC 2003	Newswire	624
DUC 2004	Newswire	500
Webis-TLDR-17	**Social Media**	**4 million**

language corpora that have been applied to training and evaluating single-document summarization networks in the past two to three years; only the two largest corpora are of sufficient size to serve as training sets by themselves. At the same time, all of these corpora cover more or less the same text genre, namely news. This is probably due to the relative ease by which news articles can be obtained as well as the fact that the news tend to contain properly written texts, usually from professional journalists. Notwithstanding the usefulness of existing corpora, we argue that the apparent lack of genre diversity currently poses an obstacle to deep learning-based summarization.

In this regard, we identified a novel, large-scale source of suitable training data from the genre of social media. We benefit from the common practice of social media users summarizing their own posts as a courtesy to their readers: the abbreviation TL;DR, originally used as a response meaning "too long; didn't read" to call out on unnecessarily long posts, has been adopted by many social media users writing long posts in anticipatory obedience and now typically indicates that a summary of the entire post follows. This provides us with a text and its summary—both written by the same person—which, when harvested at scale, is an excellent datum for developing and evaluating an automatic summarization system. In contrast to the state-of-the-art corpora, social me-

Proceedings of the Workshop on New Frontiers in Summarization, pages 59–63
Copenhagen, Denmark, September 7, 2017. ©2017 Association for Computational Linguistics

dia texts are written informally and discuss every-day topics, albeit mostly unstructured and often-times poorly written, offering new challenges to the community. Thus, we endeavored to extract a usable dataset specifically suited for abstractive summarization from Reddit, the largest discussion forum on the web, where TL;DR summaries are extensively used. In what follows, we discuss in detail how the data was obtained and preprocessed to compile the Webis-TLDR-17 corpus.

2   Related Work

The summarization community has developed a range of resources for training and evaluating ex-tractive and abstractive summarization systems geared towards a diverse set of different sum-marization tasks. Table 1 reviews the datasets most commonly used for the basic task of single-document summarization, focusing on datasets used in recent, abstractive approaches.

The English Gigaword Corpus has been the most important summarization resource in recent years, as neural network models have made great progress toward the task of generating news head-lines from article texts (Rush et al., 2015; Nal-lapati et al., 2016). The dataset consists of ap-proximately 10 million news articles along with their headlines, extracted from 7 popular news agencies: Agence France-Presse, Associated Press Worldstream, Central News Agency of Taiwan, Los Angeles Times/Washington Post Newswire Service, Washington Post/Bloomberg Newswire Service, New York Times Newswire Service, and Xinhua News Agency. About 4 million English article-title pairs have typically been used to train, evaluate and test recent summarization systems.

The famous Document Understanding Confer-ence (DUC), hosted by the US National Insti-tute of Standards and Technology (NIST) from 2001 to 2007, yielded two corpora that have been applied to single-document summarization. The DUC 2003 and DUC 2004 corpora consist of a few hundred newswire articles each, along with single-sentence summaries. Generally considered too small to train abstractive summarization sys-tems, past research has focused on the use of vari-ous optimization methods—such as non-negative matrix factorization (Lee et al., 2009), support vector regression (Ouyang et al., 2011), and evolu-tionary algorithms (Alguliev et al., 2013)—to se-lect salient sentences for an extractive summary.

Beyond that, recent works in abstractive summa-rization have used DUC corpora for validation and testing purposes.

In addition to the Gigaword and DUC corpora, whose document-summary pairs consist of only a single sentence in the summary, Nallapati et al. (2016) present a new abstractive summarization dataset based on a passage-based question answer-ing corpus constructed by Hermann et al. (2015). The data is sourced from *CNN* and *Daily Mail* news stories, which are annotated with human-generated, abstractive, multi-sentence summaries.

Next to the English resources listed in Table 1, the LCSTS dataset collected by Hu et al. (2015) is perhaps closest to our own work—both in terms of text genre and collection method. Their dataset comprises 2.5 million content-summary pairs col-lected from the Chinese social media platform Weibo, a service similar to Twitter in that a post is limited to 140 characters. Weibo users frequently start their posts with a short summary in brackets.

3   Dataset Construction

Reddit is a community centered around social news aggregation, web content rating, and discus-sion, and, as of mid-2017, one of the ten most-visited sites on the web according to Alexa.[1] Com-munity members submit and curate content con-sisting of text posts or web links, segregated into channels called *subreddits*, covering general top-ics such as Technology, Gaming, Finance, Well-being, as well as special-interest subjects that may only be relevant to a handful of users. At the time of writing, there are about 1.1 million subreddits. In each subreddit, users submit top-level posts—referred to as submissions—and others reply with comments, reflecting, contradicting, or supporting the submission. Submissions consist of a title and either a web link, or a user-supplied body text; in the latter case, the submission is also called a *self-post*. Comments always have a body text—unless subsequently deleted by the author or a moderator—which may also include inline URLs.

Large crawls of Reddit comments and submis-sions have recently been made available to the NLP community.[2] For the purpose of construct-ing our summarization corpus, we employ the set of 286 million submissions and 1.6 billion com-ments posted to Reddit between 2006 and 2016.

---

[1]http://www.alexa.com/siteinfo/reddit.com
[2]http://files.pushshift.io/reddit/

Table 2: Filtering steps to get the TL;DR corpus.

Filtering Step	Subreddits	Submissions	Comments
Raw Input	617,812	286,168,475	1,659,361,605
Contains tl.{0,3}dr	37,090	2,081,363	3,755,345
Contains tl;dr[3]	34,380	2,002,684	3,412,371
Non-bot post	34,349	1,894,094	3,379,287
Final Pairs	32,778	1,667,129	2,377,372

3.1 Corpus Construction

Given the raw data of Reddit submissions and comments, our goal is to mine for TL;DR content-summary pairs. We set up a five-step pipeline of consecutive filtering steps; Table 2 shows the number of posts remaining after each step.

An initial investigation showed that the spelling of TL;DR is not uniform, but many plausible variants exist. To boil down the raw dataset to an upper bound of submissions and comments (collectively posts) that are candidates for our corpus, we first filtered all posts that contain the two letter sequences 'tl' and 'dr' in that order, case-insensitive, allowing for up to three random letters in-between. This included a lot of instances found within URLs, which were thus ignored by default. Next, we manually reviewed a number of example posts for all of the 100 most-frequent spelling variants (covering 90% of the distribution) and found 33 variants to be highly specific to actual TL;DR summaries,[3] whereas the remaining, less frequent, variants contained too much noise to be of use.

The Reddit community has developed many bots for purposes such as content moderation, advertisement or entertainment. Posts by these bots are often well formatted but redundant and irrelevant to the topic at hand. To ensure we collect only posts made by human users—critically, some Reddit users operate TL;DR-bots that produce automatic summaries, which may introduce undesirable noise—we filter out all bot accounts with the help of an extensive list provided by the Reddit community,[4] as well as manual inspection of cases where the user name contained the substring "bot."

For the remaining posts, we attempt to split their bodies at the expression TL;DR to form the content-summary pairs for our corpus. We locate the position of the TL;DR pattern in each post, and split the text into two parts at this point, the part

Table 3: Examples of content-summary pairs.

Example Submission

Title: Ultimate travel kit
Body: Doing some traveling this year and I am looking to build the ultimate travel kit ... So far I have a Bonavita 0.5L travel kettle and AeroPress. Looking for a grinder that would maybe fit into the AeroPress. This way I can stack them in each other and have a compact travel kit.
TL;DR: What grinder would you recommend that fits in AeroPress?

Example Comment (to a different submission)

Body: Oh man this brings back memories. When I was little, around five, we were putting in a new shower system in the bathroom and had to open up the wall. The plumber opened up the wall first, then put in the shower system, and then left it there while he took a lunch break. After his break he patched up the wall and left, having completed the job. Then we couldn't find our cat. But we heard the cat. Before long we realized it was stuck in the wall, and could not get out. We called up the plumber again and he came back the next day and opened the wall. Out came our black cat, Socrates, covered in dust and filth.
TL;DR: plumber opens wall, cat climbs in, plumber closes wall, fucking meows everywhere until plumber returns the next day

before being considered as the content, and the part following as the summary. In this step, we apply a small set of rules to remove erroneous cases: multiple occurrences of TL;DRs are disallowed for their ambiguity, the length of a TL;DR must be shorter than that of the content, there must be at least 2 words in the content and 1 word in TL;DR. The last rule is very lenient; any other threshold would be artificial (i.e., a 10 word sentence may still be summarizable in 2 words). However, future users of our corpus probably might have more conservative thresholds in mind. We hence provide a subset with a 100 word content threshold.

Reddit allows Markdown syntax in post texts, and many users take advantage of this facility. As this introduces some special characters in the text, we disregard all Markdown formatting, as well as inline URLs, when searching for TL;DRs.

After filtering, we are left with approximately 1.6 million submissions and 2.4 million comments for a total of 4 million content-summary pairs. Table 3 shows one example each of content-summary pairs in submissions and comments. The development of the filtering pipeline went along with many spot-checks to ensure selection precision. As a final corpus validation, we reviewed 1000 randomly selected pairs and found 95% to be correct, a proportion that allows for realistic usage. Nevertheless, we continue on refining the filtering pipeline as systematic errors become apparent.

3.2 Corpus Statistics

For the 4 million content-summary pairs, Table 4 shows distributions of the word counts of content and summary, as well as the ratio of summary to content word count. On average, the content body of submissions tends to be nearly twice as long as

---

[3] tl dr, tl;dr, tldr, tl:dr, tl/dr, tl; dr, tl,dr, tl, dr, tl-dr, tl'dr, tl: dr, tl.dr, tl ; dr, tl_dr, tldr;dr, tl ;dr, tl\dr, tl/ dr, tld:dr, tl;;dr, tltl;dr, tl~dr, tl / dr, tl :dr, tl - dr, tl\\dr, tl. dr, tl::;dr, tl|dr, tl;sdr, tll;dr, tl : dr, tld;dr

[4] https://www.reddit.com/r/autowikibot/wiki/redditbots

Table 4: Length statistics for the TL;DR corpus.

	Min	Median	Max	Mean	σ
Comments					
Total	3	164	6,880	225.21	210.22
Content	2	144	6,597	202.99	199.19
Summary	1	15	1,816	22.21	27.81
Summ. / Cont.	0.00	0.11	1.00	0.16	0.16
Submissions					
Total	3	296	9,973	416.40	384.72
Content	2	269	9,952	382.75	366.99
Summary	1	22	3,526	33.65	47.87
Summ. / Cont.	0.00	0.08	1.00	0.12	0.13

that of comments, whereas the fraction of the total word count in the summary tends to be higher for submissions (about 11% being typical) than for comments (8%). As the length of a post increases, the length of the summary tends to increase as well (Pearson correlations of 0.40 for submissions and 0.35 for comments), while the ratio of summary to content word count increases only slightly (correlations of 0.11 and 0.07).

3.3 Corpus Verticals

The corpus allows for constructing verticals with regard to content type, content topic, and summary type. Content type refers to submissions vs. comments, the key difference being that submissions include an author-supplied title field, which can serve as an additional source of summary ground truth. Comments may perhaps inherit the title of the submission they were posted to, but topic drift may occur. The submission of the example comment in Table 3 was befittingly entitled "So I found my cat after 6 hours with some power tools...", referring to a picture of a cat stuck in a wall.

Content topic refers to the subreddit a submission or comment was posted to. While subreddits cover trending topics as well as online culture very well, thus ensuring a broader range of topics than news can deliver, there is currently no ontology grouping them for ease of selection.

In our data exploration, we observed that Reddit users write TL;DRs with various intentions, such as providing a "true" summary, asking questions or for help, or forming judgments and conclusions. Although the first kind of TL;DR posts are most important for training summarization models, yet, the latter allow for various alternative summarization-related tasks. Hence, we exemplify how the corpus may be *heuristically* split according to summary type—other summary type verticals are envisioned.

To estimate the number of true summaries, we extract noun phrases from both content and summary, and retain posts where they intersect. Only 966,430 content-summary pairs—580,391 from submissions and 386,039 from comments—pass this test, but this is a lower bound: since abstractive summaries may well be semantically relevant to a post without sharing any noun phrases.

To extract question summaries, we test for the presence of one of 21 English question words,[5] as well as a question mark, in the summary. We can isolate a subset of 78,710 content-summary pairs this way (see Table 3 top), which allow for training tailored models yielding questions for a summary.

Many posts contain abusive words in the content, the TL;DR, or both (see Table 3 bottom). While retaining vulgarity in a summary may be appropriate, it seems rarely desirable if a model introduces vulgarity of its own. To separate 299,145 vulgar summaries, we use a list of more than 500 English offensive words from Google's now defunct "What Do You Love" project.[6] Come to think of it, these may still be used to train a swearing summarizer, if only for comedic effect.

4 Conclusion

We show how social media can serve as a source of large-scale summarization training data, and mine a set of 4 million content-summary pairs from Reddit, which we make available to the research community as the Webis-TLDR-17 corpus.[7] Preliminary experiments training the models proposed by Rush et al. (2015) and Nallapati et al. (2016) on our dataset have been promising: by manual inspection of individual samples, they produce useful summaries for many Reddit posts; we leave a quantitative evaluation for future work.

Our filtering pipeline, data exploration, and vertical formation allow for fine-grained control of the data, and can be tailored to one's own needs. Other data sources should be amenable to mining TL;DRs, too: a cursory examination of the CommonCrawl and Clueweb12 web crawls unearths more than 2 million pages containing the pattern—though extracting clean content-summary pairs will likely require more effort for general web content than for self-contained social media posts.

---

[5] Extension of the word list at https://en.wikipedia.org/wiki/Interrogative_word with "can", "should", "would", "is", "could", "does", "will" after manual analysis of the corpus.

[6] Obtained via https://gist.github.com/jamiew/1112488

[7] https://www.uni-weimar.de/medien/webis/corpora/

References

Rasim M. Alguliev, Ramiz M. Aliguliyev, and Nijat R. Isazade. 2013. Multiple documents summarization based on evolutionary optimization algorithm. *Expert Syst. Appl.* 40(5):1675–1689. https://doi.org/10.1016/j.eswa.2012.09.014.

Sumit Chopra, Michael Auli, and Alexander M Rush. 2016. Abstractive Sentence Summarization with Attentive Recurrent Neural Networks. In *NAACL HLT 2016, The 2016 Conference of the North American Chapter of the Association for Computational Linguistics: Human Language Technologies, San Diego California, USA, June 12-17, 2016.* pages 93–98. http://aclweb.org/anthology/N/N16/N16-1012.pdf.

Mahak Gambhir and Vishal Gupta. 2017. Recent automatic text summarization techniques: a survey. *Artificial Intelligence Review* 47(1):1–66. https://doi.org/10.1007/s10462-016-9475-9.

Karl Moritz Hermann, Tomás Kociský, Edward Grefenstette, Lasse Espeholt, Will Kay, Mustafa Suleyman, and Phil Blunsom. 2015. Teaching machines to read and comprehend. In *Advances in Neural Information Processing Systems 28: Annual Conference on Neural Information Processing Systems 2015, December 7-12, 2015, Montreal, Quebec, Canada.* pages 1693–1701. http://papers.nips.cc/paper/5945-teaching-machines-to-read-and-comprehend.

Baotian Hu, Qingcai Chen, and Fangze Zhu. 2015. LCSTS: A Large Scale Chinese Short Text Summarization Dataset. In *Proceedings of the 2015 Conference on Empirical Methods in Natural Language Processing, EMNLP 2015, Lisbon, Portugal, September 17-21, 2015.* Association for Computational Linguistics, pages 1967–1972. http://www.aclweb.org/anthology/D15-1229.

Ju-Hong Lee, Sun Park, Chan-Min Ahn, and Daeho Kim. 2009. Automatic generic document summarization based on non-negative matrix factorization. *Inf. Process. Manage.* 45(1):20–34. https://doi.org/10.1016/j.ipm.2008.06.002.

Ramesh Nallapati, Bowen Zhou, Cícero Nogueira dos Santos, Çaglar Gülçehre, and Bing Xiang. 2016. Abstractive text summarization using sequence-to-sequence rnns and beyond. In *Proceedings of the 20th SIGNLL Conference on Computational Natural Language Learning, CoNLL 2016, Berlin, Germany, August 11-12, 2016.* pages 280–290. http://aclweb.org/anthology/K/K16/K16-1028.pdf.

You Ouyang, Wenjie Li, Sujian Li, and Qin Lu. 2011. Applying regression models to query-focused multi-document summarization. *Inf. Process. Manage.* 47(2):227–237. https://doi.org/10.1016/j.ipm.2010.03.005.

Alexander M. Rush, Sumit Chopra, and Jason Weston. 2015. A neural attention model for abstractive sentence summarization. In *Proceedings of the 2015 Conference on Empirical Methods in Natural Language Processing, EMNLP 2015, Lisbon, Portugal, September 17-21, 2015.* pages 379–389. http://aclweb.org/anthology/D/D15/D15-1044.pdf.

Abigail See, Peter J. Liu, and Christopher D. Manning. 2017. Get to the point: Summarization with pointer-generator networks. *CoRR* abs/1704.04368. To appear in ACL'17. http://arxiv.org/abs/1704.04368.

Topic Model Stability for Hierarchical Summarization

John E. Miller and **Kathleen F. McCoy**
Computer & Information Sciences
University of Delaware, Newark, DE 19711
millerje@udel.edu, mccoy@udel.edu

Abstract

We envisioned responsive generic hierarchical text summarization with summaries organized by topic and paragraph based on hierarchical structure topic models. But we had to be sure that topic models were stable for the sampled corpora. To that end we developed a methodology for aligning multiple hierarchical structure topic models run over the same corpus under similar conditions, calculating a representative centroid model, and reporting stability of the centroid model. We ran stability experiments for standard corpora and a development corpus of Global Warming articles. We found *flat* and *hierarchical* structures of two levels plus the root offer stable centroid models, but *hierarchical* structures of three levels plus the root didn't seem stable enough for use in hierarchical summarization.

1 Introduction

We envisioned a responsive generic hierarchical text summarization process for complex subjects and multiple page documents with resulting text summaries organized by topic and paragraph. Information extraction and summary construction would be based on hierarchical structure topic models learned in the analysis phase.[1] The *hierarchical* topic structure would provide the organization as well as the information quantity budget and extraction criteria for sections and paragraphs in hierarchical summarization. Initial attempts along this path offered promise for a more coherent and organized summary for a small corpus of Global Warming articles from (Live Science, 2015) versus that obtained by *flat* topic structures.

However, multiple analyses of the same Global Warming corpus and various standard corpora under similar conditions rendered seemingly different hierarchical topic models. Model differences remained even after transforming and reducing models based on required summary size and other extrinsic summary requirements. So we decided to examine topic model stability with the goal of assuring that stable, representative, and credible topic models would be produced in our analysis phase. This paper documents our effort at assuring hierarchical topic model stability for hierarchical summarization.

It is inherent in Bayesian probabilistic topic modeling and similar methods that repeat analyses of the same corpus under the same conditions give different results. But we must have substantially similar results to do credible hierarchical summarization (or other application). We require topic model stability, i.e., similar topic models for analyses performed under similar conditions. Without stable results, we do not know which analyses to believe, if any, and we mistrust the methodology itself. Furthermore, any application of the resulting topic model is not credible.

Organization of Paper Bayesian probabilisitic topic analysis (§2.1) expresses a corpus as the matrix product of topic compositions of words with document mixtures of topics. In *flat* topic analysis, the matrix of topic-word compositions is organized as a flat vector of individual topics. With *hierarchical* structure topic analysis, the topics take on a hierarchical tree structure.

Topic model quality (§2.2) is typically assessed by predictive likelihood of words for a test corpus or by assessment of topic coherence. Our stability assessment methodology seems largely com-

---

[1]Phases are the somewhat standard: corpus preparation, analysis, information extraction, summary construction.

Proceedings of the Workshop on New Frontiers in Summarization, pages 64–73
Copenhagen, Denmark, September 7, 2017. ©2017 Association for Computational Linguistics

plementary to quality assessment.

The Hungarian assignment algorithm (Kuhn, 1955) has been used for aligning *flat* topic model pairs (§2.3), based on a cost matrix of pairwise topic alignments. We will use a pairwise topic similarity measure for populating the Hungarian algorithm's cost matrix.

Topic models, including hierarchical models, are being used to construct text summaries (§2.4), including hierarchical text summaries. This provides sufficient reason to want to assure the stability of *flat* and *hierarchical* structure topic models.

We introduce the particular *flat* and *hierarchical* structure topic models (§3.1) used for this paper.

In a simple yet significant innovation, we extend topic alignment (§3.2) to hierarchical structure topic model pairs via a recursive application of the Hungarian assignment algorithm starting with root topics of the model pair. Surprisingly, we find time complexity of the *hierarchical* topic structure improves versus *flat* structure with increasing level of the hierarchy. [2]

We measure stability (§3.3) as alignment (proportion of aligned topics), similarity (weighted cosine similarity over topic compositions), and divergence (Jensen-Shannon divergence over topic distributions). Measures are defined for *flat* and then extended to *hierarchical* structure topic models.

The more topic models in the study, the more credible the stability analysis, since we are aligning more models and measuring stability based on more analyses. For complex problems, however, more models also makes it more likely we would encounter alternative topic models, just as human topic modelers might. We perform agglomerative clustering on topic model similarity (§3.4) to test whether models form a single or multiple stable topic model groups, or are unstable.

For each cluster, we align models and calculate topic frequency weighted centroids (§3.5) of topic-word compositions for aligned topics. Then we assess stability versus the centroid model (§3.6) similarly to that done previously for model pairs.

We demonstrate the methodology (§4) over *flat* and *hierarchical* structure models in an 18 run factorial experiment on three corpora, and in a separate *ad hoc* 16 run experiment on a larger corpus.

We return to our work on hierarchical summa-

---

[2]Software engineering already knows this – that hierarchical structure is less time complex than monolithic.

rization (§5) now armed with stable hierarchical topic models and examine our next steps as well as options for further research.

2   Previous Work

We use Bayesian probabilistic topic modeling in the analysis phase of our hierarchical summarization process. Here we briefly review topic modeling, topic model quality, topic model stability, and use of topic models in hierarchical summarization.

2.1   Topic Models

The Latent Dirichlet analysis (LDA) Bayesian probabilistic topic model, introduced and popularized by Blei et al. (2003); Griffiths and Steyvers (2004), factors a corpus of document-word occurrences as the matrix product of topic compositions of words and document mixtures of topics (figure 1). The topic structure is *flat* and the number of topics, K, and vocabulary size, V, are fixed. In the generative probabilistic model, topic-word compositions are distributed symmetric Dirichlet with parameter η, and document-topic mixtures are distributed Dirichlet with concentration parameter α.

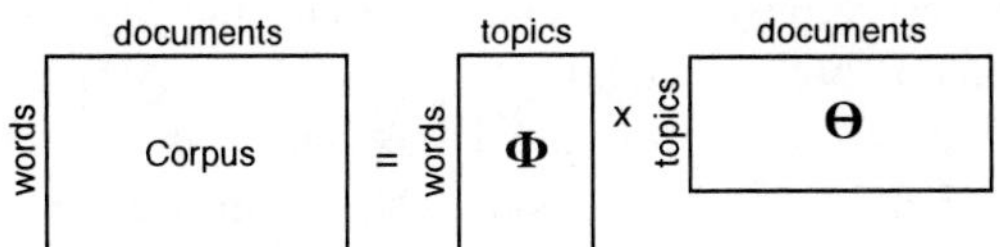

Figure 1: Topic Model Factorization of Corpus

Teh et al. (2005, 2006) generalized the LDA model in two important ways: (1) the number of topics, K, is made open ended by treating the topic model as a Dirichlet process (DP) with growth parameter γ for sampling a new topic, and (2) documents are sampled from Dirichlet processes (DPs) which are themselves sampled from corpus DPs thus forming hierarchical Dirichlet processes, HDPs, even while the topic structure remains *flat*.

Blei et al. (2010) developed *hierarchical* topic analysis where the generative model of the corpus consists of a hierarchy of nested Dirichlet processes (DPs) and each document is generated as a single non-branching path down the corpus hierarchical structure. *Stay-or-go* stochastic switches are used at each document node to determine whether to *stay* on the current topic or *go* to a topic further down the tree.

Paisley et al. (2015) extended the non-branching document paths to a nested hierarchical structure

Dirichlet process model with branching in both the document and global models. In figure 2, the grey represents the corpus tree and the black overlaid trees the individual document trees. Each document parent node is a DP sampled from its corresponding corpus node DP. Analysis infers the corpus topic structure and compositions, and document topic mixtures and *stay-or-go* switches.

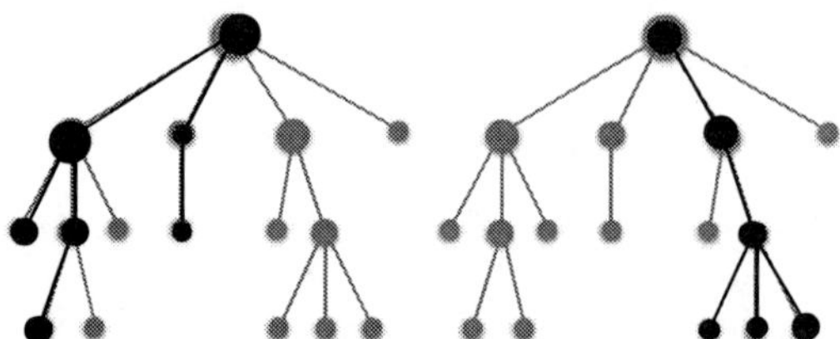

Figure 2: Hierarchical Corpus Structure

2.2 Quality

Predictive log likelihood for words, test $LL(\mathbf{x})$, is a popular measure of topic analysis quality. Test $LL(\mathbf{x})$ shows the predictability of words on test data given the model fit to training data (corpus topics and compositions). While not a stability measure, test $LL(\mathbf{x})$ does give an objective indication of predictability. Teh et al. (2007) provides formulas for calculating test $LL(\mathbf{x})$ for the *flat* topic structure in both Gibbs sampler and variational inference analysis methods.

Assessing quality of individual topics can be as simple as noting topics below a minimum frequency or comparing divergence of topics from any of uniform, corpus, or power distributions of word frequencies. More powerful methods assess individual and aggregate topic coherence. The current standard is to measure coherence by normalized pairwise mutual information (NPMI) (Aletras and Stevenson, 2013; Lau et al., 2014; Röder et al., 2015) versus pairwise probabilities calculated from some very large pertinent corpus.

We view test likelihood and topic coherence as largely complementary to topic model stability.

2.3 Topic Alignment and Stability

Topic models must be aligned on topics before assessing stability. de Wall and Barnard (2008) calculates similarity weights between topics from different models over documents, constructs a cost matrix from negative similarity weights, and applies the Hungarian assignment algorithm (Kuhn, 1955) to determine the optimal pairwise topic

model alignment. Stability is defined as the correlation between aligned topics over documents.

Greene et al. (2014) calculates the average of Jaccard scores on sets of popular word ranks between topic combinations of a topic model pair, and determines the model agreement (i.e., stability) as the average over topics of Jaccard scores resulting from the optimal topic alignment by the Hungarian assignment algorithm.

Chuang et al. (2015) notes that model alignment is "ill-defined and computationally intractable" with multiple-to-multiple mappings between topics, and adopts the solution of mapping topics *up-to-one* topic.[3]

Yang et al. (2016) aligns topics for *flat* topic structures also using the Hungarian assignment algorithm and *up-to-one* topic correspondence. Stability is measured as agreement between token topic assignments over aligned topic models.

We use the Hungarian algorithm and the *up-to-one* topic correspondence. We choose to emphasize topic correspondence based on topic word compositions, as in the generative model, and so base our cost matrix on similarity of topic word compositions between models.

2.4 Topic Model Based Summarization

Haghighi and Vanderwende (2009) examined several hybrid topic models using LDA as a building block and demonstrated the superior efficacy of their hybrid model (general topic, general content topic, detail content topics, and document specific topics) in constructing short summaries for Document Understanding Conferences (U.S. Department of Commerce: National Institute of Standards and Technology, 2015). Delort and Alfonseca (2011); Mason and Charniak (2011) used similar models in short summaries for the Text Analysis Conferences (of Commerce: National Institute of Standards and Technology, 2010, 2011). Celikyilmaz and Hakkani-Tur (2010, 2011) used a more general *hierarchical* LDA topic model structure, doing *hierarchical* summarization for longer summaries. Christensen et al. (2014) developed "hierarchical summarization" using temporal hierarchical clustering and budgeting summary component size by cluster.

We use a more general hierarchical structured Bayesian topic model similar to Paisley et al.

---

[3]Indeed, the issue of mapping 1 topic to 2+ topics would be an interesting and useful problem to solve.

(2015). Essential for any of these related hierarchical topic model or cluster based methods is the stability of the model used to drive summarization.

3   Methodology

We present a process for aligning topic models and measuring topic model stability for both *flat* and *hierarchical* structure cases. The resulting stable hierarchical structure topic centroid model would be further transformed to take into account extrinsic summarization requirements.

Stability – Measurement Process

1. Infer multiple topic models for the same corpus run under similar conditions.

2. Determine pairwise topic model alignments.

3. Calculate stability over pairs.

4. Cluster topic models using agglomerative clustering over pairwise stability.

5. For each cluster:

   (a) Align member topic models and calculate topic model centroids.

   (b) Align member topic models with topic centroid model.

   (c) Calculate stability of topic models with topic centroid model.

6. Interpret stability results.

3.1   Topic Modeling

For a *flat* topic structure, we use a Gibbs sampler implementation of Teh et al. (2006) hierarchical Dirichlet processes (HDP). For a *hierarchical* topic structure, we use a Gibbs sampler implementation of a simplified version of Paisley et al. (2015)'s nested hierarchical Dirichlet processes. Our simplified model and Gibbs sampler drops the use of *stay-or-go* stochastic switches at each document Dirichlet process (DP) node. See supplemental notes (Supplemental, 2017b).

3.2   Pairwise Topic Model Alignment

From a set of M topic models, all $M(M-1)/2$ model pairs are aligned based on topic pair assignment costs. Assignment cost between topics from distinct model pairs is calculated as

$$cost_{k,l} = -(m_k/N)(n_l/N) * cosSim(\mathbf{m_k}, \mathbf{n_l}),$$

where (k, l) indexes topics from model pairs, m_k and n_l are topic frequencies, N is corpus size, $\mathbf{m_k}$ and $\mathbf{n_l}$ are vectors of word frequencies for topic pair (k, l), and $cosSim$ calculates the cosine similarity.[4] By using topic frequency ratios in the cost, similar frequency topics are preferred. Since weak similarities are not useful, we censor $cosSim \leq .25$ and substitute zero for their cost.

***Flat* Topic Models**   Pairwise costs are assembled into a cost matrix indexed by (k, l) and the optimal cost assignment of the model pair is determined by the Hungarian assignment algorithm. For unequal numbers of topics, vectors of zero (maximum) costs are substituted for nonexistent topics.

***Hierarchical* Topic Models**   Hierarchical topic structures are single rooted branching trees of depth L where the root is depth 0. Each tree node includes a topic of word compositions, and each non-leaf tree node includes a Dirichlet process (DP) of topic mixtures. We restrict hierarchical topic structure alignment to require: (1) roots must align, and (2) aligned child branches must align in their ancestors. With these restrictions, we developed Minimize Subtree Cost (algorithm 1) applying the Hungarian algorithm to DP (non-leaf) nodes of the hierarchical topic structure.

Method $minimizeSubtreeCost$ is invoked initially for model pair roots, (σ_0, τ_0) and recursively thereafter for subtree pairs, (σ, τ). If either subtree is a leaf the topic alignment cost is returned. For internal nodes, a cost matrix is constructed between the child nodes for the subtrees, the Hungarian assignment algorithm is invoked to get the optimum cost alignment for the subtrees, the topic cost is added to the subtree costs, and this result is returned. Filling the subtree cost matrix calculates the cost of aligning properties between model pairs of subtree children by minimizing subtree costs for each child pair. Thus calculating subtree costs and filling subtree costs together ***recursively*** span the entire solution space for hierarchical topic alignment. See supplemental java snippets (Supplemental, 2017a).

Time Complexity   For *flat* topic structures, topic alignment time complexity is $O(K^2(V + K))$, where K is the number of topics and V is the vocabulary size. Preparation of the cost matrix takes K^2 topic vector cosine similarity calculations over

---

[4]Alternatively, straight cosine similarity or a divergence measure such as Hellinger distance could be used.

Algorithm 1 Minimize Subtree Cost

Require: Trees σ, τ
  Method: minimizeSubtreeCost(σ, τ)
  if isLeaf(σ) **or** isLeaf(τ) **then**
    return topicCost(σ, τ)
  else
    costs $\leftarrow$ fillSubtreeCosts(σ, τ)
    return topicCost(σ, τ)
        +HungarianAssignment(**costs**)
  end if

  Method: fillSubtreeCosts(σ, τ)
  for $k = 0$ **to** σ.children.size **do**
    for $l = 0$ **to** τ.children.size **do**
      costs$[k, l]$ $\leftarrow$ minimizeSubtreeCost
          (σ.children[k], τ.children[l])
    end for
  end for
  return costs

V words giving $O(K^2V)$, and the Hungarian assignment algorithm which minimizes cost has time complexity $O(K^3)$ (Kuhn, 1955).

Level 1 in the *hierarchical* structure is similar to the *flat* topic structure. Time complexity is $O(B^2(V+B))$, with branching factor, B, in place of number of topics, K. Each increment in level increases by a factor of B^2 the tree node pairs from the parent level. The resulting time complexity for level l beyond the root is then $O(B^{2l}(V+B))$. For $B > 1$ the final level dominates the order calculation, and so the time complexity for a *hierarchical* structure of depth L is $O(B^{2L}(V + B))$.

We compare this with the time complexity for the *flat* structure alignment problem by expressing K as though from a *flattened hierarchical* structure, $K = (1 - B^{L+1})/(1 - B)$.[5] Then, $O(K^2(V+K)) = O([[(1-B^{L+1})/(1-B)]^2(V + [(1 - B^{L+1})/(1 - B)])])$. For $B > 1$ the terms with B in the ratio dominate, and so expressing *flat* structure in *hierarchical* terms gives time complexity $O(B^{2L}(V + B^L))$. Cost of assignment for *flat* is greater by a factor of B^{L-1} versus a comparable *hierarchical* structure.

This is a surprising result! We had expected hierarchical structure to add time complexity, but instead it reduces time complexity with increasing level compared to a corresponding *flat* structure. Alignment of topics between *hierarchical* struc-

---

[5]Sum of geometric series, $\sum_{l=0}^{L} B^l$, for a branching tree.

tures is less time complex than for *flat* structures.

3.3 Pairwise Stability

Given the topic model alignment, we calculate alignment, similarity, and divergence measures. Table 1 gives *a priori* and preliminary calibration study interpretations of the stability measures.

Proportion Aligned Alignment is calculated as, $pAlign = K'/[(K_\sigma + K_\tau)/2]$, where K' is the number of aligned topics, and K_σ and K_τ are the number of topics for each model.

Weighted Similarity Similarity is calculated as topic frequency weighted similarity of the topic word compositions of the (σ, τ) model pair,[6]

$$wtSim_{\sigma,\tau} = \sum_{\substack{(k,l)\in \\ aligned}} \frac{m_k + n_l}{2N} cosSim(\mathbf{m_k}, \mathbf{n_l}),$$

where (k, l) indexes topics from the *flat* or *hierarchically* aligned model pair, m_k and n_l are topic frequencies, N is the corpus size, $\mathbf{m_k}$ and $\mathbf{n_l}$ are vectors of word frequencies for topic pair (k, l), and $cosSim$ calculates the cosine similarity. Only aligned topics are added to the $wtSim$, but the corpus size includes all observations, so the fewer aligned topics, the lower the weighted similarity. For the *hierarchical* model we require that ancestors are also aligned.

Divergence Divergence is calculated as the Jensen-Shannon divergence (JSD) between topic frequency distributions for model pairs. Distributions are calculated as follows: (1) model σ topic frequency counts are assembled in array **s** by topic index k, (2) frequencies of unaligned topics from σ are set to zero with the sum of frequencies of unaligned topics set in $\mathbf{s}_K$ where K is the maximum number of topics for the (σ, τ) model pair, (3) model τ topic frequency counts are assembled in array **t** by topic index l, (4) frequencies of unaligned topics from τ are set to zero with the sum of frequencies of unaligned topics set in $\mathbf{t}_{K+1}$, and (5) topic frequencies in **t** are reordered according to the alignment mapping between (σ, τ). Thus, aligned topics coincide with respect to their positions in $\mathbf{s}, \mathbf{t}$ and unaligned frequencies are kept separate between models. Divergence is calculated as

$$JSD(\mathbf{s}||\mathbf{t}) = 1/2(KLD(\mathbf{s}||\mathbf{m}) + KLD(\mathbf{t}||\mathbf{m})),$$

---

[6]Unweighted or other weighting could be used as well.

Basis	Value	Interpretation
a priori	$alignment = 1$	full alignment
calibration	$alignment \approx 0.6$	useful alignment
a priori	$similarity = 1$	full similarity
calibration	$similarity \approx 0.6$	useful similarity
calibration	$similarity \approx 0.25$	marginal similarity
a priori	$divergence = 0$	full convergence
calibration	$divergence \approx 0.1$	strong convergence
calibration	$divergence \approx 0.4$	strong divergence

Table 1: Preliminary interpretation of stability

where $\mathbf{m} = (\mathbf{s} + \mathbf{t})/2$ and KLD is the Kullback-Leibler divergence. For the *hierarchical* model we require that ancestors are also aligned.

3.4 Cluster Topic Models

There are multiple ways in which topics can be organized and assigned - whether performed automatically or by human experts. So we test whether model pairs align to a single stable model group, or if multiple stable groups can be identified.

We use group-average agglomerative clustering (Manning et al., 2008) on pairwise weighted similarity, $wtSim$, to form model clusters. This results in compact clusters maximizing separation between clusters while minimizing the distance between the cluster centroid and its members. Clustering begins with each model forming its own cluster and ends when either all models form a single cluster or no more clusters can be formed that meet $\overline{wtSim} > cutPoint$, where $\overline{wtSim}$ is the average weighted similarity. Output is a list of clusters where each cluster includes a list of models ordered by entry into the cluster and $\overline{wtSim}$.

Agglomerative clustering is fast and simple; pairwise similarity scores do not have to be recalculated after each clustering step. However, we don't know what are the similarities or differences between clusters without inspecting them.

3.5 Form Topic Centroid Models

With only one cluster, no unclustered models, and good similarity, the models seem stable. We form topic centroids and report this centroid model as the representative topic model. With multiple clusters, we should consider the appropriateness of multiple solutions – perhaps corresponding to multiple human solutions. We form centroids for each topic and report centroid models as representative of the clusters. The occurrence of many unclustered models would indicate instability.

Controls specify a censor limit for similarity below which topics do not merge into a centroid, and a minimum number of models and minimum topic frequency below which topics drop from the centroid topic model. While a cluster may have several models, not all topics need not be aligned across all models.

Form Topic Centroid Model (algorithm 2) forms cluster centroid models by copying the cluster centroid from the initial model and then aligning and entering individual models into the centroid iteratively based on their order of entry into the cluster. The method `optimizeSubtreeMap`, a variation on the previous `minimizeSubtreeCost` (algorithm 1), returns the topic correspondence mapping. Topics which do not meet the topic similarity censor limit ($wtSim < .25$) are not aligned. Unaligned topics are provisionally added to the centroid model in case subsequent models in the list have similar topics. After the centroid model is formed, topics which to not meet a minimum topic frequency limit or minimum number of topic models limit are dropped.

Algorithm 2 Form Topic Centroid Model

Require: Cluster list of trees λ
  Method: formCentroidModel(λ)
  $\mu \leftarrow \lambda_0$
  for $i = 1$ **to** λ.size **do**
    $mapping \leftarrow$ optimizeSubtreeMap(μ, λ_i)
    for all $topic \in \lambda_i$ **do**
      if $topic \in mapping$ **then**
        $index \leftarrow mapping.indexOf(topic)$
        aggregateTopic($\mu, \lambda_i, index, topic$)
      else
        addTopic($\mu, \lambda_i, topic$)
      end if
    end for
  end for
  for all $topic \in \mu$ **do**
    if failsDropLimits($topic$) **then**
      drop($\mu, topic$)
    end if
  end for

3.6 Centroid Model Stability

For each cluster's centroid model, we align individual models with the centroid model and estimate stability. The method is similar to that for pairwise stability with the exception that the centroid model is always one member of the pair and so only M (centroid, model) pairs are analyzed.

3.7 Use in Hierarchical Summarization

The final product is a single stable centroid model, when one exists. The stable centroid model shows the topic structure, the proportional importance of each topic, and the word composition of each topic as a discrete probability distribution. In our hierarchical summarization process, this centroid model would be further transformed (nested, pruned, aggregated) by taking into account extrinsic requirements of summary size, and paragraph and sub-paragraph structure. The resulting topic structure model would be used to extract information proportionally for each topic, and organize the section and paragraph structured summary.

If the centroid model is not stable, then hierarchical summarization would not be credible. If there are multiple identifiable stable clusters, then their centroid models become candidates for organizing the hierarchical summary.

4 Stability Experiments

The purpose of the stability experiments is to demonstrate the methodology over corpora for *flat* and *hierarchical* structures. When stable centroid models result from replicate topic analyses, they can credibly be transformed to take into account extrinsic summarization requirements, and carried forward to the information extraction phase of our hierarchical summarization process.

4.1 Corpora

Corpora used in this study are Journal of the ACM (JACM) abstracts from years 1987-2000, Global Warming (GW) articles for the year 2015 (Live Science, 2015), Proceedings of the National Academy of Sciences (PNAS) abstracts for years 1991-2001 (Ponweiser et al., 2015), Neural Information Processing Systems (NIPS) proceedings for years 1988-1999 from (Lichman, 2013). PNAS and GW texts were lemmatized. Stop words and words with frequency less than ten were removed. JACM and GW are small corpora; JACM has very small abstracts while GW has short articles; PNAS has numerous abstracts and NIPS has longer articles.

4.2 Experimental Design

An 18 run factorial design (3 corpora x 3 levels x 2 growth rates) crosses JACM, GW, and PNAS corpora, with *flat* (L=0) and *hierarchical* (L=2,3) topic structures, and topic *growth* rates to achieve

Corpus	J	V	N	D
JACM	534	1,328	33,517	62.8
GW	116	970	31,894	274.9
PNAS	27,688	9,685	2,713,006	98.0
NIPS	1,491	6,149	1,813,400	1,216.2

Table 2: Corpora Characteristics. J=document count, V=vocabulary size, N=corpus size, D=average document size.

two different topic count ranges. Four replicate topic analyses were run at each factorial setting. For training, our simplified Gibbs sampler used α=1.0 and η=0.01 with optimization. The growth parameter γ was set to create topic counts at low (L), medium (M), and high (H) ranges.

Separately, an *ad hoc* experiment was performed on a set of 16 trials on the NIPS corpus with hierarchical (L=3) model using similar training control settings. This experiment demonstrates the occurrence of multiple clusters.

4.3 Results - Factorial Design

Stability analysis was performed for each experimental group of replicates. Topics were not aligned when $wtSim < .25$, clustering terminated when when $avgWtSim < cutPoint = .5$,[7] and topics were dropped from the cluster centroid model when $nModel_k < 2$.

Table 3 shows the results for the factorial design with corpus, hierarchical topic structure (L), and growth rate (γ). Results reported are number of topics in training model (K), and stability measures of number (K') and proportion of topics aligned (pAlign) in centroid model, average weighted similarity (wtSim), and hierarchical Jensen-Shannon divergence (hJSD). Ideal results based on *a priori* values (table 1) would be $pAlign \approx 1, wtSim \approx 1, hJSD \approx 0$.

We expected simpler would be more stable (Ockham's razor), such that more levels and topics give poorer stability. This is largely confirmed by stability measures in that greater hierarchy levels and greater topic count models generally had poorer stability measures. Hierarchical L=3 models and with the JACM corpus especially showed poorer stability.

---

[7] JACM $L = 3$ model used .4 for cut point.

Model		Train	Stability			
L	γ	K	K'	pAlign	wtSim	hJSD
JACM						
0	M	70.3	70.5	1.00	0.867	0.028
2	M	78.0	66.0	0.85	0.839	0.052
3	M	84.8	48.2	0.57	0.682	0.128
0	H	106.8	106.8	1.00	0.851	0.034
2	H	104.5	87.2	0.83	0.831	0.062
3	H	108.5	46.7	0.43	0.700	0.157
GW						
0	M	65.8	65.8	1.00	0.869	0.030
2	M	73.8	72.0	0.98	0.894	0.028
3	M	82.3	59.8	0.73	0.762	0.100
0	H	99.0	98.2	0.99	0.871	0.023
2	H	108.0	89.8	0.83	0.824	0.081
3	H	105.8	62.8	0.59	0.726	0.133
PNAS						
0	L	86.8	86.5	0.99	0.930	0.013
2	L	76.8	72.3	0.94	0.905	0.052
3	L	76.3	58.8	0.77	0.732	0.137
0	M	135.0	134.0	0.99	0.920	0.017
2	M	140.3	122.5	0.87	0.875	0.071
3	M	134.3	92.2	0.69	0.752	0.143

Table 3: Experimental results - stability.

4.4 Results - *Ad hoc* Design - NIPS

We analyzed a set of 16 trials on the NIPS corpus run under somewhat similar conditions with topic counts in the 90 to 200 range with hierarchical L=3. Given the corpus size, non-equality of conditions, and diversity of topic counts, we weren't surprised to find multiple distinct clusters.

Stability analysis was performed with control settings: topics not aligned for $wtSim < .25$, clustering terminated for $\overline{wtSim} < cutPoint = .5$ or .6, and topics dropped from the cluster centroid model for $nModel_k < 2$. Results are reported in table 4. At $cutPoint = 0.5$, all models formed one cluster; at $cutPoint = 0.6$, three separate clusters were identified and six models were not joined to any cluster. Proportion of aligned topics declined ($nModel_k < 2$ is a more stringent test when there are only 2 or 3 models in the cluster), but similarity and divergence measures were substantially improved for each of the three separate clusters.

4.5 Impact on Hierarchical Summarization

For corpora in the factorial design, both *flat* and *hierarchal* L=2 topic structures resulted in good

Cluster	nModels	pAlign	wtSim	hJSD
cut point=0.5				
0	16	0.81	0.592	0.246
cut point=0.6				
0	5	0.66	0.783	0.073
1	2	0.31	0.829	0.140
2	3	0.50	0.821	0.086
*	6 models were not clustered			

Table 4: *Ad hoc* stability experiment on NIPS.

stability (high alignment and similarity with little divergence), so the centroid topic model can credibly be carried forward for use in our hierarchical summarization process. The hierarchical L=3 models are generally less stable.

The NIPS stability analysis for a single cluster shows moderate similarity of models and moderate divergence of topic distributions, while more restrictive clustering reveals three separate clusters and six unassigned models. This bears further investigation.

5 Discussion

We have:

- placed modeling hierarchical topic structure in the analysis phase of our hierarchical text summarization process;

- established the importance of a stable topic model for use in the analysis phase;

- developed a methodology for aligning and measuring stability of topic models;

- defined innovative and simple *hierarchical* topic structure model alignment via a recursive algorithm applying the Hungarian algorithm to individual Dirichlet processes;

- quantified time complexity of our hierarchical alignment algorithm and showed reduced time complexity at increasing *hierarchical* level versus *flat* topic structures;

- developed alignment, similarity, and divergence stability measures for *hierarchical* topic structures;

- applied agglomerative clustering to form coherent groups of topic models:

  - constructed representative cluster centroid models, and

– calculated centroid model stability;

- demonstrated the methodology, finding credible models for *flat* and *hierarchical* L=2 structures;

- demonstrated the methodology on a large set of *hierarchical* L=3 topic models run on the NIPS corpus, finding multiple coherent clusters plus unclustered models;

- mentioned parenthetically work on a pilot calibration study for stability measures;

Future Work   There is work to be done on topic model stability, model alignment, and stability measurement:

- apply our methodology to larger, more varied models and different inference methods;

- improve, expand, and publish calibration studies beyond our pilot;

- explore other topic model alignment cost measures;

- further improve topic alignment including options other than *up-to-one* matching;

- improve hierarchical structure topic model stability.

Summarization - Next Step   We further transform the hierarchical topic structure taking into account extrinsic summarization requirements. The product from the analysis phase is a hierarchical structure topic model where each topic includes its proportional representation of the corpus and a composition of words given as a discrete probability distribution. This structure is used in information extraction, where topic compositions match information from the corpus, e.g., sentences, and proportional representation budgets the quantity of information to be extracted for each topic. The transformed topic structure organizes summary topic and paragraph structure.

Conclusion   Our topic model stability methodology lets us diagnose and compute "usable" hierarchical topic models for collections of long documents. This is an essential and "attractive starting point towards hierarchical text summarization." [8]

---

[8]Thanks to reviewer for this concise statement of benefit.

References

Nikolaos Aletras and Mark Stevenson. 2013. Evaluating topic coherence using distributional semantics. In *Proceedings of the 10th International Conference on Computational Semantics (IWCS 2013) – Long Papers*, pages 13–22. Association for Computational Linguistics.

David M. Blei, Thomas L. Griffiths, and Michael I. Jordan. 2010. The nested chinese restaurant process and bayesian nonparametric inference of topic hierarchies. *J. ACM*, 57(2):7:1–7:30.

David M. Blei, Andrew Y. Ng, and Michael I. Jordan. 2003. Latent dirichlet allocation. *J. Mach. Learn. Res.*, 3:993–1022.

Asli Celikyilmaz and Dilek Hakkani-Tur. 2010. A hybrid hierarchical model for multi-document summarization. In *Proceedings of the 48th Annual Meeting of the Association for Computational Linguistics*, ACL '10, pages 815–824, Stroudsburg, PA, USA. Association for Computational Linguistics.

Asli Celikyilmaz and Dilek Hakkani-Tur. 2011. Discovery of topically coherent sentences for extractive summarization. In *Proceedings of the 49th Annual Meeting of the Association for Computational Linguistics: Human Language Technologies*, pages 491–499, Portland, Oregon, USA. Association for Computational Linguistics.

Janara Christensen, Stephen Soderland, Gagan Bansal, and Mausam. 2014. Hierarchical summarization: Scaling up multi-document summarization. In *Proceedings of the 52nd Annual Meeting of the Association for Computational Linguistics*. Association for Computational Linguistics.

Jason Chuang, Margaret E Roberts, Brandon M Stewart, Rebecca Weiss, Dustin Tingley, Justin Grimmer, and Jeffrey Heer. 2015. Topiccheck: Interactive alignment for assessing topic model stability. In *Proceedings of NAACL-HLT*, pages 175–184.

Jean-Yves Delort and Enrique Alfonseca. 2011. Description of the google update summarizer at TAC-2011. In *Proceedings of the Fourth Text Analysis Conference, TAC 2011, Gaithersburg, Maryland, USA, November 14-15, 2011*. NIST.

Derek Greene, Derek O'Callaghan, and Padraig Cunningham. 2014. How many topics? stability analysis for topic models. In *Machine Learning and Knowledge Discovery in Databases - European Conference, ECML PKDD 2014, Nancy, France, September 15-19, 2014. Proceedings, Part I*, volume 8724 of *Lecture Notes in Computer Science*, pages 498–513. Springer Berlin Heidelberg.

Thomas L. Griffiths and Mark Steyvers. 2004. Finding scientific topics. *Proceedings of the National Academy of Sciences*, 101(suppl 1):5228–5235.

Aria Haghighi and Lucy Vanderwende. 2009. Exploring content models for multi-document summarization. In *Proceedings of Human Language Technologies: The 2009 Annual Conference of the North American Chapter of the Association for Computational Linguistics*, NAACL '09, pages 362–370, Stroudsburg, PA, USA. Association for Computational Linguistics.

Harold W. Kuhn. 1955. The hungarian method for the assignment problem. *Naval Research Logistics Quarterly*, 2:83–97.

Jey Han Lau, David Newman, and Timothy Baldwin. 2014. Machine reading tea leaves: Automatically evaluating topic coherence and topic model quality. In *Proceedings of the 14th Conference of the European Chapter of the Association for Computational Linguistics, EACL 2014, April 26-30, 2014, Gothenburg, Sweden*, pages 530–539.

M. Lichman. 2013. UCI machine learning repository.

Live Science. 2015. Live Science. Online at livescience.com.

Christopher D. Manning, Prabhakar Raghavan, and Hinrich Schütze. 2008. *Introduction to Information Retrieval*. Cambridge University Press, Cambridge, UK.

Rebecca Mason and Eugene Charniak. 2011. Extractive multi-document summaries should explicitly not contain document-specific content. In *Proceedings of the Workshop on Automatic Summarization for Different Genres, Media, and Languages*, WASDGML '11, pages 49–54, Stroudsburg, PA, USA. Association for Computational Linguistics.

John William Paisley, Chong Wang, David M. Blei, and Michael I. Jordan. 2015. Nested hierarchical dirichlet processes. *IEEE Trans. Pattern Anal. Mach. Intell.*, 37(2):256–270.

Martin Ponweiser, Bettina Grün, and Kurt Hornik. 2015. Finding scientific topics revisited. In Maurizio Carpita, Eugenio Brentari, and El Mostafa Qannari, editors, *Advances in Latent Variables*, Studies in Theoretical and Applied Statistics, pages 93–100. Springer International Publishing.

Michael Röder, Andreas Both, and Alexander Hinneburg. 2015. Exploring the space of topic coherence measures. In *Proceedings of the Eighth ACM International Conference on Web Search and Data Mining*, WSDM '15, pages 399–408, New York, NY, USA. ACM.

U.S. Department of Commerce: National Institute of Standards and Technology. 2010. Text analysis conference 2010 – summarization track.

U.S. Department of Commerce: National Institute of Standards and Technology. 2011. Text analysis conference 2011 – summarization track.

Supplemental. 2017a. Hierarchicaltopicagreementxtra.java, hierarchicalmodelstorextra.java. Supplemental material for EMNLP Summarization workshop 2017 - java snippets on topic model alignment. Request from author by email.

Supplemental. 2017b. Topicmodeltheoryxtra.pdf. Supplemental material for EMNLP Summarization workshop 2017 - Topic model theory. Request from author by email.

Y. W. Teh, M. I. Jordan, M. J. Beal, and D. M. Blei. 2005. Sharing clusters among related groups: Hierarchical Dirichlet processes. In *Advances in Neural Information Processing Systems*, volume 17.

Yee Whye Teh, Michael I. Jordan, Matthew J. Beal, and David M. Blei. 2006. Hierarchical dirichlet processes. *Journal of the American Statistical Association*, 101(476):1566–1581.

Yee Whye Teh, Kenichi Kurihara, and Max Welling. 2007. Collapsed variational inference for hdp. In *NIPS*, pages 1481–1488. Curran Associates, Inc.

U.S. Department of Commerce: National Institute of Standards and Technology. 2015. Document understanding conferences.

Alta de Wall and Etienne Barnard. 2008. Evaluating topic models with stability. In *19th Annual Symposium of the Pattern Recognition Association of South Africa*. Pattern Recognition Association of South Africa.

Yi Yang, Shimei Pan, Jie Lu, Mercan Topkara, and Yangqiu Song. 2016. The stability and usability of statistical topic models. *ACM Trans. Interact. Intell. Syst.*, 6(2):14:1–14:23.

Learning to Score System Summaries for Better Content Selection Evaluation.

Maxime Peyrard and **Teresa Botschen** and **Iryna Gurevych**

Research Training Group AIPHES and UKP Lab
Computer Science Department, Technische Universität Darmstadt
`www.aiphes.tu-darmstadt.de, www.ukp.tu-darmstadt.de`

Abstract

The evaluation of summaries is a challenging but crucial task of the summarization field. In this work, we propose to learn an automatic scoring metric based on the human judgements available as part of classical summarization datasets like TAC-2008 and TAC-2009. Any existing automatic scoring metrics can be included as features, the model learns the combination exhibiting the best correlation with human judgments. The reliability of the new metric is tested in a further manual evaluation where we ask humans to evaluate summaries covering the whole scoring spectrum of the metric. We release the trained metric as an open-source tool.

1 Introduction

The task of automatic multi-document summarization is to convert source documents into a condensed text containing the most important information. In particular, the question of evaluation is notably difficult due to the inherent lack of gold standard.

The evaluation can be done manually by involving humans in the process of scoring a given system summary. For example, with the *Responsiveness* metric, human annotators score summaries on a LIKERT scale ranging from 1 to 5. Later, the *Pyramid* scheme was introduced to evaluate content selection with high inter-annotator agreement (Nenkova et al., 2007).

Manual evalations are meaningful and reliable but are also expensive and not reproducible. This makes them unfit for systematic comparison.

Due to the necessity of having cheap and reproducible metrics, a significant body of research was dedicated to the study of automatic evaluation metrics. Automatic metrics aim to produce a semantic similarity score between the candidate summary and a pool of reference summaries previously written by human annotators (Lin, 2004; Yang et al., 2016; Ng and Abrecht, 2015). Some variants rely only on the source documents and the candidate summary ignoring the reference summaries (Louis and Nenkova, 2013; Steinberger and Ježek, 2012).

In order to select the best automatic metric, we typically consider manual evalution metrics as our gold standard, then a good automatic metric should reliably predict how well a summarizer would perform if human evaluation was conducted (Owczarzak et al., 2012; Lin, 2004; Rankel et al., 2013).

In practice, we use the human judgment datasets like the ones constructed during the manual evaluation of the Text Analysis Conference (TAC). The system summaries submitted to the shared tasks were manually scored by trained human annotators following the Responsiveness and/or the Pyramid schemes. An automatic metric is considered good if it ranks the system summaries similarly as humans did.

Currently, ROUGE (Lin, 2004) is the accepted standard for automatic evaluation of content selection because of its simplicity and its good correlation with human judgments. However, previous works on evaluation metrics comparison averaged scores of summaries over topics for each system and then computed the correlation with averaged scores given by humans. ROUGE works well in this scenario which compares only systems after aggregating their scores for many summaries. We call this scenario *system-level correlation analysis*.

A more natural analysis, which we use in this work, is to compute the correlation between the

Proceedings of the Workshop on New Frontiers in Summarization, pages 74–84
Copenhagen, Denmark, September 7, 2017. ©2017 Association for Computational Linguistics

candidate metric and human judgments for each topic indivually and then average these correlations over topics. In this scenario, which we call *summary-level correlation analysis*, the performance of ROUGE significantly drops meaning that on average ROUGE does not really identify summary quality, it can only rank systems after aggregation of many topics.

In order to advance the field of summarization we need to have more consistent metrics correlating well with humans on every topic and capable of estimating the quality of individual summaries (not just systems).

We propose to rely on human judgment datasets to learn an automatic scoring metric. The learned metric presents the advantage of being explicitly trained to exhibit high correlation with the "gold-standard" human judgments at the summary level (and not just at the system level). The setup is also convenient because any already existing automatic metric can be incorporated as a feature and the model learns the best combination of features matching human judgments.

We should worry whether the learned metric is reliable. Indeed, typical human judgment datasets (like the ones from TAC-2008 or TAC-2009) contain manual scores only for several system summaries which have a limited range of quality. We conduct a manual evaluation specifically designed to test the metric accross its whole scoring spectrum.

To summarize our contributions: We performed a summary-level correlation analysis to compare a large set of existing evaluation metrics. We learned a new evaluation metric as a combination of existing ones to maximize the summary-level correlation with human judgments. We conducted a manual evaluation to test whether learning from available human judgment datasets yields a reliable metric accross its whole scoring spectrum.

2 Related Work

Automatic evaluation of content has been the subject of a lot of research. Many automatic metrics have been developed and we present here some of the most important ones.

ROUGE (Lin, 2004) simply computes the n-gram overlap between a system summary and a pool of reference summaries. It has become a de-facto standard metric because of its simplicity and high correlation with human judgments at the system-level. Afterwards, Ng and Abrecht (2015) extended ROUGE with word embeddings. Instead of hard lexical matching of n-grams, ROUGE-WE uses soft matching based on the cosine similarity of word embedding.

Recently, a line of research aimed at creating strong automatic metrics by automating the Pyramid scoring scheme (Harnly et al., 2005). Yang et al. (2016) proposed PEAK, a metric where the components requiring human input in the original Pyramid annotation scheme are replaced by state-of-the-art NLP tools. It is more semantically motivated than ROUGE and approximates correctly the manual Pyramid scores but it is computationally expensive making it difficult to use in practice.

Some other metrics do not make use of the reference summaries, they compute a score based only on the candidate summary and the source documents (Lin et al., 2006; Louis and Nenkova, 2013). One representative of this class is the Jensen Shannon (JS) divergence, an information-theoretic measure comparing system summaries and source documents with their underlying probability distributions of n-grams. JS divergence is simply the symmetric version of the well-known Kullback-Leibler (KL) divergence (Haghighi and Vanderwende, 2009).

Little work has been done on the topic of learning an evaluation metric. Conroy and Dang (2008) previously investigated the performances of ROUGE metrics in comparison with human judgments and proposed ROSE (ROUGE Optimal Summarization Evaluation) a linear combination of ROUGE metrics to maximize correlation with human responsiveness. We also look for a combination of features which correlates well with human judgements but, in contrast to Conroy and Dang (2008), we include a wider set of metrics: ROUGE scores, other evaluation metrics (like Jensen-Shannon divergence) and features typically used by summarization systems.

Hirao et al. (2007) also proposed a related approach. They used a voting based regression to score summaries with human judgments as gold standard. Our setup is different because we train and evaluate our metric with the summary-level correlation analysis instead of the system-level one. Our experiments are done on multi-document datasets whereas they use single-documents. Finally, we also perform a further manual evaluation to test the metric outside of its training domain.

3   Approach

Let a dataset D contain m topics. A given topic t_i consists of a set of documents $\mathcal{D}_i$, a set of reference summaries θ_i, a set of n system summaries $\mathcal{S}_i$ and the scores given by humans to the n summaries of $\mathcal{S}_i$ noted $\mathcal{R}_i$. We note $s_{i,j}$ the j-th summary of the i-th topic and $r_{i,j}^h$ the score it received from manual evaluation:

$$t_i = (\mathcal{D}_i, \theta_i, \mathcal{S}_i, \mathcal{R}_i)$$
$$\mathcal{S}_i = [s_{i,1}, \dots, s_{i,n}] \qquad (1)$$
$$\mathcal{R}_i = [r_{i,1}^h, \dots, r_{i,n}^h]$$

An automatic evaluation metric is a function taking as input a document set $\mathcal{D}_i$, a set of reference summaries θ_i and a candidate system summary s and outputs a score. For simplicity, we note: $\sigma(\mathcal{D}_i, \theta_i, s) = \sigma_i(s)$ the score of s as a summary of the i-th topic according to some scoring metric σ.

We search an automatic scoring function σ such that $\sigma_i(s_{i,j})$ correlates well with the manual scores $r_{i,j}^h$.

The final score can be computed at the system-level by aggregating scores over topics before and then computing the correlation or at the summary-level by computing the correlation for each topic and then averaging over topics. We briefly present the difference between the two in the following paragraphs.

System-level correlation   Let K be any correlation metric operating on two lists of scored elements, then the system-level correlation is computed by the following formula:

$$K_{avg}^{sys} = K([\sum_i^m \sigma_i(s_{i,1}), \dots, \sum_i^m \sigma_i(s_{i,n})],$$
$$[\sum_i^m r_{i,1}^h, \dots, \sum_i^m r_{i,n}^h]) \qquad (2)$$

Both terms in K are lists of size n. The scores for the summaries of the l-th summarizer are aggregated to form the l-th element of the lists. The correlation is computed on the two aggregated lists. Therefore, K_{avg}^{sys} only indicates whether the evaluation metrics can rank systems correctly after aggregation of many summary scores but it ignores individual summaries. It has been used before because evaluation metrics were initially tasked to compare systems.

Summary-level correlation   Instead, we advocate for the summary-level correlation which is computed by the following formula:

$$K_{avg}^{summ} = \frac{1}{m} \cdot \sum_{t_i \in D} K([\sigma_i(s_{i,1}), \dots, \sigma_i(s_{i,n})],$$
$$[r_{i,1}^h, \dots, r_{i,n}^h]) \qquad (3)$$

Here, we compute the correlation between human judgments and automatic scores for each topic and then average the correlation scores over topics. This measures how well evaluation metrics correlate with human judgments for summaries and not only for systems which is important in order to have finer grain of understanding.

From now on, when we refer to correlation with human judgments we will refer to the summary-level correlation.

Correlation metrics   There exist many possible choices for K. As different correlation metrics measure different properties, we use three complementary metrics: Pearson's r, Spearman's ρ and Normalized Discounted Cumulative Gain (Ndcg).

Pearson's r is a value correlation metric which depicts linear relationships between the scores produced by the automatic metric and the human judgments.

Spearman's ρ is a rank correlation metric which compares the ordering of systems induced by the automatic metric and the ordering of systems induced by human judgments.

Ndcg is a metric that compares ranked lists and puts more emphasis on the top elements by logarithmic decay weighting. Intuitively, it captures how well the automatic metric can recognize the best summaries.

3.1   Features

The choice of features is a crucial part of every learning setup. Here, we can benefit from the large amount of previous works studying signals of summary quality. We can classify these signals in three categories.

First, any existing automatic scoring metric can be a feature. These metrics use the candidate summary and the reference summary to output a score.

The second category contains the previous summarization systems having an explicit formulation of summary quality. These systems can implicitly score any summary, then they extract the summary with maximal score via optimization techniques

(Gillick and Favre, 2009; Haghighi and Vander-wende, 2009). Optimization-based systems have recently become popular (McDonald, 2007). Such features score the candidate summary based only on the document sources and the summary itself.

The last category contains the metrics producing a score based only on the summary. Examples of such metrics include readability or redundancy.

Clearly, features using reference summaries (existing automatic metrics) are expected to be more useful for our task. However, it has been shown that some metrics of the second category (like JS divergence) also contain useful signal to approximate human judgments (Louis and Nenkova, 2013). Therefore, we use features coming from all three categories expecting that they are sensitive to different properties of a good summary.

We considered only features cheap to compute in order to deliver a simple and efficient tool. We now briefly present the selected features.

Features using reference summaries ROUGE-N (Lin, 2004) computes the n-gram overlap between the candidate summary and the pool of reference summaries. We include as features the variants identified by Owczarzak et al. (2012) as strongly correlating with humans: ROUGE-2 recall with stemming and stopwords not removed (giving the best agreement with human evaluation), and ROUGE-1 recall (the measure with the highest ability to identify the better summary in a pair of system summaries).

ROUGE-L (Lin, 2004) considers each sentence of the candidate and reference summaries as sequences of words (after stemming). It interprets the longest common subsequence between sentences as a similarity measure. An overall score for the candidate summary is given by combining the scores of individual sentences. One advantage of using ROUGE-L is that it does not require consecutive matches but in-sequence matches reflecting sentence-level word order.

JS divergence measures the dissimilarity between two probability distributions. In summarization, it was also used to compare the n-gram probability distribution of a summary and souce documents (Louis and Nenkova, 2013), but here we employ it for comparing the n-gram probability distribution of the candidate summary with the reference summaries. Thus, it yields an information-theoretic measure of the dissimilarity between the candidate summary and the reference summaries.

If θ_i is the set of reference summaries for the i-th topic, then we compute the following score:

$$JS_{ref}(s, \theta_i) = \frac{1}{|\theta_i|} \sum_{ref \in \theta_i} JS(s, ref) \quad (4)$$

ROUGE-WE (Ng and Abrecht, 2015) is the variant of ROUGE-N replacing the hard lexical matching by a soft matching based on the cosine similarity of word embeddings. We use ROUGE-WE-1 and ROUGE-WE-2 as part of our features.

FrameNet-based metrics ROUGE-WE proposes a statistical approach (word embeddings) to alleviate the hard lexical matching of ROUGE. We also include a linguistically motivated one. We replace all nouns and verbs of the reference and candidate summaries with their FrameNet (Baker et al., 1998) frames. This frame annotation is done with the best-performing system configuration from Hartmann et al. (2017) pre-trained on all FrameNet data. It assigns a frame to a word based on the word itself and the surrounding context in the sentence.

Frames are more abstract than words, thus different but related words might be associated with the same frames depending on the meaning of the words in the respective context. ROUGE-N can now match related words through their frames. We also use the unigram and bigram variants (Frame-N).

Semantic Vector Space Similarities In general, automatic evaluation metrics comparing system summaries with reference summaries propose a kind of semantic similarity between summaries. Finding good automatic evaluation metric is hard because the task of textual semantic similarity is challenging. With the development of word embeddings (Mikolov et al., 2013), several semantic similarities have arisen exploiting the inherent similarities built in vector space models. We include one such metric: AVG_{SIM}, the cosine similarity between the average word embeddings of the system summary and the reference summaries. To reduce noise, we exclude stopwords.

Features using document sources are inspired by existing summarization systems:

TF⋆IDF comes from the seminal work from Luhn (1958). Each sentence in the summary is scored according to the TF*IDF of its term. The score of the summary is the sum of the scores of its sentences. We computed the version based on unigrams and bigrams (TF*IDF-N).

N-gram Coverage is inspired by the strong summarizer ICSI (Gillick and Favre, 2009). Each n-gram in the summary is scored with the frequency it has in the source documents. The final score of the system summary is the sum of the scores of its n-grams. We also use the variants based on unigrams and bigrams (Cov-N).

KL and JS measures the KL or JS divergence between the word distributions in the summary and source documents. We use as features both KL and JS based on unigram and bigram distributions (KL-N and JS-N).

Features using the candidate summary only Finally, we also include a redundancy metric based on n-gram repetition in the summary. It is the number of unique n-grams divided by the total number of n-grams in the summary. We also use unigrams and bigrams (Red-N).

3.2 Model

For a given topic t_i, let ϕ be the function taking as input a document set $\mathcal{D}_i$, a set of reference summaries θ_i and a system summary s and outputing the set of features described earlier. We note $\phi(\mathcal{D}_i, \theta_i, s) = \phi_i(s)$, the feature set representing s as a summary of the topic i.

We aim to learn a function σ_ω with parameters ω scoring summaries similarly as humans would. If $\sigma_\omega(\phi_i(s))$ is the score given by the learned metric to the summary s, we look for the set of parameters ω which maximizes the summary-level correlation defined by equation 3. It means we are trying to solve the following problem:

$$\operatorname*{argmax}_\omega \sum_{t_i \in D} K([\sigma_\omega(\phi_i(s_{i,1})), \ldots, \sigma_\omega(\phi_i(s_{i,n}))],$$
$$[r_{i,1}^h, \ldots, r_{i,n}^h]) \quad (5)$$

We can approach this problem either with a *learning-to-rank* or with a *regression* framework. Learning-to-rank seems well suited because it captures the fact that we are interested in ranking summaries, however we selected the regression approach in order to keep the model simple. It solves a different but closely related problem:

$$\operatorname*{argmax}_\omega \sum_{t_i \in D} \sum_j^n \frac{\|\sigma_\omega(\phi_i(s_{i,j})) - r_{i,j}^h\|^2}{2} \quad (6)$$

The regression finds the parameters predicting the scores closest to the ones given by humans. We use an off-the-shelf implementation of Support Vector Regression (SVR) from scikit-learn (Pedregosa et al., 2011).

4 Experiments

We conducted both automatic and manual testing of the learned metric. We present here the datasets and results of the experiments.

4.1 Datasets

We use two multi-document summarization datasets from the Text Analysis Conference (TAC) shared tasks: TAC-2008 and TAC-2009.[1] TAC-2008 and TAC-2009 contain 48 and 44 topics, respectively. Each topic consists of 10 news articles to be summarized in a maximum of 100 words. We use only the so-called initial summaries (A summaries), but not the update part.

For each topic, there are 4 human reference summaries. In both editions, all system summaries and the 4 reference summaries were manually evaluated by NIST assessors for readability, content selection (with Pyramid) and overall responsiveness. At the time of the shared tasks, 57 systems were submitted to TAC-2008 and 55 to TAC-2009. For our experiments, we use the Pyramid and the responsiveness annotations.

With our notations, for example with TAC-2009, we have $n = 55$ scored system summaries, $m = 44$ topics, $\mathcal{D}_i$ contains 10 documents and θ_i contains 4 reference summaries.

We also use the recently created German dataset DBS-corpus (Benikova et al., 2016). It contains 10 topics consisting of 4 to 14 documents each. The summaries have variable sizes and are about 500 words long. For each topic, 5 summaries were evaluated by trained human annotators but only for content selection with Pyramid.

We experiment with this dataset because it contains heterogeneous sources (different text types) in German about the educational domain. This contrasts with the English homogeneous news documents from TAC-2008 and TAC-2009. Thus, we can test our technique in a different summarization setup.

---

[1] http://tac.nist.gov/2009/ Summarization/, http://tac.nist.gov/2008/ Summarization/

4.2 Correlation Analysis

Baselines Each feature presented earlier is evaluated individually. [2] Indeed, they all produce scores for summaries meaning we can measure their correlation with human judgments. Classical evaluation metrics, like ROUGE-N variants, are therefore also included in this analysis and serve as baselines. Identifying which metrics have high correlation with human judgments constitutes an initial feature analysis.

Most of the features do not need language dependent information, except those requiring word embeddings or frame identification based on a frame inventory. We do not include the frame identification features when experimenting with the German DBS-corpus. However, for the other language dependent features, we used the German word embeddings developed by Reimers et al. (2014). For the English datasets, we use dependency-based word embeddings (Levy and Goldberg, 2014).

The performances of the baselines on TAC-2008 and TAC-2009 are displayed in Table 1, and Table 2 depicts scores for the DBS-corpus. In order to have an insightful view, we report the scores for the three correlation metrics presented in the previous section: Pearson's r, Spearman's ρ and Ndcg.

Feature Analysis There are fewer scored summaries per topic in the DBS-corpus (5 compared to 55 in TAC-2008). Shorter ranked lists generally have higher scores which explains the overall higher correlation scores in the DBS-corpus. It also contains longer summaries (500 words compared to 100 words for TAC) which provides a reason behind the better performances of JS features. Indeed, word frequency distributions are more representative for longer texts.

First, we see that classical evaluation metrics like ROUGE-N have lower correlation when computed at the summary-level. Here the correlations are around 0.60 spearman's ρ while they often surpass 0.90 in the system-level scenario (Lin, 2004).

However, the experiments confirm that ROUGE-N, especially ROUGE-2, are strong when compared to other available metrics. Even the more semantically motivated metrics like ROUGE-N-WE or Frame-N (ROUGE-N enriched with frame annotations) can not outperform the simple ROUGE-N. The added semantic information might be too noisy to really give improvements. Simple lexical comparison still seems to be better for evaluation of summaries.

Interestingly, it is the other simple evaluation metric $JS_{ref} - N$ which competes with ROUGE-N. This metric only compares the distribution of n-grams in the reference summaries with the distribution of n-grams in the candidate summary and it outperforms ROUGE-N for pearson's r. However, ROUGE-N still outperforms $JS_{ref} - N$ for Ndcg. It indicates that this metric can be complementary with ROUGE-N even though it was rarely used for evaluation before.

Finally, we observe that the features not using the reference summaries have poor performances. It is troubling because these are the strategies used by classical summarization systems in order to decide which summary to extract. Overall, they have Ndcg scores higher than 0.5 meaning they can decently identify some of the best summaries explaining why these systems can produce good summaries.

Our Models For each dataset, we trained two models. The first model (S^3_{full} for *Supervised Summarization Scorer*) uses all the available features for training. However, the previous feature analysis revealed that some features are poor. We hypothesized that they might harm the learning process. Therefore we trained a second model S^3_{best} using only 6 of the best features. [3] We normalize human scores so that they every topic has the same mean.

Both models are trained and tested in a leave-one-out cross-validation scenario ensuring proper testing of the approach. The results for TAC-2008 and TAC-2009 are presented in Table 1 while the results for the DBS-corpus are in Table 2. For comparison we also added the correlation between pyramid and responsiveness when both annotations are available.

Model analysis As expected we observe that using the restricted set of non-noisy features gives stronger results. S^3_{best} is the best metric and outperforms the classical ROUGE-N. Thanks to the combination of ROUGE-N and $JS_{ref} - N$, it gets the best of both worlds and has consistent performances accross datasets and correlation measures.

---

[2]We do not include Red-N in the result table because it does not aim to measure content selection

[3]ROUGE-1, ROUGE-2, ROUGE-WE-1, ROUGE-WE-2, $JS_{ref} - 1$ and $JS_{ref} - 2$

| | TAC-2008 | | | | | | TAC-2009 | | | | | |
| | responsiveness | | | Pyramid | | | responsiveness | | | Pyramid | | |
	r	ρ	Ndcg	r	ρ	Ndcg	r	ρ	Ndcg	r	ρ	Ndcg
TF*IDF-1	.1760	.2248	.5040	.1833	.2376	.3594	.1874	.2226	.3912	.2423	.2845	.2349
TF*IDF-2	.0478	.1540	.5962	.0496	.1827	.4833	.0476	.1674	.5079	.0972	.2337	.3949
Cov-1	.2552	.2635	.6137	.2812	.3035	.5140	.2267	.2212	.5627	.2765	.2871	.4776
Cov-2	.1056	.1878	.6154	.1136	.2287	.5228	.1382	.0787	.5602	.1170	.1336	.4936
KL-1	.1774	.2240	.4922	.1996	.2682	.3470	.1696	.2220	.4139	.2328	.2939	.2568
KL-2	.0042	.1654	.6188	.0038	.1921	.5160	.0602	.1373	.6311	.0355	.2011	.5641
JS-1	.2517	.2771	.4411	.2811	.3214	.2839	.2160	.2352	.3896	.2742	.3119	.2273
JS-2	.0409	.1708	.5874	.0447	.2058	.4804	.0013	.1548	.5646	.0310	.2166	.4734
ROUGE-1	.7035	.5786	.9304	.7479	.6329	**.9125**	.7043	.5657	.8901	.8085	.6922	.9323
ROUGE-2	.6955	.5725	.9333	.7184	.6358	.9064	.7271	.5837	.9039	.8031	.6949	.9272
ROUGE-1-WE	.5714	.4503	.9042	.5798	.4587	.8434	.5865	.4377	.8724	.6534	.5163	.8792
ROUGE-2-WE	.5665	.3971	.8972	.5563	.3888	.8258	.6072	.4130	.8749	.6712	.4811	.8709
ROUGE-L	.6815	.5207	.9300	.7028	.5688	.8937	.7305	.5631	**.9083**	.7799	.6529	.9159
AVG_{SIM}	.1351	.0904	.6890	.0747	.0543	.5521	.2389	.1557	.6861	.2306	.1597	.5956
Frame-1	.6587	.5083	.9174	.6861	.5294	.8867	.6786	.5270	.8827	.7626	.6280	.9158
Frame-2	.6769	.5190	.9194	.6917	.5560	.8885	.7152	.5555	.9000	.7814	.6486	.9191
$JS_{ref}-1$	.6907	.5642	.3786	.7527	.6481	.1862	.7125	.5834	.3091	.8328	.7286	.1214
$JS_{ref}-2$	.6943	.5579	.3961	.7187	.6253	.2101	.7291	.5862	.3195	.8105	.7007	.1342
S^3_{full}	.6960	.5582	.9256	.7537	.6520	.9073	.7310	.5522	.9002	.8384	.7240	.9373
S^3_{best}	**.7154**	**.5954**	**.9330**	**.7545**	**.6527**	.9077	**.7386**	**.5952**	.9015	**.8429**	**.7315**	**.9354**
Pyramid	.7030	.6604	.8528	—	—	—	.7152	.6386	.8520	—	—	—

Table 1: Correlation of automatic metrics with human judgments for TAC-2008 and TAC-2009.

Thanks to the combination of metrics, our model has more consistent performances accross different correlation metrics. It especially benefits from the complementarity of ROUGE and JS_{ref}.

While the improvements are sometimes good, they are not dramatic. A bigger and more diverse training data should give further improvements. With a better training set, it might even not be necessary to manually remove the noisy features as the model will learn when to ignore which features.

4.3 Percentage of failure

By analysing the average correlation between the different metrics and human judgments over all topics, we only get an average overview. It would be useful to estimate the number of topics on which a metric *fails* or *works*. One could plot cumulative distribution graphs where the x-axis is the correlation range (from 0 to 1 in absolute values) and the y-axis indicates the number of topics on which the metric's correlation with humans was above the given x point. However, this would require 460 plots (3 datasets * 20 metrics * 6 correlations measures) which would not be readable.

Instead, we define a threshold for each correlation measure and count the percentage of topics for which the metric's correlation with humans was below the threshold. The threshold value is

| | Pyramid | | |
	r	ρ	Ndcg
TF*IDF-1	.2902	.2016	.8077
TF*IDF-2	.2903	.2396	.8181
Cov-1	.0997	.0544	.8891
Cov-2	.0991	.0638	.8965
KL-1	.7299	.6992	.7348
KL-2	.3089	.1967	.8316
JS-1	.2909	.1680	.8324
JS-2	.1531	.1385	.8496
ROUGE-1	.7016	.7412	.9841
ROUGE-2	.8272	**.8892**	.9985
ROUGE-1-WE	.6842	.7140	.9782
ROUGE-2-WE	.7643	.7937	.9914
ROUGE-L	.7908	.8268	.9957
AVG_{SIM}	.7844	.8309	.9924
$JS_{ref}-1$	**.9712**	.8732	.6881
$JS_{ref}-2$	.9689	.8793	.6879
S^3_{full}	.9077	.8781	.9988
S^3_{best}	.9483	.8755	**.9988**

Table 2: Correlation of automatic metrics with human judgments for the DBS-corpus.

| | TAC-2008 | | | | | | TAC-2009 | | | | | |
| | responsiveness | | | Pyramid | | | responsiveness | | | Pyramid | | |
	r	ρ	Ndcg	r	ρ	Ndcg	r	ρ	Ndcg	r	ρ	Ndcg
ROUGE-1	**.2500**	.3958	**.0208**	.1250	.3125	**.1250**	.2727	.4318	**.2272**	.0455	.1364	.0223
ROUGE-2	.3125	.4167	.0208	.2708	**.2292**	.1667	.2500	.3864	**.2272**	.0682	.1591	**.0000**
ROUGE-1-WE	.7083	.7708	.1042	.6875	.6875	.4583	.5455	.7500	.2500	.4318	.5682	.2955
ROUGE-2-WE	.6667	.8333	.1667	.6667	.8333	.6458	.5455	.7727	.2500	.3409	.6364	.3636
$JS_{ref} - 1$	.2917	.4375	1.000	**.1042**	.2917	1.000	**.2045**	.4091	1.000	**.0227**	.1136	1.000
$JS_{ref} - 2$	.3542	.4375	1.000	.2708	.3125	1.000	.2500	.3864	1.000	**.0227**	**.0909**	1.000
S_{best}^{3}	**.2500**	**.2917**	**.0208**	.1458	.2708	.1458	.2272	**.3409**	**.2272**	**.0227**	.1136	.0227

Table 3: Percentage of topics for which the correlation between the metric and human judgments is below the chosen thresholds for TAC-2008 and TAC-2009.

an indicator of when the metrics fails to correctly model human judgments on a given topic. We chose: 0.65 for pearson's r, 0.55 for spearman's ρ and 0.85 for Ndcg. The values are chosen arbitrarily but in order to get a meaningful picture, if we choose a threshold too low then all metrics are always above, if the threshold is too high all metrics are always below. We report the scores for the set of best features and our best metric S_{best}^{3} on TAC datasets in Table 3.

We observe that our metric performs well and has low percentage of *failure*. It exhibits again its robustness accross different correlation measures. We also observe the strong performances of the JS_{ref} especially the unigram version, however it fails completely for the Ndcg metrics which indicates that it always has problems to identify the top best summaries even though its overall correlation is good. Again this confirms that our metric benefits from the complementarity of JS_{ref} and ROUGE because ROUGE has performs well with Ndcg.

4.4 Manual annotation

Our models are trained with human judgment datasets constructed during the shared tasks, meaning that only some system summaries and the 4 references summaries have been evaluated by humans. Systems have a limited range of quality as they rarely propose excellent summaries, and bad summaries are usually due to unrelated errors (like empty summaries). This is a concern because our learned metric will certainly perform well in this quality range, but it should also perform well outside of this range. It has to be capable to correctly recognize the new and better summaries that will be proposed by future systems.

As the learning is constrained to a specific quality range, we need to check that the whole scoring spectrum of the metric correlates well with humans. We check that what is considered upper-bound (resp. random) by the metric is also considered as excellent (resp. bad) by humans.

Annotation setup We collect summaries by employing a meta-heuristic solver introduced recently for extractive MDS by Peyrard and Eckle-Kohler (2016). Specifically, we use the tool published with their paper.[4]

Their meta-heuristic solver implements a *Genetic Algorithm* to create and iteratively optimize summaries over time. In this implementation, the individuals of the population are the candidate solutions which are valid extractive summaries. Each summary is represented by a binary vector indicating for each sentence in the source document whether it is included in the summary or not. The size of the population is a hyper-parameter that we set to 100. Two evolutionary operators are applied: the mutation and the reproduction. Mutations happen to several randomly chosen summaries by randomly removing one of its sentences and adding a new one that does not violate the length constraint. The reproduction is performed by randomly extracting a valid summary from the union of sentences of randomly selected parent summaries. Both operators are controlled by hyper-parameters which we set to their default values.

We use our metric S_{best}^{3} as the fitness function and, after the algorithm converges, the final population is a set of summaries ranging from almost random to almost upper-bound. For 15 topics of TAC-2009, we automatically selected 10 summaries of various quality from the final population and asked two humans to score them following the

<hr>

[4]`https://github.com/UKPLab/coling2016-genetic-swarm-MDS`

	Responsiveness		
	r	ρ	Ndcg
Best baseline	.6945	.6701	.9210
S^3_{full}	.7198	.6818	.9323
S^3_{best}	**.7318**	**.6936**	**.9355**

Table 4: Correlation of automatic metrics with human accross the whole scoring spectrum of S^3_{best}.

guidelines used during DUC and TAC for assessing responsiveness. To select the summaries, we ranked them according to their S^3_{best} scores and for a population of 100 we picked 10 evenly spaced summaries (the first, the tenth and so on). We observe an inter-annotator agreement of 0.74 Cohen's κ. The results are displayed in Table 4 where S^3_{best} is compared to the best baseline (ROUGE-2) and S^3_{full}.

The S^3_{best} metric gets consistent correlation scores with human judgments as it had with responsiveness in the previous experiements (on TAC-2009, for responsiveness, S^3_{best} has 0.7386 pearson's r, 0.5952 spearman's ρ and 0.9015 Ndcg) . It is a strong indicator that the metric is reliable even outside of its training domain. It also outperforms ROUGE-2 in this experiment.

5 Discussion

The experiments showed that even semantically motivated metrics struggle to outperform ROUGE-N. However, the simple JS_{ref} and ROUGE-N using only n-gram are the best baselines. Reporting these two metrics together might be more insightful than simply reporting ROUGE-N because they are complementary. Our learned metric is benefiting from this complementarity to achieve its scores.

However, finding a good evaluation metric for summarization is a challenging task which is still not solved. We proposed to tackle this problem by learning the metric to approximate human judgments with a regression framework. A learning-to-rank approach could give stronger results because it might be easier to rank summaries. Even after normalization human scores are noisy and topic-dependent. We expect ranking to be more transferable from one topic to another. Here, we constrained ourselves to a simple approach in order to provide a user-friendly tool and the regression offered a simple and effective solution.

Our experiments revealed that the available

human judgment datasets are somehow limited. While it is possible to learn a reliable combination of existing metrics, one would need better and bigger human judgment datasets to really get strong improvements. In particular, it is important to extend the coverage of these datasets because we rely on them to compare evaluation metrics. These annotations are the key to understand what humans consider to be good summaries. Statistical analysis on such datasets will likely be beneficial to develop both evaluation metrics and summarization systems (Peyrard and Eckle-Kohler, 2017).

The metric was evaluated on English news datasets and on a German dataset of heterogeneous sources but a wider study might be needed in order to measure the generalization of the learned metric to other datasets and domains. Such generalization capabilities would be interesting because one would not need to re-train a new metric for every domain.

We believe it is important to develop evaluation metrics correlating well with human judgments at the summary-level. This gives a more insightful and reliable metric. If the metric is reliable enough, one can use it as a target to train supervised summarization systems (Takamura and Okumura, 2010; Sipos et al., 2012) and approach summarization as a principled machine learning task.

6 Conclusion

We presented an approach to learn an automatic evaluation metrics correlating well with human judgments at the summary-level. The metric is a combination of existing automatic scoring strategies learned via regression. We release the metric as an open-source tool. [5] We hope this study will encourage more work on learning evaluation metrics and improving the human judgement datasets. Better human judgment datasets will be greatly beneficial for improving both evaluation metrics and summarization systems.

Acknowledgments

This work has been supported by the German Research Foundation (DFG) as part of the Research Training Group "Adaptive Preparation of Information from Heterogeneous Sources" (AIPHES) under grant No. GRK 1994/1, and via the German-Israeli Project Cooperation (DIP, grant No. GU 798/17-1).

---

[5] https://github.com/UKPLab/emnlp-ws-2017-s3

References

Collin F. Baker, Charles J. Fillmore, and John B. Lowe. 1998. The Berkeley FrameNet Project. In *Proceedings of the 36th Annual Meeting of the Association for Computational Linguistics and 17th International Conference on Computational Linguistics*, pages 86–90. Association for Computational Linguistics.

Darina Benikova, Margot Mieskes, Christian M. Meyer, and Iryna Gurevych. 2016. Bridging the gap between extractive and abstractive summaries: Creation and evaluation of coherent extracts from heterogeneous sources. In *Proceedings of the 26th International Conference on Computational Linguistics (COLING)*, pages 1039 – 1050.

John M. Conroy and Hoa Trang Dang. 2008. Mind the Gap: Dangers of Divorcing Evaluations of Summary Content from Linguistic Quality. In *Proceedings of the 22Nd International Conference on Computational Linguistics (COLING)*, volume 1, pages 145–152.

Dan Gillick and Benoit Favre. 2009. A Scalable Global Model for Summarization. In *Proceedings of the Workshop on Integer Linear Programming for Natural Language Processing*, pages 10–18, Boulder, Colorado. Association for Computational Linguistics.

Aria Haghighi and Lucy Vanderwende. 2009. Exploring Content Models for Multi-document Summarization. In *Proceedings of Human Language Technologies: The 2009 Annual Conference of the North American Chapter of the Association for Computational Linguistics*, pages 362–370, Boulder, Colorado. Association for Computational Linguistics.

Aaron Harnly, Rebecca Passonneau, and Owen Rambow. 2005. Automation of Summary Evaluation by the Pyramid Method. In *Proceedings of the International Conference Recent Advances in Natural Language Processing (RANLP)*, pages 226–232, Borovets, Bulgaria.

Silvana Hartmann, Ilia Kuznetsov, Teresa Martin, and Iryna Gurevych. 2017. Out-of-domain FrameNet Semantic Role Labeling. In *Proceedings of the 15th Conference of the European Chapter of the Association for Computational Linguistics (EACL 2017)*, pages 471–482. Association for Computational Linguistics.

Tsutomu Hirao, Manabu Okumura, Norihito Yasuda, and Hideki Isozaki. 2007. Supervised Automatic Evaluation for Summarization with Voted Regression Model. *Information Processing and Management*, 43(6):1521–1535.

Omer Levy and Yoav Goldberg. 2014. Dependency-Based Word Embeddings. In *Proceedings of the 52nd Annual Meeting of the Association for Computational Linguistics (ACL)*, volume 2, pages 302–308.

Chin-Yew Lin. 2004. ROUGE: A Package for Automatic Evaluation of Summaries. In *Text Summarization Branches Out: Proceedings of the ACL-04 Workshop*, pages 74–81, Barcelona, Spain. Association for Computational Linguistics.

Chin-Yew Lin, Guihong Cao, Jianfeng Gao, and Jian-Yun Nie. 2006. An Information-Theoretic Approach to Automatic Evaluation of Summaries. In *Proceedings of the Human Language Technology Conference at NAACL*, pages 463–470, New York City, USA.

Annie Louis and Ani Nenkova. 2013. Automatically Assessing Machine Summary Content Without a Gold Standard. *Computational Linguistics*, 39(2):267–300.

Hans Peter Luhn. 1958. The Automatic Creation of Literature Abstracts. *IBM Journal of Research Development*, 2:159–165.

Ryan McDonald. 2007. A Study of Global Inference Algorithms in Multi-document Summarization. In *Proceedings of the 29th European Conference on IR Research*, pages 557–564, Rome, Italy. Springer-Verlag.

Tomas Mikolov, Ilya Sutskever, Kai Chen, Greg S Corrado, and Jeff Dean. 2013. Distributed Representations of Words and Phrases and their Compositionality. In *Advances in Neural Information Processing Systems 26*, pages 3111–3119.

Ani Nenkova, Rebecca Passonneau, and Kathleen McKeown. 2007. The Pyramid Method: Incorporating Human Content Selection Variation in Summarization Evaluation. *ACM Transactions on Speech and Language Processing (TSLP)*, 4(2).

Jun-Ping Ng and Viktoria Abrecht. 2015. Better summarization evaluation with word embeddings for rouge. In *Proceedings of the 2015 Conference on Empirical Methods in Natural Language Processing*, pages 1925–1930, Lisbon, Portugal. Association for Computational Linguistics.

Karolina Owczarzak, John M. Conroy, Hoa Trang Dang, and Ani Nenkova. 2012. An Assessment of the Accuracy of Automatic Evaluation in Summarization. In *Proceedings of Workshop on Evaluation Metrics and System Comparison for Automatic Summarization*, pages 1–9, Montreal, Canada. Association for Computational Linguistics.

Fabian Pedregosa, Gael Varoquaux, Alexandre Gramfort, Vincent Michel, Bertrand Thirion, Olivier Grisel, Mathieu Blondel, Peter Prettenhofer, Ron Weiss, Vincent Dubourg, Jake Vanderplas, Alexandre Passos, David Cournapeau, Matthieu Brucher, Matthieu Perrot, and Edouard Duchesnay. 2011. Scikit-learn: Machine Learning in Python. *Journal of Machine Learning Research*, 12:2825–2830.

Maxime Peyrard and Judith Eckle-Kohler. 2016. A General Optimization Framework for Multi-Document Summarization Using Genetic Algorithms and Swarm Intelligence. In *Proceedings of the 26th International Conference on Computational Linguistics (COLING 2016)*, pages 247 – 257, Osaka, Japan. The COLING 2016 Organizing Committee.

Maxime Peyrard and Judith Eckle-Kohler. 2017. A principled framework for evaluating summarizers: Comparing models of summary quality against human judgments. In *Proceedings of the 55th Annual Meeting of the Association for Computational Linguistics (ACL 2017)*, volume Volume 2: Short Papers. Association for Computational Linguistics.

Peter A. Rankel, John M. Conroy, Hoa Trang Dang, and Ani Nenkova. 2013. A Decade of Automatic Content Evaluation of News Summaries: Reassessing the State of the Art. In *Proceedings of the 51st Annual Meeting of the Association for Computational Linguistics*, pages 131–136, Sofia, Bulgaria. Association for Computational Linguistics.

Nils Reimers, Judith Eckle-Kohler, Carsten Schnober, Jungi Kim, and Iryna Gurevych. 2014. GermEval-2014: Nested Named Entity Recognition with Neural Networks. In *Workshop Proceedings of the 12th Edition of the KONVENS Conference*, pages 117–120.

Ruben Sipos, Pannaga Shivaswamy, and Thorsten Joachims. 2012. Large-margin Learning of Submodular Summarization Models. In *Proceedings of the 13th Conference of the European Chapter of the Association for Computational Linguistics*, pages 224–233, Avignon, France. Association for Computational Linguistics.

Josef Steinberger and Karel Ježek. 2012. Evaluation measures for text summarization. *Computing and Informatics*, 28(2):251–275.

Hiroya Takamura and Manabu Okumura. 2010. Learning to Generate Summary as Structured Output. In *Proceedings of the 19th ACM international Conference on Information and Knowledge Management*, pages 1437–1440, Toronto , ON, Canada. Association for Computing Machinery.

Qian Yang, Rebecca Passonneau, and Gerard de Melo. 2016. PEAK: Pyramid Evaluation via Automated Knowledge Extraction. In *Proceedings of the 30th AAAI Conference on Artificial Intelligence (AAAI 2016)*, Phoenix, AZ, USA. AAAI Press.

Revisiting the Centroid-based Method: A Strong Baseline for Multi-Document Summarization

Demian Gholipour Ghalandari
Aylien Ltd., Dublin, Ireland
demian@aylien.com

Abstract

The centroid-based model for extractive document summarization is a simple and fast baseline that ranks sentences based on their similarity to a centroid vector. In this paper, we apply this ranking to possible summaries instead of sentences and use a simple greedy algorithm to find the best summary. Furthermore, we show possibilities to scale up to larger input document collections by selecting a small number of sentences from each document prior to constructing the summary. Experiments were done on the DUC2004 dataset for multi-document summarization. We observe a higher performance over the original model, on par with more complex state-of-the-art methods.

1 Introduction

Extractive multi-document summarization (MDS) aims to summarize a collection of documents by selecting a small number of sentences that represent the original content appropriately. Typical objectives for assembling a summary include information coverage and non-redundancy. A wide variety of methods have been introduced to approach MDS.

Many approaches are based on sentence ranking, i.e. assigning each sentence a score that indicates how well the sentence summarizes the input (Erkan and Radev, 2004; Hong and Nenkova, 2014; Cao et al., 2015). A summary is created by selecting the top entries of the ranked list of sentences. Since the sentences are often treated separately, these models might allow redundancy in the summary. Therefore, they are often extended by an anti-redundancy filter while de-queuing ranked sentence lists.

Other approaches work at summary-level rather than sentence-level and aim to optimize functions of sets of sentences to find good summaries, such as KL-divergence between probability distributions (Haghighi and Vanderwende, 2009) or submodular functions that represent coverage, diversity, etc. (Lin and Bilmes, 2011)

The centroid-based model belongs to the former group: it represents sentences as bag-of-word (BOW) vectors with TF-IDF weighting and uses a centroid of these vectors to represent the whole document collection (Radev et al., 2004). The sentences are ranked by their cosine similarity to the centroid vector. This method is often found as a baseline in evaluations where it usually is outperformed (Erkan and Radev, 2004; Hong et al., 2014).

This baseline can easily be adapted to work at the summary-level instead the sentence level. This is done by representing a summary as the centroid of its sentence vectors and maximizing the similarity between the summary centroid and the centroid of the document collection. A simple greedy algorithm is used to find the best summary under a length constraint.

In order to keep the method efficient, we outline different methods to select a small number of candidate sentences from each document in the input collection before constructing the summary.

We test these modifications on the DUC2004 dataset for multi-document summarization. The results show an improvement of Rouge scores over the original centroid method. The performance is on par with state-of-the-art methods which shows that the similarity between a summary centroid and the input centroid is a well-suited function for global summary optimization.

The summarization approach presented in this paper is fast, unsupervised and simple to implement. Nevertheless, it performs as well as more

Proceedings of the Workshop on New Frontiers in Summarization, pages 85–90
Copenhagen, Denmark, September 7, 2017. ©2017 Association for Computational Linguistics

complex state-of-the-art approaches in terms of Rouge scores on the DUC2004 dataset. It can be used as a strong baseline for future research or as a fast and easy-to-deploy summarization tool.

2 Approach

2.1 Original Centroid-based Method

The original centroid-based model is described by Radev et al. (2004). It represents sentences as BOW vectors with TF-IDF weighting. The centroid vector is the sum of all sentence vectors and each sentence is scored by the cosine similarity between its vector representation and the centroid vector. Cosine similarity measures how close two vectors A and B are based on their angle and is defined as follows:

$$sim(A, B) = \frac{A \cdot B}{|A||B|} \tag{1}$$

A summary is selected by de-queuing the ranked list of sentences in decreasing order until the desired summary length is reached.

Rossiello et al. (2017) implement this original model with the following modifications:

1. In order to avoid redundant sentences in the summary, a new sentence is only included if it does not exceed a certain maximum similarity to any of the already included sentences.

2. To focus on only the most important terms of the input documents, the values in the centroid vector which fall below a tuned threshold are set to zero.

This model, which includes the anti-redundancy filter and the selection of top-ranking features, is treated as the "original" centroid-based model in this paper.

We implement the selection of top-ranking features for both the original and modified models slightly differently to Rossiello et al. (2017): all words in the vocabulary are ranked by their value in the centroid vector. On a development dataset, a parameter is tuned that defines the proportion of the ranked vocabulary that is represented in the centroid vector and the rest is set to zero. This variant resulted in more stable behavior for different amounts of input documents.

2.2 Modified Summary Selection

The similarity to the centroid vector can also be used to score a summary instead of a sentence. By representing a summary as the sum of its sentence vectors, it can be compared to the centroid, which is different from adding centroid-similarity scores of individual sentences.

With this modification, the summarization task is explicitly modelled as finding a combination of sentences that summarize the input well together instead of finding sentences that summarize the input well independently. This strategy should also be less dependent on anti-redundancy filtering since a combination of redundant sentences is probably less similar to the centroid than a more diverse selection that covers different prevalent topics.

In the experiments, we will therefore call this modification the "global" variant of the centroid model. The same principle is used by the *KL-Sum* model (Haghighi and Vanderwende, 2009) in which the optimal summary minimizes the KL-divergence of the probability distribution of words in the input from the distribution in the summary. *KLSum* uses a greedy algorithm to find the best summary. Starting with an empty summary, the algorithm includes at each iteration the sentence that maximizes the similarity to the centroid when added to the already selected sentences. We also use this algorithm for sentence selection. The procedure is depicted in Algorithm 1 below.

Algorithm 1 Greedy Sentence Selection

1: **Input:** input sentences D, centroid c, $limit$
2: **Output:** summary sentences S
3: $S \leftarrow \emptyset$
4: $length \leftarrow 0$
5: **while** $length < limit$ **and** $D \neq \emptyset$ **do**
6:     $s_{best} \leftarrow \arg\max_{s \in D} sim(S \cup \{s\}, c)$
7:     $S \leftarrow S \cup \{s_{best}\}$
8:     $D \leftarrow D \setminus \{s_{best}\}$
9:     $length \leftarrow length + 1$

2.3 Preselection of Sentences

The modified sentence selection method is less efficient than the orginal method since at each iteration the score of a possible summary has to be computed for all remaining candidate sentences. It may not be noticeable for a small number of input sentences. However, it would have an impact if the amount of input documents was larger, e.g. for the summarization of top-100 search results in document retrieval.

Therefore, we explore different methods for reducing the number of input sentences before applying the greedy sentence selection algorithm to make the model more suited for larger inputs. It is also important to examine how this affects Rouge scores.

We test the following methods of selecting N sentences from each document as candidates for the greedy sentence selection algorithm:

N-first

The first N sentences of the document are selected. This results in a mixture of a lead-N baseline and the centroid-based method.

N-best

The sentences are ranked separately in each document by their cosine similarity to the centroid vector, in decreasing order. The N best sentences of each document are selected as candidates.

New-TF-IDF

Each sentence is scored by the sum of the TF-IDF scores of the terms that are mentioned in that sentence for the first time in the document. The intuition is that sentences are preferred if they introduce new important information to a document.

Note that in each of these candidate selection methods, the centroid vector is always computed as the sum of all sentence vectors, including the ones of the ignored sentences.

3 Experiments

Datasets

For testing, we use the DUC2004 Task 2 dataset from the Document Understanding Conference (DUC). The dataset consists of 50 document clusters containing 10 documents each. For tuning hyperparameters, we use the CNN/Daily Mail dataset (Hermann et al., 2015) which provides summary bulletpoints for individual news articles. In order to adapt the dataset for MDS, 50 CNN articles were randomly selected as documents to initialize 50 clusters. For each of these seed articles, 9 articles with the highest word-overlap in the first 3 sentences were added to that cluster. This resulted in 50 documents clusters, each containing 10 topically related articles. The reference summaries for each cluster were created by interleaving the sentences of the article summaries until a length contraint (100 words) was reached.

Baselines & Evaluation

Hong et al. (2014) published SumRepo, a repository of summaries for the DUC2004 dataset generated by several baseline and state-of-the-art methods [1]. We evaluate summaries generated by a selection of these methods on the same data that we use for testing. We calculate Rouge scores with the Rouge toolkit (Lin, 2004). In order to compare our results to Hong et al. (2014) we use the same Rouge settings as they do[2] and report results for Rouge-1, Rouge-2 and Rouge-4 recall. The baselines include a basic centroid-based model without an anti-redundancy filter and feature reduction.

Preprocessing

In the summarization methods proposed in this paper, the preprocessing includes sentence segmentation, lowercasing and stopword removal.

Parameter Tuning

The similarity threshold for avoiding redundancy (r) and the vocabulary-included-in-centroid ratio (v) are tuned with the original centroid model on our development set. Values from 0 to 1 with step size 0.1 were tested using a grid search. The optimal values for r and v were 0.6 and 0.1, respectively. These values were used for all tested variants of the centroid model. For the different methods of choosing N sentences of each document before summarization, we tuned N separately for each, with values from 1 to 10, using the global model. The best N found for N-first, N-best, new-tfidf were 7, 2 and 3 respectively.

Results

Table 1 shows the Rouge scores measured in our experiments. The first two sections show results for baseline and SOTA summaries from SumRepo. The third section shows the summarization variants presented in this paper. "G" indicates that the global greedy algorithm was used instead of sentence-level ranking. In the last section, "- R" indicates that the method was tested without the anti-redundancy filter.

[1] http://www.cis.upenn.edu/~nlp/corpora/sumrepo.html

[2] ROUGE-1.5.5 with the settings -n 4 -m -a -l 100 -x -c 95 -r 1000 -f A -p 0.5 -t 0

Model	R-1	R-2	R-4
Centroid	36.03	7.89	1.20
LexRank	35.49	7.42	0.81
KLSum	37.63	8.50	1.26
CLASSY04	37.23	8.89	1.46
ICSI	38.02	**9.72**	**1.72**
Submodular	38.62	9.19	1.34
DPP	**39.41**	9.57	1.56
RegSum	38.23	9.71	1.59
Centroid	37.91	9.53	1.56
Centroid + N-first	38.04	9.56	1.56
Centroid + N-best	37.86	9.67	**1.67**
Centroid + new-tf-idf	38.27	9.64	1.54
Centroid + G	38.55	9.73	1.53
Centroid + G + N-first	38.85	**9.86**	1.62
Centroid + G + N-best	38.86	9.77	1.53
Centroid + G + new-tf-idf	**39.11**	9.81	1.58
Centroid - R	35.54	8.73	1.42
Centroid + G - R	38.58	9.73	1.53

Table 1: Rouge scores on DUC2004.

Both the global optimization and the sentence preselection have a positive impact on the performance.

The global + new-TF-IDF variant outperforms all but the DPP model in Rouge-1 recall. The global + N-first variant outperforms all other models in Rouge-2 recall. However, the Rouge scores of the SOTA methods and the introduced centroid variants are in a very similar range.

Interestingly, the original centroid-based model, without any of the new modifications introduced in this paper, already shows quite high Rouge scores in comparison to the other baseline methods. This is due to the anti-redundancy filter and the selection of top-ranking features.

In order to see whether the global sentence selection alleviates the need for an anti-redundancy filter, the original method and the global method (without N sentences per document selection) were tested without it (section 4 in Table 1). In terms of Rouge-1 recall, the original model is clearly very dependent on checking for redundancy when including sentences, while the global variant does not change its performance much without the anti-redundancy filter. This matches the expectation that the globally motivated method handles redundancy implicitly.

4 Example Summaries

Table 2 shows generated example summaries using the global centroid method with the three sentence preselection methods. For readability, truncated sentences (due to the 100-word limit) at the end of the summaries are excluded. The original positions of the summary sentences, i.e. the indices of the document and the sentence inside the document are given. As can be seen in the examples, the N-first method is restricted to sentences appearing early in documents. In the new-TF-IDF example, the second and third sentences were preselected because high ranking features such as "robot" and "arm" appeared for the first time in the respective documents.

5 Related Work

In addition to various works on sophisticated models for multi-document summarization, other experiments have been done showing that simple modifications to the standard baseline methods can perform quite well.

Rossiello et al. (2017) improved the centroid-based method by representing sentences as sums of word embeddings instead of TF-IDF vectors so that semantic relationships between sentences that have no words in common can be captured. Mackie et al. (2016) also evaluated summaries from SumRepo and did experiments on improving baseline systems such as the centroid-based and the KL-divergence method with different anti-redundancy filters. Their best optimized baseline obtained a performance similar to the ICSI method in SumRepo.

6 Conclusion

In this paper we show that simple modifications to the centroid-based method can bring its performance to the same level as state-of-the-art methods on the DUC2004 dataset. The resulting summarization methods are unsupervised, efficient and do not require complicated feature engineering or training.

Changing from a ranking-based method to a global optimization method increases performance and makes the summarizer less dependent on explicitly checking for redundancy. This can be useful for input document collections with differing levels of content diversity.

The presented methods for restricting the input to a maximum of N sentences per document

Example Summaries
N-first (N=7)
For the second day in a row, astronauts boarded space shuttle Endeavour on Friday for liftoff on NASA's first space station construction flight. Endeavour and its astronauts closed in Sunday to capture the first piece of the international space station, the Russian-made Zarya control module that had to be connected to the Unity chamber aboard the shuttle. Mission Control gave the astronauts plenty of time for the tasks. On their 12-day flight, Endeavour's astronauts are to locate a Russian part already in orbit, grasp it with the shuttle's robot arm and attach the new U.S. module.   **Sentence positions (doc, sent):** (0, 0), (1, 0), (1, 5), (8, 5)
N-best (N=2)
For the second day in a row, astronauts boarded space shuttle Endeavour on Friday for liftoff on NASA's first space station construction flight. The astronauts will use the shuttle robot arm to capture the Russian space station piece and attach it to Unity. Mission Control ordered the pilots to fire the shuttle thrusters to put an extra three miles between Endeavour and the space junk, putting Endeavour a total of five miles from the orbiting debris. On their 12-day flight, Endeavour's astronauts are to locate a Russian part already in orbit, grasp it with the shuttle's robot arm and attach the new U.S. module.   **Sentence positions (doc, sent):** (0, 0), (0, 20), (2, 19), (8, 5)
New-TF-IDF (N=3)
For the second day in a row, astronauts boarded space shuttle Endeavour on Friday for liftoff on NASA's first space station construction flight. The astronauts will use the shuttle robot arm to capture the Russian space station piece and attach it to Unity. The shuttle's 50-foot robot arm had never before been assigned to handle an object as massive as the 44,000-pound Zarya, a power and propulsion module that was launched from Kazakhstan on Nov. 20. Endeavour's astronauts connected the first two building blocks of the international space station on Sunday, creating a seven-story tower in the shuttle cargo bay.   **Sentence positions (doc, sent):** (0, 0), (0, 20), (1, 12), (5, 0)

Table 2: Summaries of the cluster **d30031** in DUC2004 generated by the modified centroid method using different sentence preselection methods.

lead to additional improvements while reducing computation effort, if global optimization is being used. These methods could be useful for other summarization models that rely on pairwise similarity computations between all input sentences, or other properties which would slow down summarization of large numbers of input sentences.

The modified methods can also be used as strong baselines for future experiments in multi-document summarization.

References

Ziqiang Cao, Furu Wei, Li Dong, Sujian Li, and Ming Zhou. 2015. Ranking with recursive neural networks and its application to multi-document summarization. In *AAAI*. pages 2153–2159.

Günes Erkan and Dragomir R. Radev. 2004. Lexrank: Graph-based lexical centrality as salience in text summarization. *Journal of Artificial Intelligence Research* 22:457–479.

Aria Haghighi and Lucy Vanderwende. 2009. Exploring content models for multi-document summarization. In *Proceedings of Human Language Technologies: The 2009 Annual Conference of the North American Chapter of the Association for Computational Linguistics*. Association for Computational Linguistics, pages 362–370.

Karl Moritz Hermann, Tomas Kocisky, Edward Grefenstette, Lasse Espeholt, Will Kay, Mustafa Suleyman, and Phil Blunsom. 2015. Teaching machines to read and comprehend. In *Advances in Neural Information Processing Systems*. pages 1693–1701.

Kai Hong, John M. Conroy, Benoit Favre, Alex Kulesza, Hui Lin, and Ani Nenkova. 2014. A repository of state of the art and competitive baseline summaries for generic news summarization. In *LREC*. pages 1608–1616.

Kai Hong and Ani Nenkova. 2014. Improving the estimation of word importance for news multi-document summarization. In *EACL*. pages 712–721.

Chin-Yew Lin. 2004. Rouge: A package for automatic evaluation of summaries. In *Text summarization branches out: Proceedings of the ACL-04 workshop*. Barcelona, Spain, volume 8.

Hui Lin and Jeff Bilmes. 2011. A class of submodular functions for document summarization. In *Proceedings of the 49th Annual Meeting of the Association for Computational Linguistics: Human Language Technologies-Volume 1*. Association for Computational Linguistics, pages 510–520.

Stuart Mackie, Richard McCreadie, Craig Macdonald, and Iadh Ounis. 2016. Experiments in newswire summarisation. In *European Conference on Information Retrieval*. Springer, pages 421–435.

Dragomir R. Radev, Hongyan Jing, Małgorzata Styś, and Daniel Tam. 2004. Centroid-based summarization of multiple documents. *Information Processing & Management* 40(6):919–938.

Gaetano Rossiello, Pierpaolo Basile, and Giovanni Semeraro. 2017. Centroid-based text summarization through compositionality of word embeddings. *MultiLing 2017* page 12.

Reader-Aware Multi-Document Summarization: An Enhanced Model and The First Dataset[*]

Piji Li[†]   Lidong Bing[‡]   Wai Lam[†]
[†]Department of Systems Engineering and Engineering Management,
The Chinese University of Hong Kong
[‡]AI Lab, Tencent Inc., Shenzhen, China
[†]{pjli, wlam}@se.cuhk.edu.hk, [‡]lyndonbing@tencent.com

Abstract

We investigate the problem of reader-aware multi-document summarization (RA-MDS) and introduce a new dataset for this problem. To tackle RA-MDS, we extend a variational auto-encodes (VAEs) based MDS framework by jointly considering news documents and reader comments. To conduct evaluation for summarization performance, we prepare a new dataset. We describe the methods for data collection, aspect annotation, and summary writing as well as scrutinizing by experts. Experimental results show that reader comments can improve the summarization performance, which also demonstrates the usefulness of the proposed dataset. The annotated dataset for RA-MDS is available online[1].

1   Introduction

The goal of multi-document summarization (MDS) is to automatically generate a brief, well-organized summary for a topic which describes an event with a set of documents from different sources. (Goldstein et al., 2000; Erkan and Radev, 2004; Wan et al., 2007; Nenkova and McKeown, 2012; Min et al., 2012; Bing et al., 2015; Li et al., 2017). In the typical setting of MDS, the input is a set of news documents about the same topic. The output summary is a piece of short text document containing several sentences, generated only based on the input original documents.

With the development of social media and mobile equipments, more and more user generated

NEWS: The most important announcements from Google's big developers' conference

Figure 1: Reader comments of the news "The most important announcements from Google's big developers' conference (May, 2017)".

content is available. Figure 1 is a snapshot of reader comments under the news report "The most important announcements from Google's big developers' conference"[2]. The content of the original news report talks about some new products based on AI techniques. The news report generally conveys an enthusiastic tone. However, while some readers share similar enthusiasms, some others express their worries about new products and technologies and these comments can also reflect their interests which may not be very salient in the original news reports. Unfortunately, existing MDS approaches cannot handle this issue. We investigate this problem known as reader-aware multi-document summarization (RA-MDS). Under the RA-MDS setting, one should jointly consider news documents and reader comments when generating the summaries.

One challenge of the RA-MDS problem is how to conduct salience estimation by jointly considering the focus of news reports and the reader interests revealed by comments. Meanwhile, the model should be insensitive to the availability of diverse aspects of reader comments. Another challenge is that reader comments are very noisy, not fully grammatical and often expressed in infor-

[*]The work described in this paper is supported by a grant from the Grant Council of the Hong Kong Special Administrative Region, China (Project Code: 14203414).

[1]http://www.se.cuhk.edu.hk/~textmine/dataset/ra-mds/

[2]https://goo.gl/DdU0vL

Proceedings of the Workshop on New Frontiers in Summarization, pages 91–99
Copenhagen, Denmark, September 7, 2017. ©2017 Association for Computational Linguistics

mal expressions. Some previous works explore the effect of comments or social contexts in single document summarization such as blog summarization (Hu et al., 2008; Yang et al., 2011). However, the problem setting of RA-MDS is more challenging because the considered comments are about an event which is described by multiple documents spanning a time period. Another challenge is that reader comments are very diverse and noisy. Recently, Li et al. (2015) employed a sparse coding based framework for RA-MDS jointly considering news documents and reader comments via an unsupervised data reconstruction strategy. However, they only used the bag-of-words method to represent texts, which cannot capture the complex relationship between documents and comments.

Recently, Li et al. (2017) proposed a sentence salience estimation framework known as *VAESum* based on a neural generative model called Variational Auto-Encoders (VAEs) (Kingma and Welling, 2014; Rezende et al., 2014). During our investigation, we find that the Gaussian based VAEs have a strong ability to capture the salience information and filter the noise from texts. Intuitively, if we feed both the news sentences and the comment sentences into the VAEs, commonly existed latent aspect information from both of them will be enhanced and become salient. Inspired by this consideration, to address the sentence salience estimation problem for RA-MDS by jointly considering news documents and reader comments, we extend the VAESum framework by training the news sentence latent model and the comment sentence latent model simultaneously by sharing the neural parameters. After estimating the sentence salience, we employ a phrase based compressive unified optimization framework to generate a final summary.

There is a lack of high-quality dataset suitable for RA-MDS. Existing datasets from DUC[3] and TAC[4] are not appropriate. Therefore, we introduce a new dataset for RA-MDS. We employed some experts to conduct the tasks of data collection, aspect annotation, and summary writing as well as scrutinizing. To our best knowledge, this is the first dataset for RA-MDS.

Our contributions are as follows: (1) We investigate the RA-MDS problem and introduce a new dataset for the problem of RA-MDS. To our best

---

[3]http://duc.nist.gov/
[4]http://tac.nist.gov/

knowledge, it is the first dataset for RA-MDS. (2) To tackle the RA-MDS, we extend a VAEs-based MDS framework by jointly considering news documents and reader comments. (3) Experimental results show that reader comments can improve the summarization performance, which also demonstrates the usefulness of the dataset.

2 Framework

2.1 Overview

As shown in Figure 2, our reader-aware news sentence salience framework has three main components: (1) latent semantic modeling; (2) comment weight estimation; (3) joint reconstruction. Consider a dataset X_d and X_c consisting of n_d news sentences and n_c comment sentences respectively from all the documents in a topic (event), represented by bag-of-words vectors. Our proposed news sentence salience estimation framework is extended from VAESum (Li et al., 2017), which can jointly consider news documents and reader comments. One extension is that, in order to absorb more useful information and filter the noisy data from comments, we design a weight estimation mechanism which can assign a real value ρ_i for a comment sentence $\mathbf{x}_c^i$. The comment weight $\rho \in \mathbb{R}^{n_c}$ is integrated into the VAEs based sentence modeling and data reconstruction component to handle comments.

2.2 Reader-Aware Salience Estimation

Variational Autoencoders (VAEs) (Kingma and Welling, 2014; Rezende et al., 2014) is a generative model based on neural networks which can be used to conduct latent semantic modeling. Li et al. (2017) employ VAEs to map the news sentences into a latent semantic space, which is helpful in improving the MDS performance. Similarly, we also employ VAEs to conduct the semantic modeling for news sentences and comment sentences. Assume that both the prior and posterior of the latent variables are Gaussian, i.e., $p_\theta(\mathbf{z}) = \mathcal{N}(0, \mathbf{I})$ and $q_\phi(\mathbf{z}|\mathbf{x}) = \mathcal{N}(\mathbf{z}; \boldsymbol{\mu}, \boldsymbol{\sigma}^2 \mathbf{I})$, where $\boldsymbol{\mu}$ and $\boldsymbol{\sigma}$ denote the variational mean and standard deviation respectively, which can be calculated with a multilayer perceptron (MLP). VAEs can be divided into two phases, namely, encoding (inference), and decoding (generation). All the operations are de-

92

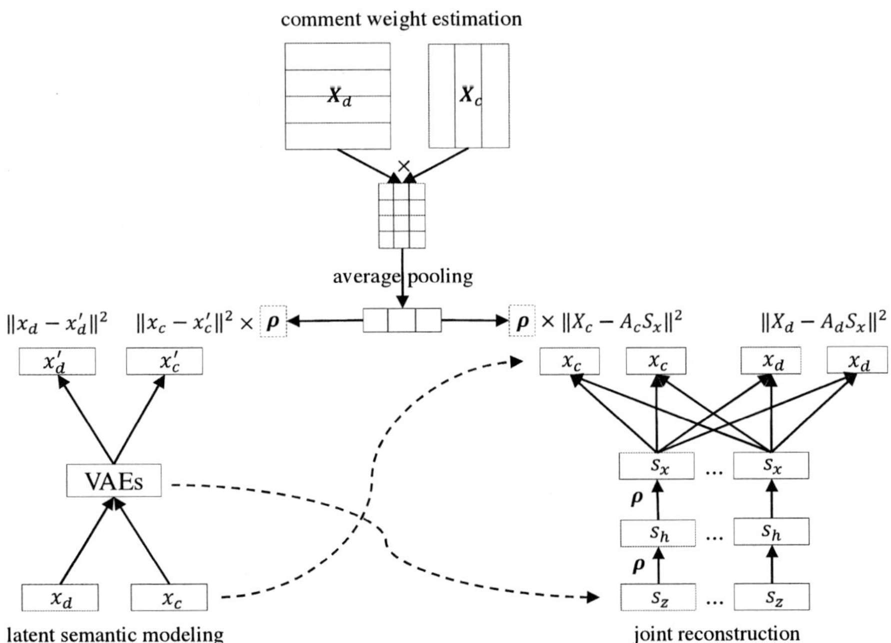

Figure 2: Our proposed framework. **Left**: Latent semantic modeling via variation auto-encoders for news sentence $\mathbf{x}_d$ and comment sentence $\mathbf{x}_c$. **Middle**: Comment sentence weight estimation. **Right**: Salience estimation by a joint data reconstruction method. $\mathbf{A}_d$ is a news reconstruction coefficient matrix which contains the news sentence salience information.

picted as follows:

$$
\begin{aligned}
h_{enc} &= relu(W_{xh}x + b_{xh}) \\
\mu &= W_{h\mu}h_{enc} + b_{h\mu} \\
\log(\sigma^2) &= W_{h\sigma}h_{enc} + b_{h\sigma} \\
\varepsilon &\sim \mathcal{N}(0, \mathbf{I}), \quad z = \mu + \sigma \otimes \varepsilon \\
h_{dec} &= relu(W_{zh}z + b_{zh}) \\
x' &= sigmoid(W_{hx}h_{dec} + b_{hx})
\end{aligned}
\tag{1}
$$

Based on the reparameterization trick in Equation 1, we can get the analytical representation of the variational lower bound $\mathcal{L}(\theta, \varphi; \mathbf{x})$:

$$
\log p(x|z) = \sum_{i=1}^{|V|} x_i \log x_i' + (1 - x_i) \cdot \log(1 - x_i')
$$

$$
-D_{KL}[q_\varphi(z|x)\|p_\theta(z)] = \frac{1}{2}\sum_{i=1}^{K}(1 + \log(\sigma_i^2) - \mu_i^2 - \sigma_i^2)
$$

where $\mathbf{x}$ denotes a general sentence, and it can be a news sentence $\mathbf{x}_d$ or a comment sentnece $\mathbf{x}_c$.

By feeding both the news documents and the reader comments into VAEs, we equip the model a ability of capturing the information from them jointly. However, there is a large amount of noisy information hidden in the comments. Hence we design a weighted combination mechanism for fusing news and comments in the VAEs. Precisely, we split the variational lower bound $\mathcal{L}(\theta, \varphi; \mathbf{x})$

into two parts and fuse them using the comment weight ρ:

$$
\mathcal{L}(\theta, \varphi; \mathbf{x}) = \mathcal{L}(\theta, \varphi; \mathbf{x}_d) + \rho \times \mathcal{L}(\theta, \varphi; \mathbf{x}_c) \tag{2}
$$

The calculation of ρ will be discussed later.

The news sentence salience estimation is conducted by an unsupervised data reconstruction framework. Assume that $\mathbf{S}_z = \{\mathbf{s}_z^1, \mathbf{s}_z^2, \cdots, \mathbf{s}_z^m\}$ are m latent aspect vectors used for reconstructing all the latent semantic vectors $\mathbf{Z} = \{\mathbf{z}^1, \mathbf{z}^2, \cdots, \mathbf{z}^n\}$. Thereafter, the variational-decoding progress of VAEs can map the latent aspect vector $\mathbf{S}_z$ to $\mathbf{S}_h$, and then produce m new aspect term vectors $\mathbf{S}_x$:

$$
\begin{aligned}
s_h &= relu(W_{zh}s_z + b_{zh}) \\
s_x &= sigmoid(W_{hx}s_h + b_{hx})
\end{aligned}
\tag{3}
$$

VAESum (Li et al., 2017) employs an alignment mechanism (Bahdanau et al., 2015; Luong et al., 2015) to recall the lost detailed information from the input sentence. Inspired this idea, we design a jointly weighted alignment mechanism by considering the news sentence and the comment sentence simultaneously. For each decoder hidden state s_h^i, we align it with each news encoder hidden state h_d^j

by an alignment vector $a^d \in \mathbb{R}^{n_d}$. We also align it with each comments encoder hidden state h_c^j by an alignment vector $a^c \in \mathbb{R}^{n_c}$. In order to filter the noisy information from the comments, we again employ the comment weight ρ to adjust the alignment vector of comments:

$$\tilde{a}^c = a^c \times \rho \qquad (4)$$

The news-based context vector c_d^i and the comment-based context vector c_c^i can be obtained by linearly blending the input hidden states respectively. Then the output hidden state can be updated based on the context vectors:

$$\tilde{s}_h^i = \tanh(W_{dh}^h c_d^i + W_{ch}^h c_c^i + W_{hh}^a s_h^i) \qquad (5)$$

Then we can generate the updated output aspect vectors based on $\tilde{s}_h^i$. We add a similar alignment mechanism into the output layer.

$\mathbf{S}_z$, $\mathbf{S}_h$, and $\mathbf{S}_x$ can be used to reconstruct the space to which they belong respectively. In order to capture the information from comments, we design a joint reconstruction approach here. Let $\mathbf{A}_d \in \mathbb{R}^{n_d \times m}$ be the reconstruction coefficient matrix for news sentences, and $\mathbf{A}_c \in \mathbb{R}^{n_c \times m}$ be the reconstruction coefficient matrix for comment sentences. The optimization objective contains three reconstruction terms, jointly considering the latent semantic reconstruction and the term vector space reconstruction for news and comments respectively:

$$\mathcal{L}_A = (\|Z_d - A_d S_z\|_2^2 + \|H_d - A_d S_h\|_2^2$$
$$+ \|X_d - A_d S_x\|_2^2) + \rho \times (\|Z_c - A_c S_z\|_2^2 \qquad (6)$$
$$+ \|H_c - A_c S_h\|_2^2 + \|X_c - A_c S_x\|_2^2)$$

This objective is integrated with the variational lower bound of VAEs $\mathcal{L}(\theta, \varphi; \mathbf{x})$ and optimized in a multi-task learning fashion. Then the new optimization objective is:

$$\mathcal{J} = \min_{\Theta}(-\mathcal{L}(\theta, \varphi; x) + \mathcal{L}_A) \qquad (7)$$

where Θ is a set of all the parameters related to this task. We define the magnitude of each row of $\mathbf{A}_d$ as the salience scores for the corresponding news sentences.

We should note that the most important variable in our framework is the comment weight vector ρ, which appears in all the three components of our framework. The basic idea for calculating ρ is that if the comment sentence is more similar to

the news content, then it contains less noisy information. For all the news sentences X_d and all the comment sentences X_c, calculate the relation matrix $R \in \mathbb{R}^{n_d \times n_c}$ by:

$$R = X_d \times X_c^T \qquad (8)$$

Then we add an average pooling layer to get the coefficient value for each comment sentence:

$$\mathbf{r} = \frac{1}{n_c} \sum_{i=1}^{n_c} R[i, :] \qquad (9)$$

Finally, we add a sigmoid function to adjust the coefficient value to $(0, 1)$:

$$\rho = sigmoid(\mathbf{r}) \qquad (10)$$

Because we have different representations from different vector space for the sentences, therefore we can calculate the comment weight in different semantic vector space. Here we use two spaces, namely, latent semantic space obtained by VAEs, and the original bag-of-words vector space. Then we can merge the weights by a parameter λ_p:

$$\rho = \lambda_p \times \rho_z + (1 - \lambda_p) \times \rho_x \qquad (11)$$

where ρ_z and ρ_x are the comment weight calculated from latent semantic space and term vector space. Actually, we can regard ρ as some gates to control the proportion of each comment sentence absorbed by the framework.

2.3 Summary Construction

In order to produce reader-aware summaries, inspired by the phrase-based model in Bing et al. (2015) and Li et al. (2015), we refine this model to consider the news sentences salience information obtained by our framework. Based on the parsed constituency tree for each input sentence, we extract the noun-phrases (NPs) and verb-phrases (VPs). The overall objective function of this optimization formulation for selecting salient NPs and VPs is formulated as an integer linear programming (ILP) problem:

$$\max\{\sum_{i} \alpha_i S_i - \sum_{i<j} \alpha_{ij}(S_i + S_j)R_{ij}\}, \qquad (12)$$

where α_i is the selection indicator for the phrase P_i, S_i is the salience scores of P_i, α_{ij} and R_{ij} is co-occurrence indicator and the similarity a pair of phrases (P_i, P_j) respectively. The similarity is calculated with the Jaccard Index based method. In order to obtain coherent summaries with good readability, we add some constraints into the ILP framework. For details, please refer to Woodsend and Lapata (2012), Bing et al. (2015), and Li et al. (2015). The objective function and constraints are linear. Therefore the optimization can be solved by existing ILP solvers such as simplex algorithms (Dantzig and Thapa, 2006). In the implementation, we use a package called lp_solve[5].

3 Data Description

In this section, we describe the preparation process of the dataset. Then we provide some properties and statistics.

3.1 Background

The definition of the terminology related to the dataset is given as follows.[6]

Topic: A topic refers to an event and it is composed of a set of news documents from different sources.

Document: A news article describing some aspects of the topic. The set of documents in the same topic typically span a period, say a few days.

Category: Each topic belongs to a category. There are 6 predefined categories: (1) Accidents and Natural Disasters, (2) Attacks (Criminal/Terrorist), (3) New Technology, (4) Health and Safety, (5) Endangered Resources, and (6) Investigations and Trials (Criminal/Legal/Other).

Aspect: Each category has a set of predefined aspects. Each aspect describes one important element of an event. For example, for the category "Accidents and Natural Disasters", the aspects are "WHAT", "WHEN", "WHERE", "WHY", "WHO_AFFECTED", "DAMAGES", and "COUNTERMEASURES".

Aspect facet: An aspect facet refers to the actual content of a particular aspect for a particular topic. Take the topic "Malaysia Airlines Disappearance" as an example, facets for the aspect "WHAT" include "missing Malaysia Airlines Flight 370", "two passengers used passports stolen in Thailand from an Austrian and an Italian." etc. Facets for the aspect "WHEN" are " Saturday morning",

"about an hour into its flight from Kuala Lumpur", etc.

Comment: A piece of text written by a reader conveying his or her altitude, emotion, or any thought on a particular news document.

3.2 Data Collection

The first step is to select topics. The selected topics should be in one of the above categories. We make use of several ways to find topics. The first way is to search the category name using Google News. The second way is to follow the related tags on Twitter. One more useful method is to scan the list of event archives on the Web, such as earthquakes happened in 2017 [7].

For some news websites, in addition to provide news articles, they offer a platform to allow readers to enter comments. Regarding the collection of news documents, for a particular topic, one consideration is that reader comments can be easily found. Another consideration is that all the news documents under a topic must be collected from different websites as far as possible. Similar to the methods used in DUC and TAC, we also capture and store the content using XML format.

Each topic is assigned to 4 experts, who are major in journalism, to conduct the summary writing. The task of summary writing is divided into two phases, namely, aspect facet identification, and summary generation. For the aspect facet identification, the experts read and digested all the news documents and reader comments under the topic. Then for each aspect, the experts extracted the related facets from the news document. The summaries were generated based on the annotated aspect facets. When selecting facets, one consideration is those facets that are popular in both news documents and reader comments have higher priority. Next, the facets that are popular in news documents have the next priority. The generated summary should cover as many aspects as possible, and should be well-organized using complete sentences with a length restriction of 100 words.

After finishing the summary writing procedure, we employed another expert for scrutinizing the summaries. Each summary is checked from five linguistic quality perspectives: grammaticality, non-redundancy, referential clarity, focus, and coherence. Finally, all the model summaries are stored in XML files.

---

[5]http://lpsolve.sourceforge.net/5.5/

[6]In fact, for the core terminology, namely, topic, document, category, and aspect, we follow the MDS task in TAC (`https://tac.nist.gov/ /2011/Summarization/Guided-Summ.2011. guidelines.html`).

[7]https://en.wikipedia.org/wiki/Category:2017_earthquakes

3.3 Data Properties

The dataset contains 45 topics from those 6 predefined categories. Some examples of topics are "Malaysia Airlines Disappearance", "Flappy Bird", "Bitcoin Mt. Gox", etc. All the topics and categories are listed in Appendix A. Each topic contains 10 news documents and 4 model summaries. The length limit of the model summary is 100 words (slitted by space). On average, each topic contains 215 pieces of comments and 940 comment sentences. Each news document contains an average of 27 sentences, and each sentence contains an average of 25 words. 85% of non-stop model summary terms (entities, unigrams, bigrams) appeared in the news documents, and 51% of that appeared in the reader comments. The dataset contains 19k annotated aspect facets.

4 Experimental Setup

4.1 Dataset and Metrics

The properties of our own dataset are depicted in Section 3.3. We use ROUGE score as our evaluation metric (Lin, 2004) with standard options[8]. F-measures of ROUGE-1, ROUGE-2 and ROUGE-SU4 are reported.

4.2 Comparative Methods

To evaluate the performance of our dataset and the proposed framework **RAVAESum** for RA-MDS, we compare our model with the following methods:

- **RA-Sparse** (Li et al., 2015): It is a framework to tackle the RA-MDS problem. A sparse-coding-based method is used to calculate the salience of the news sentences by jointly considering news documents and reader comments.

- **Lead** (Wasson, 1998) : It ranks the news sentences chronologically and extracts the leading sentences one by one until the length limit.

- **Centroid** (Radev et al., 2000): It summarizes clusters of news articles automatically grouped by a topic detection system, and then it uses information from the centroids of the clusters to select sentences.

- **LexRank** (Erkan and Radev, 2004) and **TextRank** (Mihalcea and Tarau, 2004): Both methods are graph-based unsupervised framework for sentence salience estimation based on PageRank algorithm.

- **Concept** (Bing et al., 2015): It generates abstractive summaries using phrase-based optimization framework with concept weight as salience estimation. The concept set contains unigrams, bigrams, and entities. The weighted term-frequency is used as the concept weight.

We can see that only the method RA-Sparse can handle RA-MDS. All the other methods are only for traditional MDS without comments.

4.3 Experimental Settings

The input news sentences and comment sentences are represented as BoWs vectors with dimension $|V|$. The dictionary V is created using unigrams, bigrams and named entity terms. n_d and n_c are the number of news sentences and comment sentences respectively. For the number of latent aspects used in data reconstruction, we let $m = 5$. For the neural network framework, we set the hidden size $d_h = 500$ and the latent size $K = 100$. For the parameter λ_p used in comment weight, we let $\lambda_p = 0.2$. Adam (Kingma and Ba, 2014) is used for gradient based optimization with a learning rate 0.001. Our neural network based framework is implemented using Theano (Bastien et al., 2012) on a single GPU[9].

5 Results and Discussions

5.1 Results on Our Dataset

The results of our framework as well as the baseline methods are depicted in Table 1. It is obvious that our framework RAVAESum is the best among all the comparison methods. Specifically, it is better than RA-Sparse significantly ($p < 0.05$), which demonstrates that VAEs based latent semantic modeling and joint semantic space reconstruction can improve the MDS performance considerably. Both RAVAESum and RA-Sparse are better than the methods without considering reader comments.

---

[8]ROUGE-1.5.5.pl -n 4 -w 1.2 -m -2 4 -u -c 95 -r 1000 -f A -p 0.5 -t 0

Table 1: Summarization performance.

System	R-1	R-2	R-SU4
Lead	0.384	0.110	0.144
TextRank	0.402	0.122	0.159
LexRank	0.425	0.135	0.165
Centroid	0.402	0.141	0.171
Concept	0.422	0.149	0.177
RA-Sparse	0.442	0.157	0.188
RAVAESum	**0.443***	**0.171***	**0.196***

Table 2: Further investigation of RAVAESum.

System	R-1	R-2	R-SU4
RAVAESum-noC	0.437	0.162	0.189
RAVAESum	**0.443***	**0.171***	**0.196***

5.2 Further Investigation of Our Framework

To further investigate the effectiveness of our proposed RAVAESum framework, we adjust our framework by removing the comments related components. Then the model settings of RAVAESum-noC are similar to VAESum (Li et al., 2017). The evaluation results are shown in Table 2, which illustrate that our framework with reader comments RAVAESum is better than RAVAESum-noC significantly($p < 0.05$).

Moreover, as mentioned in VAESum (Li et al., 2017), the output aspect vectors contain the word salience information. Then we select the top-10 terms for event "Sony Virtual Reality PS4", and "'Bitcoin Mt. Gox Offlile'" for model RAVAESum (+C) and RAVAESum-noC (-C) respectively, and the results are shown in Table 3. It is obvious that the rank of the top salience terms are different. We check from the news documents and reader comments and find that some terms are enhanced by the reader comments successfully. For example, for the topic "Sony Virtual Reality PS4", many readers talked about the product of "Oculus", hence the word "oculus" is assigned a high salience by our model.

5.3 Case Study

Based on the news and comments of the topic "Sony Virtual Reality PS4", we generate two summaries with our model considering comments (RAVAESum) and ignoring comments

(RAVAESum-noC) respectively. The summaries and ROUGE evaluation are given in Table 4. All the ROUGE values of our model considering comments are better than those ignoring comments with large gaps. The sentences in ***italic bold*** of the two summaries are different. By reviewing the comments of this topic, we find that many readers talked about "Oculus", the other product with virtual reality techniques. This issue is well identified by our model and select the sentence "*Mr. Yoshida said that Sony was inspired and encouraged to do its own virtual reality project after the enthusiastic response to the efforts of Oculus VR and Valve, another game company working on the technology.*".

6 Conclusions

We investigate the problem of reader-aware multi-document summarization (RA-MDS) and introduce a new dataset. To tackle the RA-MDS, we extend a variational auto-encodes (VAEs) based MDS framework by jointly considering news documents and reader comments. The methods for data collection, aspect annotation, and summary writing and scrutinizing by experts are described. Experimental results show that reader comments can improve the summarization performance, which demonstrate the usefulness of the proposed dataset.

References

Dzmitry Bahdanau, Kyunghyun Cho, and Yoshua Bengio. 2015. Neural machine translation by jointly learning to align and translate. In *ICLR*.

Frédéric Bastien, Pascal Lamblin, Razvan Pascanu, James Bergstra, Ian Goodfellow, Arnaud Bergeron, Nicolas Bouchard, David Warde-Farley, and Yoshua Bengio. 2012. Theano: new features and speed improvements. *arXiv preprint arXiv:1211.5590*.

Lidong Bing, Piji Li, Yi Liao, Wai Lam, Weiwei Guo, and Rebecca Passonneau. 2015. Abstractive multi-document summarization via phrase selection and merging. In *ACL*, pages 1587–1597.

George B Dantzig and Mukund N Thapa. 2006. *Linear programming 1: introduction*. Springer Science & Business Media.

Günes Erkan and Dragomir R Radev. 2004. Lexpagerank: Prestige in multi-document text summarization. In *EMNLP*, volume 4, pages 365–371.

---

[9]Tesla K80, 1 Kepler GK210 is used, 2496 Cuda cores, 12G GDDR5 memory.

Table 3: Top-10 terms extracted from each topic according to the word salience values

Topic	±C	Top-10 Terms
"Sony Virtual	−C	Sony, headset, game, virtual, morpheus, reality, vr, project, playstation, Yoshida
Reality PS4"	+C	Sony, game, vr, virtual, headset, reality, morpheus, ***oculus***, project, playstation
"Bitcoin Mt.	−C	bitcoin, gox, exchange, mt., currency, Gox, virtual, company, money, price
Gox Offlile"	+C	bitcoin, currency, money, exchange, gox, mt., virtual, company, price, world

Table 4: Generated summaries for the topic "Sony Virtual Reality PS4".

System	R-1	R-2	R-SU4
RAVAESum-noC	0.482	0.184	0.209

A virtual reality headset that's coming to the PlayStation 4. ***Today announced the development of "Project Morpheus" (Morpheus) "a virtual reality (VR) system that takes the PlayStation4 (PS4)".*** Shuhei Yoshida, president of Sony Computer Entertainment, revealed a prototype of Morpheus at the Game Developers Conference in San Francisco on Tuesday. Sony showed off a prototype device V called Project Morpheus V that can be worn to create a virtual reality experience when playing games on its new PlayStation 4 console. ***The camera on the Playstation 4 using sensors that track the player's head movements.***

System	R-1	R-2	R-SU4
RAVAESum	**0.490**	**0.230**	**0.243**

Shuhei Yoshida, president of Sony Computer Entertainment, revealed a prototype of Morpheus at the Game Developers Conference in San Francisco on Tuesday. A virtual reality headset that's coming to the PlayStation 4. Sony showed off a prototype device V called Project Morpheus V that can be worn to create a virtual reality experience when playing games on its new PlayStation 4 console. ***Mr. Yoshida said that Sony was inspired and encouraged to do its own virtual reality project after the enthusiastic response to the efforts of Oculus VR and Valve, another game company working on the technology.***

Jade Goldstein, Vibhu Mittal, Jaime Carbonell, and Mark Kantrowitz. 2000. Multi-document summarization by sentence extraction. In *NAACL-ANLPWorkshop*, pages 40–48.

Meishan Hu, Aixin Sun, and Ee-Peng Lim. 2008. Comments-oriented document summarization: Understanding documents with readers' feedback. In *SIGIR*, pages 291–298.

Diederik Kingma and Jimmy Ba. 2014. Adam: A method for stochastic optimization. In *ICLR*.

Diederik P Kingma and Max Welling. 2014. Auto-encoding variational bayes. In *ICLR*.

Piji Li, Lidong Bing, Wai Lam, Hang Li, and Yi Liao. 2015. Reader-aware multi-document summarization via sparse coding. In *IJCAI*, pages 1270–1276.

Piji Li, Zihao Wang, Wai Lam, Zhaochun Ren, and Lidong Bing. 2017. Salience estimation via variational auto-encoders for multi-document summarization. In *AAAI*, pages 3497–3503.

Chin-Yew Lin. 2004. Rouge: A package for automatic evaluation of summaries. In *Text summarization branches out: Proceedings of the ACL-04 workshop*, volume 8.

Minh-Thang Luong, Hieu Pham, and Christopher D Manning. 2015. Effective approaches to attention-based neural machine translation. In *EMNLP*, pages 1412–1421.

Rada Mihalcea and Paul Tarau. 2004. Textrank: Bringing order into texts. Association for Computational Linguistics.

Ziheng Lin Min, Yen Kan Chew, and Lim Tan. 2012. Exploiting category-specific information for multi-document summarization. *COLING*, pages 2093–2108.

Ani Nenkova and Kathleen McKeown. 2012. A survey of text summarization techniques. In *Mining Text Data*, pages 43–76. Springer.

Dragomir R Radev, Hongyan Jing, and Malgorzata Budzikowska. 2000. Centroid-based summarization of multiple documents: sentence extraction, utility-based evaluation, and user studies. In *Proceedings of the 2000 NAACL-ANLP Workshop on Automatic summarization*, pages 21–30. Association for Computational Linguistics.

Danilo Jimenez Rezende, Shakir Mohamed, and Daan Wierstra. 2014. Stochastic backpropagation and approximate inference in deep generative models. In *ICML*, pages 1278–1286.

Xiaojun Wan, Jianwu Yang, and Jianguo Xiao. 2007. Manifold-ranking based topic-focused multi-document summarization. In *IJCAI*, volume 7, pages 2903–2908.

Mark Wasson. 1998. Using leading text for news summaries: Evaluation results and implications for commercial summarization applications. In *ACL*, pages 1364–1368.

Kristian Woodsend and Mirella Lapata. 2012. Multiple aspect summarization using integer linear programming. In *EMNLP-CNLL*, pages 233–243.

Zi Yang, Keke Cai, Jie Tang, Li Zhang, Zhong Su, and Juanzi Li. 2011. Social context summarization. In *SIGIR*, pages 255–264.

Appendices

A Topics

Table 5: All the topics and the corresponding categories. The 6 predefined categories are: (1) Accidents and Natural Disasters, (2) Attacks (Criminal/Terrorist), (3) New Technology, (4) Health and Safety, (5) Endangered Resources, and (6) Investigations and Trials (Criminal/Legal/Other).

Topic	Category
Boston Marathon Bomber Sister Arrested	6
iWatch	3
Facebook Offers App With Free Access in Zambia	3
441 Species Discovered in Amazon	5
Beirut attack	2
Great White Shark Choked by Sea Lion	1
Sony virtual reality PS4	3
Akademik Shokalskiy Trapping	1
Missing Oregon Woman Jennifer Huston Committed Suicide	6
Bremerton Teen Arrested Murder 6-year-old Girl	6
Apple And IBM Team Up	3
California Father Accused Killing Family	6
Los Angeles Earthquake	1
New Species of Colorful Monkey	5
Japan Whaling	5
Top Doctor Becomes Latest Ebola Victim	4
New South Wales Bushfires	1
UK David Cameron Joins Battle Against Dementia	4
UK Cameron Calls for Global Action on Superbug Threat	4
Karachi Airport Attack	2
Air Algerie Plane Crash	1
Flappy Bird	3
Moscow Subway Crash	1
Rick Perry Lawyers Dismissal of Charges	6
New York Two Missing Amish Girls Found	6
UK Contaminated Drip Poisoned Babies	4
Taiwan Police Evict Student Protesters	2
US General Killed in Afghan	5
Monarch butterflies drop	5
UN Host Summit to End Child Brides	4
Two Tornadoes in Nebraska	1
Global Warming Threatens Emperor Penguins	5
Malaysia Airlines Disappearance	1
Google Conference	3
Africa Ebola Out of Control in West Africa	4
Shut Down of Malaysia Airlines mh17	1
Sochi Terrorist Attack	2
Fire Phone	3
ISIS executes David Haines	2
UK Rotherham 1400 Child Abuse Cases	6
Rare Pangolins Asians eating Extinction	5
Kunming Station Massacre	2
Bitcoin Mt. Gox	3
UK Jimmy Savile Abused Victims in Hospital	6
ISIS in Iraq	2

A Pilot Study of Domain Adaptation Effect for Neural Abstractive Summarization

Xinyu Hua and **Lu Wang**
College of Computer and Information Science
Northeastern University
Boston, MA 02115
hua.x@husky.neu.edu   luwang@ccs.neu.edu

Abstract

We study the problem of domain adaptation for neural abstractive summarization. We make initial efforts in investigating what information can be transferred to a new domain. Experimental results on news stories and opinion articles indicate that neural summarization model benefits from pre-training based on extractive summaries. We also find that the combination of in-domain and out-of-domain setup yields better summaries when in-domain data is insufficient. Further analysis shows that, the model is capable to select salient content even trained on out-of-domain data, but requires in-domain data to capture the style for a target domain.

1 Introduction

Recent text summarization research moves towards producing abstractive summmaries, which better emulates human summarization process and produces more concise summaries (Nenkova et al., 2011). Built on the success of sequence-to-sequence learning with encoder-decoder neural networks (Bahdanau et al., 2014), there has been growing interest in utilizing this framework for generating abstractive summaries (Rush et al., 2015; Wang and Ling, 2016; Takase et al., 2016; Nallapati et al., 2016; See et al., 2017). The end-to-end learning framework circumvents efforts in feature engineering and template construction as done in previous work (Ganesan et al., 2010; Wang and Cardie, 2013; Gerani et al., 2014; Pighin et al., 2014), by directly learning to detect summary-worthy content as well as generate fluent sentences.

Nevertheless, training such systems requires large amounts of labeled data, which creates a big hurdle for new domains where training data is scant and expensive to acquire. Consequently, we raise the following research questions:

Input (News):The Department of Defense has identified 441 American service members who have died since the start of the Iraq war. It confirmed the death of the following American yesterday: DAVIS, Raphael S., 24, specialist, Army National Guard; Tutwiler, Miss.; 223rd Engineer Battalion.
Abstract: Name of American newly confirmed dead in Iraq ; 441 American service members have died since start of war.

Input (Opinion): WHEN the 1999 United States Ryder Cup team trailed the Europeans, 10-6, going into Sunday's 12 singles matches at the Country Club outside Boston, Ben Crenshaw, the United States captain, issued a declaration of confidence in his golfers. "I'm a big believer in faith ," Crenshaw said firmly in his Texas twang . " I have a good feeling about this." The next day , Crenshaw' cavalry won the firsts even singles matches. With a sudden 13-10 lead , the turnaround put unexpected pressure on the Europeans, ...
Abstract: Dave Anderson Sports of The Times column discusses US team's poor performance against Europe in Ryder Cup.

Figure 1: A snippet of sample news story and opinion article from The New York Times Annotated Corpus (Sandhaus, 2008).

- *domain adaptation*: whether we can leverage available out-of-domain abstracts or extractive summaries to help train a neural summarization system for a new domain?

- *transferable component*: what information is transferable and what are the limitations?

In this paper, we attempt to shed some light on the above questions by investigating neural summarization on two types of documents with major difference: news stories and opinion articles from The New York Times Annotated Corpus (Sandhaus, 2008). Sample articles and human written abstracts are shown in Figure 1. We select a reasonably simple task on generating short news summary for multi-paragraph documents.

Proceedings of the Workshop on New Frontiers in Summarization, pages 100–106
Copenhagen, Denmark, September 7, 2017. ©2017 Association for Computational Linguistics

Contributions. We first investigate the effect of parameter initialization via pre-training on extractive summaries. A large-scale dataset consisting of 1 million article-extract pairs is collected from The New York Times for use. Experimental results show that this step improves summarization performance measured by ROUGE (Lin, 2004) and BLEU (Papineni et al., 2002).

We then treat news stories as source domain and opinion articles as target domain, and make initial tries for understanding the feasibility of domain adaptation. Importantly, by testing on opinion article summarization, the model leveraging data from both source and target domains yields better performance than in-domain trained model when in-domain training data is rare.

Furthermore, we interpret the learned model to understand what information is transferred to a new domain. In general, a model trained on out-of-domain data can learn to detect summary-worthy content, but may not match the generation style in the target domain. Concretely, we observe that the model trained on news domain pays similar amount of attention to summary-worthy content (i.e., words reused by human abstracts) when tested on news and opinion articles. On the other hand, human writers tend to employ new words unseen from the input when constructing opinion abstracts. End-to-end evaluation results imply that the model trained on out-of-domain data fails to capture this aspect.

The above observations suggest that the neural summarization model learns to 1) identify salient content, and 2) generate summaries with a style as in the training data. The first element might be transferable to a new domain, while not so much for the second.

2 The Neural Summarization Model

In this work, we choose the attentional sequence-to-sequence model with pointer-generator mechanism (See et al., 2017) for study. Briefly, the model learns to generate a sequence of tokens $\{y_i\}$ based on the following conditional probability: $p(y_i = w|y_1, \ldots, y_{i-1}, x) = p_{gen}P_{vocab}(w) + (1 - p_{gen})\sum_{i:w_i=w} a_i^t$

Here $P_{vocab}(w)$ denotes the probability to generate a new word from vocabulary, p_{gen} is a learned parameter that chooses between generating and copying, depending on the hidden states and attention distribution. This model enhances

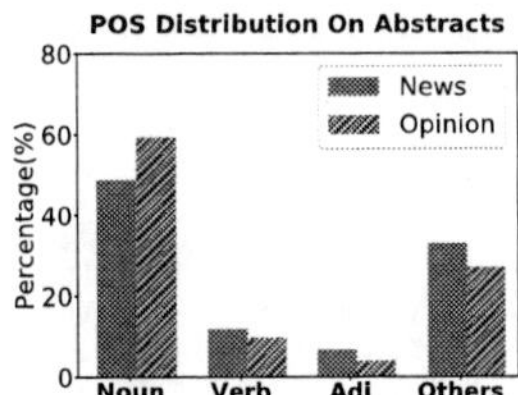

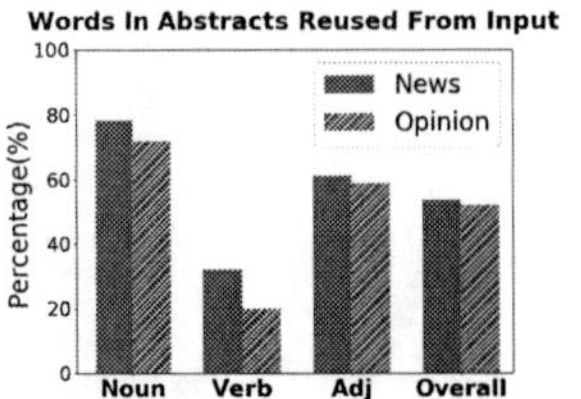

Figure 2: [Left] Part-of-speech (POS) distribution for words in abstracts. [Right] Percentage of words in abstracts that are reused from input, per POS and all words. OPINION abstracts generally reuse less words.

the original attention model (Bahdanau et al., 2014) by incorporating pointer-network (Vinyals et al., 2015), which allows the decoder to copy accurate information from input. Due to space limitation, we refer the readers to original paper (See et al., 2017) for model details.

For experiments, we employ bidirectional recurrent neural network (RNN) as encoder and unidirectional RNN as decoder, both implemented by Long Short Term Memory (LSTM) with 256 hidden units. Input and output data are lowercased as described in (See et al., 2017).

3 Datasets and Experimental Setup

Primary Data. Our primary data source is The New York Times Annotated Corpus (Sandhaus, 2008) (henceforth called NYT-annotated). Compared with other commonly used dataset for abstractive summarization, NYT-annotated has more variation in its abstracts, such as paraphrase and generalization. It also comes with other human labels we could use to characterize the type of articles. The whole dataset consists of 1.8 million articles, of which 650,000 are annotated with human constructed abstracts. Articles longer than 15 tokens and abstracts longer than 10 tokens are extracted for use in our study (as in Figure 1).

The resulting dataset are further separated into two types based on their taxonomy tags[1]: NEWS stories and OPINION articles. We believe these two types of documents are different enough in terms of topics, summary style, and lexical level language use, that they could be treated as different domains for our study. We collected 100,824

---

[1] The corpus comes with taxonomic classifiers tags. Articles with tag "News" are treated as news stories; for the rest, the ones with "Opinion","Editorial", or "Features" are treated as opinion articles.

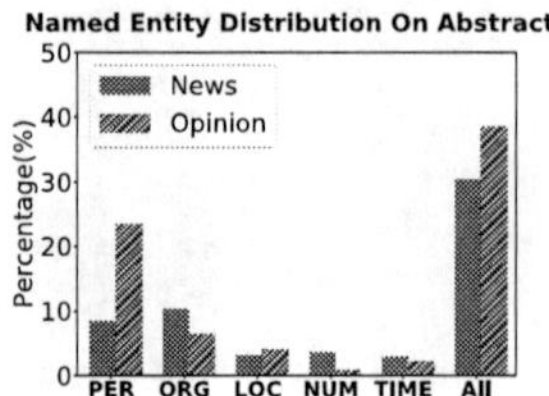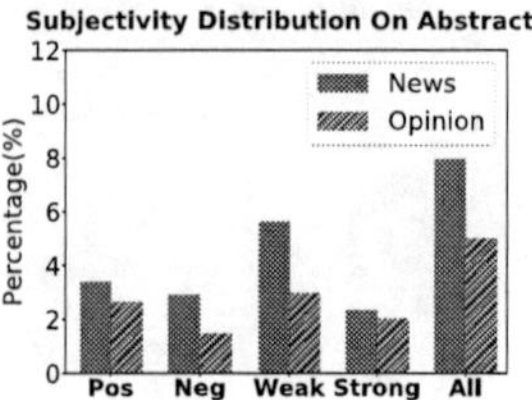

Figure 3: Named Entities distribution (left) and subjective words distribution (right) in abstracts. More PERSON, less ORGANIZATION, and less subjective words are observed in OPINION.

articles for NEWS which is treated as source domain, and 51,214 for OPINION as target domain. The average length for documents of NEWS is 680.8 tokens, and 785.6 tokens for OPINION. The average lengths for abstracts are 23.14 and 19.13 for NEWS and OPINION.

We also make use of the section tag, such as *Business, Sports, Arts*, to calculate the topic distribution for these two domains. About 57% of the documents of NEWS are about *Sports*, whereas more than 78% documents of OPINION are about *Arts*. We also observe different levels of subjectivity based on the percentage of strong subjective words taken from MPQA lexicon (Wilson et al., 2005). On average 4.1% of the tokens in OPINION articles are strong subjective, compared to 2.9% for NEWS stories. This shows the topics and word usage are essentially different between these two domains.

Characterizing Two Domains. Here we characterize the difference between NEWS and OPINION by analyzing the distribution of word types in abstracts and how often human reuse words from input text to construct the summaries. Overall, 81.3% of the words in NEWS abstracts are reused from input, compared with 75.8% for OPINION. The distribution for words of different part-of-speech is displayed on the left of Figure 2, which shows that there are relatively more Nouns in OPINION. In the same figure, we display the percentage of words in abstract that are reused from input, which suggests that human tends to reuse more nouns and verbs for NEWS abstracts. Furthermore, the distribution of Named Entities words and subjective words in abstracts are depicted in Figure 3.

Model Pre-training Dataset. We further collect lead paragraphs and article descriptions for 1,435,735 articles from The New York Times API[2]. About 71% of these descriptions are the first sentences in the lead paragraphs, and thus can be considered as extractive summaries. About one million lead paragraph and description pairs are retained for pre-training[3] (henceforth NYT-extract).

Training Setup. We randomly divide NYT-annotated into training (75%), validation (15%), and test (10%) for both news and opinion. Experiments are conducted with the following setups:
1) IN-DOMAIN: Training and testing are done in the same domain, for NEWS and OPINION;
2) OUT-OF-DOMAIN: training on source domain NEWS, and testing on target domain OPINION; and 3) MIX-DOMAIN: training on source domain NEWS and then on target domain OPINION, and testing on OPINION. Training stops when the trend of loss function on validation set starts increasing.

Evaluation Metrics. We use automatic evaluation on recall-oriented ROUGE (Lin, 2004) and precision-oriented BLEU (Papineni et al., 2002). We consider ROUGE-2 which measures bigram recall, and ROUGE-L which takes into account the longest common subsequence. We also evaluate on BLEU which measures precision up to bi-grams.

4 Results

Effect of Pre-training with Extracts. We first evaluate whether pre-training can improve summarization performance for IN-DOMAIN setups, where we initialize model parameters by training on NYT-extract for about 20,000 iterations. Otherwise, parameters are randomly initialized. Results are displayed in Table 1. We also consider two baselines, BASELINE1 outputs the first sentence, BASLINE2 selects the first 22 (news) and 15 (opinion) tokens (with similar lengths as human summaries).

As can be seen, the pre-training step improves performance for NEWS, whereas the performance on OPINION remains roughly the same. This might be due to the fact that news abstracts reuse more

---

[2]https://developer.nytimes.com

[3]Unsupervised language model (Ramachandran et al., 2016) can also be used for parameter initialization before our pre-training step. Here our goal is to allow the model to learn searching for summary-worthy content, in addition to grammaticality and language fluency.

words from input, which are closer to extractive summaries than opinion abstracts.

	R-2	R-L	BLEU	Avg Len
Test on News				
BASELINE1	23.5	**35.4**	19.9	28.94
BASELINE2	19.5	30.1	19.5	22.00
IN-DOMAIN	23.3	34.1	21.3	22.08
IN-DOMAIN + pre-train	**24.2**	34.5	**22.4**	21.59
Test on Opinion				
BASELINE1	17.9	26.6	11.4	28.18
BASELINE2	12.9	20.5	11.7	15.00
IN-DOMAIN	19.8	**31.9**	**19.9**	14.60
IN-DOMAIN + pre-train	**19.9**	31.8	19.4	14.22

Table 1: Evaluation based on ROUGE-2 (R-2), ROUGE-L (R-L), and BLEU (multiplied by 100) for in-domain training.

Effect of Domain Adaptation. Here we evaluate on domain adaptation, where OPINION is the target domain. From Figure 4, we can see that when In-domain data is insufficient Mix-domain training yields better performance. As more In-domain training data becomes available, it outperforms Mix-domain training. Baseline for selecting the first sentence as summary is also displayed. Sample summaries in Figure 5 also shows that OUT-OF-DOMAIN training tends to generate summary in similar style to the source domain, while MIX-DOMAIN training introduces the style of the target domain. In our dataset, the first sentences of summaries for OPINION are usually in the form of *[PERSON] reviews/criticizes/columns [EVENT]*, but the summaries for NEWS usually start with event descriptions directly. Such style difference is reflected in OUT-OF-DOMAIN and MIX-DOMAIN too.

We further classify the words in gold-standard summaries based on if they are seen in abstracts during training and then whether they are taken from the input text. We examine whether they are generated correctly. Full training set of opinion is used for in-domain and mix-domain training. Table 2 shows that among in-domain models, the model trained for news are superior at generating tokens mentioned in the input, compared to the model trained for opinion (33.7% v.s. 22.0%). Nonetheless, model trained for opinion is better at generating new words not in the input (8.2% vs. 2.6%). This is consistent with our observation that in opinion domain human editors favors

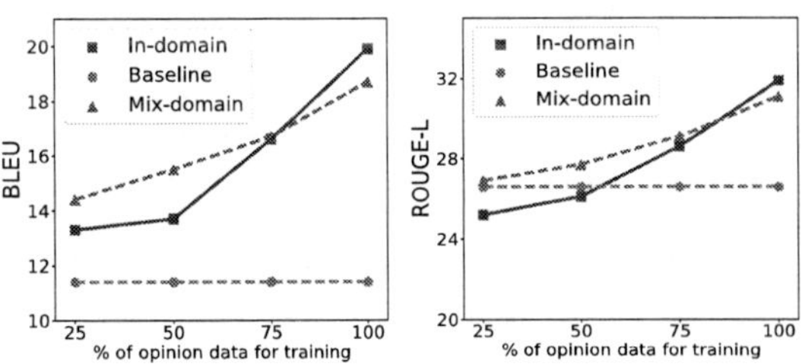

Figure 4: BLEU (left) and ROUGE-L (right) performance on In-domain and Mix-domain setup over different amount of training data. As the training data increases, In-domain outperforms Mix-domain training.

	Seen in Training (%)					Unseen (%)
	In Input			*Not In Input*		
	Gen	Mis	Total	Gen	Mis	Total	
Test on News							
IN-DOMAIN	33.7	40.9	74.6	2.6	19.3	21.9	3.5
Test on Opinion							
IN-DOMAIN	22.0	43.3	65.3	8.2	22.1	30.3	
OUT-OF-DOMAIN	19.9	45.3	65.2	1.1	29.2	30.3	4.5
MIX-DOMAIN	18.6	46.6	65.2	6.3	23.9	30.2	

Table 2: Comparison of generated (Gen) and missed (Mis) tokens for different training setups. We divide token in goldstandard summaries by 1) if it is seen in abstracts during training, and 2) if it is in the input text.

new words different from the input.

Further Analysis. Here we study what information is transferable cross domains by investigating the attention weights assigned to the input text.

What can be transferred. We start with input words with highest attention weights when generating the summaries. Among these, we show the percentage over different word categories as in Table 3. For named entities, model trained on out-of-domain data pays more attention to PERSON and less attention to ORGANIZATION, while the in-domain trained model does reverse . This is consistent with the fact that opinion abstracts contains more PERSON and less ORGANIZATION than news abstracts (see Figure 3). This suggests that the identification of summary-worthy named entities might be transferable from NEWS to OPINION. Similar effect is also observed for nouns and verbs, though less significant.

Attention change for domain adaptation. We also examine the percentage of attention paid to summary-worthy words. For every output token we pick the input token with highest attention weight, and count the ones reused by hu-

Human: stephen holden reviews carnegie hall concert celebrating music of judy garland. singers include her daughter, lorna luft.
Out-of-Domain: article discusses possibility of carnegie hall in carnegie hall golf tournament.
Mix-Domain: stephen holden reviews performance by jazz singer celebration by rainbow and garland at carnegie, part of tribute hall.

Human: janet maslin reviews john grisham book the king of torts .
Out-of-Domain: interview with john grisham of legal thriller is itself proof for john grisham 376 pages.
Mix-Domain: janet maslin reviews book the king of torts by john grisham .

Human: anthony tommasini reviews 23d annual benefit concert of richard tucker music foundation , featuring members of metropolitan opera orchestra led by leonard slatkin .
Out-of-Domain: final choral society and richard tucker music foundation , on sunday night in [UNK] fisher hall , will even longer than substantive 22d gala last year .
Mix-Domain: anthony tommasini reviews 23d annual benefit concert of benefit of richard tucker music.

Figure 5: Sample summaries based on OUT-OF-DOMAIN and MIX-DOMAIN training on opinion articles.

man. For IN-DOMAIN test on NEWS, on average 29.57% of the output tokens have highest attention on summary-worthy words. For OUT-OF-DOMAIN test on OPINION, the number is 15.93%; for MIX-DOMAIN, it is 26.08%. This shows the ability to focus on salient words is largely kept for MIX-DOMAIN training. Additionally, as can be seen in Table 3, model trained on MIX-DOMAIN puts more attention weights on PERSON (and all named entities) and nouns, but less attention on verbs and subjective words, compared with the model trained OUT-OF-DOMAIN. This again aligns with our observation for the domain difference based on abstracts as in Figures 2 and 3.

5 Related Work

Domain adaptation has been studied for a wide range of natural language processing tasks (Blitzer et al., 2007; Florian et al., 2004; Daume III, 2007; Foster et al., 2010). However, little has been done for investigating summarization systems (Sandu et al., 2010; Wang and Cardie, 2013). To the best of our knowledge, we are the first to study the adaptation of neural summarization models for

	IN-DOMAIN	OUT-OF-DOMAIN	MIX-DOMAIN
$Src \rightarrow Trt$	$News \rightarrow News$	$News \rightarrow Opin$	$News + Opin \rightarrow Opin$
PER	7.9%	8.7%	15.1% ↑
ORG	10.9%	6.9%	8.2% ↑
All NEs	26.7%	23.6%	31.6% ↑
Noun	41.2%	36.2%	43.3% ↑
Verb	10.3%	6.7%	5.5% ↓
Positive	5.6%	5.1%	4.5% ↓
Negative	2.5%	2.2%	2.1% ↓

Table 3: Attention distribution on different word categories. We consider input words with highest attention weights when generating the summaries, and characterize them by Named Entity, POS tag, and Subjectivity. The arrows shows the change with regard to OUT-OF-DOMAIN.

new domain. Furthermore, Recent work in neural summarization mainly focuses on specfic extensions to improve system performance (Rush et al., 2015; Takase et al., 2016; Gu et al., 2016; Nallapati et al., 2016; Ranzato et al., 2015). It is unclear how to adapt the existing neural summarization systems to a new domain when the training data is limited or not available. This is a question we aim to address in this work.

6 Conclusion

We investigated domain adaptation for abstractive neural summarization. Experimental results showed that pre-training model with extractive summaries helps. By analyzing the attention weight distribution over input tokens, we found the model was capable to select salient information even trained on out-of-domain data. This points to future direcions where domain adaptation techniques can be developed to allow a summarization system to learn content selection from out-of-domain data while acquiring language generating behavior with in-domain data.

Acknowledgments

This work was supported in part by National Science Foundation Grant IIS-1566382 and a GPU gift from Nvidia. We thank three anonymous reviewers for their valuable suggestions on various aspects of this work.

References

Dzmitry Bahdanau, Kyunghyun Cho, and Yoshua Bengio. 2014. Neural machine translation by jointly learning to align and translate. *arXiv preprint arXiv:1409.0473* .

John Blitzer, Mark Dredze, Fernando Pereira, et al. 2007. Biographies, bollywood, boom-boxes and blenders: Domain adaptation for sentiment classification. In *ACL*. volume 7, pages 440–447.

Hal Daume III. 2007. Frustratingly easy domain adaptation. In *Proceedings of the 45th Annual Meeting of the Association of Computational Linguistics*. Association for Computational Linguistics, Prague, Czech Republic, pages 256–263. http://www.aclweb.org/anthology/P07-1033.

R Florian, H Hassan, A Ittycheriah, H Jing, N Kambhatla, X Luo, N Nicolov, and S Roukos. 2004. A statistical model for multilingual entity detection and tracking. In Daniel Marcu Susan Dumais and Salim Roukos, editors, *HLT-NAACL 2004: Main Proceedings*. Association for Computational Linguistics, Boston, Massachusetts, USA, pages 1–8.

George Foster, Cyril Goutte, and Roland Kuhn. 2010. Discriminative instance weighting for domain adaptation in statistical machine translation. In *Proceedings of the 2010 Conference on Empirical Methods in Natural Language Processing*. Association for Computational Linguistics, Stroudsburg, PA, USA, EMNLP '10, pages 451–459. http://dl.acm.org/citation.cfm?id=1870658.1870702.

Kavita Ganesan, ChengXiang Zhai, and Jiawei Han. 2010. Opinosis: a graph-based approach to abstractive summarization of highly redundant opinions. In *Proceedings of the 23rd international conference on computational linguistics*. Association for Computational Linguistics, pages 340–348.

Shima Gerani, Yashar Mehdad, Giuseppe Carenini, Raymond T Ng, and Bita Nejat. 2014. Abstractive summarization of product reviews using discourse structure. In *EMNLP*. pages 1602–1613.

Jiatao Gu, Zhengdong Lu, Hang Li, and Victor O.K. Li. 2016. Incorporating copying mechanism in sequence-to-sequence learning. In *Proceedings of the 54th Annual Meeting of the Association for Computational Linguistics (Volume 1: Long Papers)*. Association for Computational Linguistics, Berlin, Germany, pages 1631–1640. http://www.aclweb.org/anthology/P16-1154.

Chin-Yew Lin. 2004. Rouge: A package for automatic evaluation of summaries. In *Text summarization branches out: Proceedings of the ACL-04 workshop*. Barcelona, Spain, volume 8.

Ramesh Nallapati, Bowen Zhou, Cicero dos Santos, Ça glar Gulçehre, and Bing Xiang. 2016. Abstractive text summarization using sequence-to-sequence rnns and beyond. *CoNLL 2016* page 280.

Ani Nenkova, Kathleen McKeown, et al. 2011. Automatic summarization. *Foundations and Trends® in Information Retrieval* 5(2–3):103–233.

Kishore Papineni, Salim Roukos, Todd Ward, and Wei-Jing Zhu. 2002. Bleu: a method for automatic evaluation of machine translation. In *Proceedings of the 40th annual meeting on association for computational linguistics*. Association for Computational Linguistics, pages 311–318.

Daniele Pighin, Marco Cornolti, Enrique Alfonseca, and Katja Filippova. 2014. Modelling events through memory-based, open-ie patterns for abstractive summarization. In *Proceedings of the 52nd Annual Meeting of the Association for Computational Linguistics (Volume 1: Long Papers)*. Association for Computational Linguistics, Baltimore, Maryland, pages 892–901. http://www.aclweb.org/anthology/P14-1084.

Prajit Ramachandran, Peter J Liu, and Quoc V Le. 2016. Unsupervised pretraining for sequence to sequence learning. *arXiv preprint arXiv:1611.02683* .

Marc'Aurelio Ranzato, Sumit Chopra, Michael Auli, and Wojciech Zaremba. 2015. Sequence level training with recurrent neural networks. *arXiv preprint arXiv:1511.06732* .

Alexander M. Rush, Sumit Chopra, and Jason Weston. 2015. A neural attention model for abstractive sentence summarization. In *Proceedings of the 2015 Conference on Empirical Methods in Natural Language Processing*. Association for Computational Linguistics, Lisbon, Portugal, pages 379–389. http://aclweb.org/anthology/D15-1044.

Evan Sandhaus. 2008. The new york times annotated corpus, 2008. *Linguistic Data Consortium, PA* .

Oana Sandu, Giuseppe Carenini, Gabriel Murray, and Raymond Ng. 2010. Domain adaptation to summarize human conversations. In *Proceedings of the 2010 Workshop on Domain Adaptation for Natural Language Processing*. Association for Computational Linguistics, pages 16–22.

Abigail See, Peter J Liu, and Christopher D Manning. 2017. Get to the point: Summarization with pointer-generator networks. *arXiv preprint arXiv:1704.04368* .

Sho Takase, Jun Suzuki, Naoaki Okazaki, Tsutomu Hirao, and Masaaki Nagata. 2016. Neural headline generation on abstract meaning representation. In *Proceedings of the 2016 Conference on Empirical Methods in Natural Language Processing*. Association for Computational Linguistics, Austin, Texas, pages 1054–1059. https://aclweb.org/anthology/D16-1112.

Oriol Vinyals, Meire Fortunato, and Navdeep Jaitly. 2015. Pointer networks. In *Advances in Neural Information Processing Systems*. pages 2692–2700.

Lu Wang and Claire Cardie. 2013. Domain-independent abstract generation for focused meeting summarization. In *Proceedings of the 51st Annual*

Meeting of the Association for Computational Linguistics (Volume 1: Long Papers). Association for Computational Linguistics, Sofia, Bulgaria, pages 1395–1405. http://www.aclweb.org/anthology/P13-1137.

Lu Wang and Wang Ling. 2016. Neural network-based abstract generation for opinions and arguments. In *Proceedings of the 2016 Conference of the North American Chapter of the Association for Computational Linguistics: Human Language Technologies*. Association for Computational Linguistics, San Diego, California, pages 47–57. http://www.aclweb.org/anthology/N16-1007.

Theresa Wilson, Janyce Wiebe, and Paul Hoffmann. 2005. Recognizing contextual polarity in phrase-level sentiment analysis. In *Proceedings of the conference on human language technology and empirical methods in natural language processing*. Association for Computational Linguistics, pages 347–354.

Author Index

Association for Computational Linguistics
209 N. Eighth Street
Stroudsburg, Pennsylvania 18360

ISBN 978-1-5108-4761-3